Never Quit the Fight

Books by Ralph Peters

Nonfiction

New Glory
Beyond Baghdad
Beyond Terror
Fighting for the Future

Fiction

Traitor
The Devil's Garden
Twilight of Heroes
Flames of Heaven
The Perfect Soldier
The War in 2020
Red Army
Bravo Romeo

Writing as Owen Parry

Fiction

Rebels of Babylon
Bold Sons of Erin
Honor's Kingdom (Hammett Award)
Call Each River Jordan
Shadows of Glory
Faded Coat of Blue (Herodotus Award)
Our Simple Gifts
Strike the Harp

NEVER QUIT
THE FIGHT

Ralph Peters

STACKPOLE
BOOKS

Published by
STACKPOLE BOOKS
5067 Ritter Road
Mechanicsburg, PA 17055
www.stackpolebooks.com

Printed in the United States

First edition

10 9 8 7 6 5 4 3 2

Library of Congress Cataloging-in-Publication Data
Peters, Ralph, 1952-
   Never quit the fight / Ralph Peters.
      p. cm.
   ISBN-13: 978-0-8117-3328-1 (hardcover)
   ISBN-10: 0-8117-3328-9 (hardcover)
   1. United States—Military policy. 2. United States—Politics and
government—2001- 3. World politics—21st century. 4. War on Terrorism,
2001- 5. Counterinsurgency. I. Title.

UA23.P4695 2006
355' .033573—dc22

2006004555

*To those who wore our country's uniform
and died defending civilization
in Iraq and Afghanistan*

Contents

"This war, like the next war, is a war to end war."

—David Lloyd George

Introduction

Savage Days

This book focuses on a period of slightly more than two years in our recent history, from the late summer of 2003 to the autumn of 2005. Despite glances backward and projections into the distant future, the themes addressed here were dictated by this brief, turbulent, inspiring, and disheartening period. A nation at war pretended that it was not. A presidential administration insisted that we were at war but acted as though the greed-spurred 1990s had never ended. A national election offered the American people one of the poorest choices in our history, between an incumbent administration that stood for arrogance, corruption, and security, and a challenger who emanated fecklessness, weakness, and a spirit of surrender. We gritted our teeth and chose the man who would fight over a man who didn't seem to stand for anything at all.

At home, this was a period of political polarization, when both of our major political parties fell captive to extremists. The Democratic party went through an intellectual and moral collapse, allowing an intolerant minority among Republicans to harden their prejudices and insist that their morality was the only morality. Most Americans were left politically homeless as neofascist organizations, such as moveon.org, battled over our heads with a religious right that appeared to have discarded the Gospels in favor of Old Testament cruelty.

Abroad, our men and women in uniform fought remarkably well despite poor national leadership on one hand and a hard-left minority on the other that seemed to feel more empathy for Islamist terrorists than for our own troops. "Support our troops, bring them home!" became the most cynical political mantra since the McCarthy era. Yet our troops never wavered. They deserve far more respect and recognition than an insincere political class and our toxic media will grant them.

As the events of 9/11 receded, many Americans appeared to lose touch with the implacable and merciless nature of our enemies. Our government was penalized for performing too well in the wake of terror's high watermark: As further attacks on our country were frustrated and our troops carried the war into terror's homelands, citizens relaxed into a business-as-usual attitude. Yet we face opponents who would wait a generation, if need be, to exterminate myriad Americans, Europeans, Christians, Jews, Hindus, Buddhists, less-devout Muslims, and adherents of any other faith that did not conform to the severe interpretation of God's will insisted upon by Islamist madmen. The stakes are all or nothing to our enemies. Their visions may seem preposterous and absurd, but history suggests that philosophical absurdities are far more apt to kill masses of the innocent than reason.

This new age of endless war is profoundly different from any previous experience of conflict within living memory. After the titanic industrial-war struggles of the twentieth century, when the alliance that produced the most materiel won the big wars and conflicts were about competitions for power and rival theories of government, we now find ourselves in a death struggle with demons from the dawn of time, engaged in Cain-and-Abel warfare waged against us by opponents whose view of God is superstitious, soaked in blood, and obsessed with behavior rather than transcendent faith. We are *not* at war with ideas, but with beliefs. And those beliefs are a throwback to ancient eras of human sacrifice and carnivorous gods.

One of the few moral triumphs of the modern age was the ability to doubt and still believe (although much of Europe has elevated doubt above belief, leaving a continent bereft of meaning and spirit). The religious extremists who threaten civilization today permit no doubt—and ultimately care less about faith than about conformity. From atheist Europe to the maddened Islamic realms of the Middle East, this is not an age of religious revival, but of religious degeneration, the age of the small, mean god. While the struggle for the soul of Islam is the conflict immediately before us, every major religion appears to be at war with itself. We may have entered an age of religious fragmentation, when great faiths divide into factions of those who believe in a merciful deity and those who would form their religions into militant engines to serve a vengeful bogeyman. It will be up to those who believe in God's benevolence to rescue their faiths from the geniuses of hate.

This is the fatal issue of our time.

Even those who despise religion had best pay attention: The issue of God's will, as interpreted by discontented human beings, will reshape the governance of continents in the coming decades. We insist that our wars are not religious wars. But they are. Because our enemies believe them to be so.

The old strategic factors, such as demography, economics, natural resources, and political systems, continue to matter, but they are largely played out as tools for understanding the deepest currents at work in this disturbed world. The new factors range from collective jealousy and religious psychosis to a culture-crippling dread of female sexuality and the poisonous effects of the undisciplined, unscrupulous, and breathtakingly irresponsible global media. Virtually all that the academics and diplomats, the politicians and generals thought they knew about the sources of mass unrest, massacre, and war is obsolete. The age in which we live is utterly different than that to which we were able to cling—at increasing cost—as late as the year 2000.

Ours is the age of barbarians with microchips, of zealots who cannily exploit the civilized world's rules in their attempts to destroy it. 9/11 did not merely mark the end of yet another form of American innocence. It brought the Victorian era's belief that progress is irreversible and that men instinctively crave enlightenment to a much belated close. We are learning that many human beings prefer certainty, no matter how oppressive and primitive, to the risks and responsibilities of freedom.

Civilizations are massive organisms as different one from the other as individual human beings. The comfortable relativism of the past fifty years was a fantasy. Entire civilizations fail. Even within robust civilizations, some cultures yearn for—and can cope with—far greater degrees of social and political liberty than others. This is an age in which some humans seek ever fewer limits on individual opportunity, while others long for the determinism of the prison cell.

Whatever we learn about civilizations, governments, and man's relationship to the divine in the coming decades, we shall certainly hear a great deal about military matters. Although the military is not always an ideal tool with which to respond to incipient or immediate crises, it is all too often the only tool available with the resources, organization, and sense of responsibility to act—whether we speak of foreign wars or domestic disasters. We have already learned (or relearned) a great deal, not least that, for all the extravagant claims of technology hawkers, the nature of warfare *never* changes. Weapons, uniforms, organizations, and even battlefield rules may change, but warfare remains essentially the same endeavor it was when the first tribes went at each other with rocks and spears. It is not pleasing to think so, yet it is undeniable that warfare is an integral part of humankind's heritage. And after thousands of years of practice, we are very, very good at it. Tragically, making war may be what humans do best.

Much of this book focuses on the experiences and lessons of our recent military endeavors. There will be more to come.

— Ralph Peters, Northern Virginia,
October 24, 2005

PART I

Guns Up

In Praise of Attrition

Parameters

Summer 2004

"Who dares to call the child by its true name?"

—GOETHE, *FAUST*

In our military, the danger of accepting the traditional wisdom has become part of the traditional wisdom. Despite our lip service to creativity and innovation, we rarely pause to question fundamentals. Partly, of course, this is because officers in today's Army or Marine Corps operate at a wartime tempo, with little leisure for reflection. Yet, even more fundamentally, deep prejudices have crept into our military—as well as into the civilian world—that obscure elementary truths.

There is no better example of our unthinking embrace of an error than our rejection of the term "war of attrition." The belief that attrition, as an objective or a result, is inherently negative is simply wrong. A soldier's job is to kill the enemy. All else, however important it may appear at the moment, is secondary. And to kill the enemy is to attrit the enemy. All wars in which bullets—or arrows—fly are wars of attrition.

Of course, the term "war of attrition" conjures the unimaginative slaughter of the Western Front, with massive casualties on both sides. Last year, when journalists wanted to denigrate our military's occupation efforts in Iraq, the term bubbled up again and again. The notion that killing even the enemy is a bad thing in war has been exacerbated by the defense industry's claims, seconded by glib military careerists, that precision weapons and technology in general had irrevocably changed the nature of warfare. But the nature of warfare never changes—only its superficial manifestations.

3

The U.S. Army also did great harm to its own intellectual and practical grasp of war by trolling for theories, especially in the 1980s. Theories don't win wars. Well-trained, well-led soldiers in well-equipped armies do. And they do so by killing effectively. Yet we heard a great deal of nonsense about "maneuver warfare" as the solution to all our woes, from our numerical disadvantage vis-à-vis the Warsaw Pact to our knowledge that the "active defense" on the old inner-German border was political tomfoolery and a military sham—and, frankly, the best an Army gutted by Vietnam and its long hangover could hope to do.

Maneuver is not a solution unto itself, any more than technology is. It exists in an ever-readjusting balance with fires. Neither fires nor maneuver can be dispensed with. This sounds obvious, but that which is obvious is not always that which is valued or pursued. Those who would be theorists always prefer the arcane to the actual.

Precious few military campaigns have been won by maneuver alone—at least not since the Renaissance and the days of chessboard battles between corporate condottieri. Napoleon's Ulm campaign, the Japanese march on Singapore, and a few others make up the short list of "bloodless" victories.

Even campaigns that appear to be triumphs of maneuver prove, on closer inspection, to have been successful because of a dynamic combination of fire and maneuver. The opening, conventional phase of the Franco-Prussian War, culminating in the grand envelopment at Sedan, is often cited as an example of brilliant maneuver at the operational level—yet the road to Paris was paved with more German than French corpses. It was a bloody war that happened to be fought on the move. Other campaigns whose success was built on audacious maneuvers nonetheless required attrition battles along the way or at their climax, from Moltke's brilliant concentration on multiple axes at Koenigsgraetz (urgent marches to a gory day), to the German blitzkrieg efforts against the Poles, French, and Russians, and on to Operation Desert Storm, in which daring operational maneuvers positioned tactical firepower for a series of short, convincingly sharp engagements. Even the Inchon landing, one of the two or three most daring operations led by an American field commander, failed to bring the Korean War to a conclusion.

More often than not, an overreliance on bold operational maneuvers to win a swift campaign led to disappointment, even disaster. One may argue for centuries about the diversion of a half dozen German divisions from the right flank of the Schlieffen Plan in 1914, but the attempt to win the war in one swift sweep led to more than four years of stalemate on the Western Front. In the same campaign season, Russian attempts at grand maneuver in the vicinity of the Masurian lakes collapsed in the face of counter-maneuvers and sharp encounter battles—a German active defense that drew on Napoleon's "strategy of the central position"—while, in Galicia, aggressive maneuvering proved to be exactly the wrong approach for the Austro-Hungarian military—which was ill-prepared for encounter battles.

There is no substitute for shedding the enemy's blood.

Despite initial maneuver victories against Russia and in the Western Desert, a German overreliance on maneuver as a substitute for adequate firepower ultimately led to the destruction of Nazi armies. Time and again, from Lee's disastrous Gettysburg campaign to the race to the Yalu in Korea, overconfidence in an army's capabilities to continue to assert its power during grand maneuvers led to stunning reverses. The results were not merely a matter of Clausewitzian culminating points, but of fundamentally flawed strategies.

Operation Iraqi Freedom, one of the most successful military campaigns in history, was intended to be a new kind of war of maneuver, in which aerial weapons would "shock and awe" a humbled opponent into surrender while ground forces did a little light dusting in the house of war. But instead of being decided by maneuvered technologies, the three-week war was fought and won—triumphantly—by soldiers and marines employing both aggressive operational maneuvers *and* devastating tactical firepower.

The point is not that maneuver is the stepbrother of firepower, but that there is no single answer to the battlefield, no formula. The commander's age-old need to balance incisive movements with the application of weaponry is unlikely to change even well beyond our lifetimes. It's not an either-or matter, but about getting the integration right in each specific case.

Although no two campaigns are identical, the closest we can come to an American superpower model of war would be this:

strategic maneuver, then operational maneuver to deliver fires, then tactical fires to enable further maneuver. Increasingly, strategic fires play a role—although they do not win wars or decide them. Of course, no battlefield is ever quite so simple as this proposition, but any force that loses its elementary focus on killing the enemy swiftly and relentlessly until that enemy surrenders unconditionally cripples itself.

Far from entering an age of maneuver, we have entered a new age of attrition warfare in two kinds: First, the war against religious terrorism is unquestionably a war of attrition—if one of your enemies is left alive or unimprisoned, he will continue trying to kill you and destroy your civilization. Second, Operation Iraqi Freedom, for all its dashing maneuvers, provided a new example of a postmodern war of attrition—one in which the casualties are overwhelmingly on one side.

Nothing says that wars of attrition have to be fair.

It's essential to purge our minds of the clichéd images the term "war of attrition" evokes. Certainly, we do not and will not seek wars in which vast casualties are equally distributed between our own forces and the enemy's. But a one-sided war of attrition, enabled by our broad range of superior capabilities, is a strong model for a twenty-first-century American way of war.

No model is consistently applicable. That is—or should be—a given. Wars create exceptions, to the eternal chagrin of military commanders and the consistent embarrassment of theorists. One of our greatest national and military strengths is our adaptability. Unlike many other cultures, we have an almost-primal aversion to wearing the straitjacket of theory, and our independence of mind serves us very well indeed. But the theorists are always there, like devils whispering in our ears, telling us that airpower will win this war, or that satellite "intelligence" obviates the need for human effort, or that a mortal enemy will be persuaded to surrender by a sound-and-light show.

Precision weapons unquestionably have value, but they are expensive and do not cause adequate destruction to impress a hardened enemy. The first time a guided bomb hits the deputy's desk, it will get his chief's attention, but if precision weaponry fails both to annihilate the enemy's leadership and to somehow convince the army and population it has been defeated, it leaves the job to the soldier once again. Those who live in the technological clouds simply do not grasp the importance of graphic, extensive destruction in convincing an opponent of his defeat.

Focus on killing the enemy. With fires. With maneuver. With sticks and stones and polyunsaturated fats. In a disciplined military, aggressive leaders and troops can always be restrained. But it's difficult to persuade leaders schooled in caution that their mission is not to keep an entire corps' tanks on line, but to rip the enemy's heart out. We have made great progress from the ballet of Desert Storm—"spoiled" only by then-Major General Barry McCaffrey's insistence on breaking out of the chorus line and kicking the enemy instead of thin air—to the close-with-the-enemy spirit of last year's race to Baghdad.

In the bitter years after Vietnam, when our national leaders succumbed to the myth that the American people would not tolerate casualties, elements within our military—although certainly not everyone—grew morally and practically timid. By the mid-1990s, the U.S. Army's informal motto appeared to be "We won't fight, and you can't make us."

There were obvious reasons for this. Our military—especially the Army and Marine Corps—felt betrayed by our national leadership over Vietnam. Then President Reagan evacuated Beirut shortly after the bombing of our Marine barracks on the city's outskirts—beginning a long series of bipartisan retreats in the face of terror that ultimately led to 9/11. We hit a low point in Mogadishu, when Army Rangers, Special Operations elements, and line troops delivered a devastating blow against General Aideed's irregulars—only to have President Clinton declare defeat by pulling out. One may argue about the rationale for our presence in Somalia and about the dangers of mission creep, but once we're in a fight, we need to win it—and remain on the battlefield long enough to convince our enemies they've lost on every count.

Things began to change less than two weeks into our campaign in Afghanistan. At first, there was caution—would the new president run as soon as we suffered casualties? Then, as it dawned on our commanders that the administration would stand behind our forces, we saw one of the most innovative campaigns in military history unfold with stunning speed.

Our military, and especially our Army, has come a long way. But we're still in recovery—almost through our Cold War hangover, but still too vulnerable to the nonsense concocted by desk-bound theoreticians. Evaluating lessons learned in Iraq, a recent draft study for a major joint command spoke of the need for "discourses" between commanders at various levels and their staffs.

Trust me. We don't need discourses. We need plain talk, honest answers, and the will to close with the enemy and kill him. And to keep on killing him until it is unmistakably clear to the entire world who won. When military officers start speaking in academic gobbledygook, it means they have nothing to contribute to the effectiveness of our forces. They badly need an assignment to Fallujah.

Consider our enemies in the War on Terror. Men who believe, literally, that they are on a mission from God to destroy your civilization and who regard death as a promotion are not impressed by elegant maneuvers. You must find them, no matter how long it takes, and then kill them. If they surrender, you must accord them their rights under the laws of war and international conventions. But, as we have learned so painfully from all the mindless, left-wing nonsense spouted about the prisoners at Guantanamo, you are much better off killing them before they have a chance to surrender.

We have heard no end of blather about network-centric warfare, to the great profit of defense contractors. If you want to see a superb—and cheap—example of "net-war," look at al Qa'eda. The mere possession of technology does not ensure that it will be used effectively. And effectiveness is what matters.

It isn't a question of whether or not we *want* to fight a war of attrition against religion-fueled terrorists. We're *in* a war of attrition with them. We have no realistic choice. Indeed, our enemies are, in some respects, better suited to both global and local wars of maneuver than we are. They have a world in which to hide, and the world is full of targets for them. They do not heed laws or boundaries. They make and observe no treaties. They do not expect the approval of the United Nations Security Council. They do not face election cycles. And their weapons are largely provided by our own societies.

We have the technical capabilities to deploy globally, but, for now, we are forced to watch as Pakistani forces fumble efforts to surround and destroy concentrations of terrorists; we cannot enter any country (except, temporarily, Iraq) without the permission of its government. We have many tools—military, diplomatic, economic, cultural, law enforcement, and so on—but we have less freedom of maneuver than our enemies.

But we do have superior killing power, once our enemies have been located. Ultimately, the key advantage of a superpower is super power. Faced with implacable enemies who would kill every man, woman, and child in our country and call the killing good (the ultimate war of attrition), we must be willing to use that power wisely, but remorselessly.

We are, militarily and nationally, in a transition phase. Even after 9/11, we do not fully appreciate the cruelty and determination of our enemies. We will learn our lesson, painfully, because the terrorists will not quit. The only solution is to kill them and keep on killing them: a war of attrition. But a war of attrition fought on our terms, not theirs.

Of course, we shall hear no end of fatuous arguments to the effect that we can't kill our way out of the problem. Well, until a better methodology is discovered, killing every terrorist we can find is a good interim solution. The truth is that even if you can't kill yourself out of the problem, you can make the problem a great deal smaller by effective targeting.

And we shall hear that killing terrorists only creates more terrorists. This is sophomoric nonsense. The surest way to swell the ranks of terror is to follow the approach we did in the decade before 9/11 and do nothing of substance. Success breeds success. Everybody loves a winner. The clichés exist because they're true. Al Qa'eda and related terrorist groups metastasized because they were viewed in the Muslim world as standing up to the West successfully and handing the Great Satan America embarrassing defeats with impunity. Some fanatics will flock to the standard of terror no matter what we do. But it's far easier for Islamic societies to purge themselves of terrorists if the terrorists are on the losing end of the global struggle than if they're allowed to become triumphant heroes to every jobless, unstable teenager in the Middle East and beyond.

Far worse than fighting such a war of attrition aggressively is to pretend you're not in one while your enemy keeps on killing you.

Even the occupation of Iraq is a war of attrition. We're doing remarkably well, given the restrictions under which our forces operate. But no grand maneuvers, no gestures of humanity, no offers of conciliation, and no compromises will persuade the terrorists to halt their efforts to disrupt the development of a democratic, rule-of-law Iraq. On the contrary, anything less than relentless pursuit, with both preemptive and retaliatory action, only encourages the terrorists and remaining Ba'athist gangsters.

With hardcore terrorists, it's not about PSYOP or jobs or deploying dental teams. It's about killing them. Even regarding the general population, which benefits from our reconstruction and development efforts, the best thing we can do for them is to kill terrorists and insurgents. Until the people of Iraq are secure, they are not truly free. The terrorists know that. We pretend otherwise.

This will be a long war, stretching beyond many of our lifetimes. And it will be a long war of attrition. We must ensure that the casualties are always disproportionately on the other side.

Curiously, although our military avoids a "body count" in Iraq—body counts have at least as bad a name as wars of attrition—the media insist on one. Sad to say, the body count cherished by the media is the number of our own troops dead and wounded. With our overcaution, we have allowed the media to create a perception that the losses are consistently on our side. By avoiding an enemy body count, we create an impression of our own defeat.

In a war of attrition, numbers matter.

Regarding the other postmodern form of wars of attrition—the high-velocity conventional operations in which maneuver and firepower, speed and violent systemic shock combine to devastate an opposing force—the Army and Marine Corps need to embrace it, instead of allowing the technical services, the Air Force and Navy, to define the future of war (which the Air Force, especially, is defining wrongly). We will not live to see a magical suite of technologies achieve meaningful victories at no cost in human life. We need to oppose that massive lie at every opportunity. The twenty-first century's opening decades, at least, will be dominated by the up-gunned

Cain-and-Abel warfare we have seen from Manhattan to Bali, from Afghanistan's Shamali Plain to Nasiriyeh, from Fallujah to Madrid.

The problem is that the Department of Defense combines two fundamentally different breeds of military services. In the Air Force and the Navy, people support machines. In the Army and Marine Corps, machines support people. Although expensive technologies can have great utility—and Air Force and Navy assets made notable contributions to the Army-Marine victory in Operation Iraqi Freedom—the technical services have a profoundly diminished utility in the extended range of operations we are required to perform, from urban raids to extended occupations, from foot patrols in remote environments to peacemaking.

The Navy is struggling hard with these issues, but the Air Force is the strongest opponent of admitting that we face wars of attrition, since it has invested overwhelmingly in precision weapons designed to win a war by "deconstructing" the enemy's command networks. But the only way you can decisively cripple the command networks of terrorist organizations is by killing terrorists. Even in Operation Iraqi Freedom, airpower made an invaluable contribution, but attacking military and governmental infrastructure targets proved no substitute for destroying enemy forces. When, in midwar, the focus of the air effort shifted from trying to persuade Saddam Hussein to wave a white handkerchief (which he had no incentive to do) to destroying Iraqi military equipment and killing enemy troops, the utility of airpower soared.

It cannot be repeated often enough: Whatever else you aim to do in wartime, never lose your focus on killing the enemy.

A number of the problems we have faced in the aftermath of Operation Iraqi Freedom arose because we tried to moderate the amount of destruction we inflicted on the Iraqi military. The only result was the rise of an Iraqi *Dolchstosslegende*, the notion that they weren't really defeated, but betrayed. Combined with insufficient numbers of Coalition troops to blanket the country—especially the Sunni triangle—in the weeks immediately following the toppling of the regime, crucial portions of the population never really felt America's power.

It is not enough to materially defeat your enemy. You must convince your enemy that he has been defeated. You cannot do that by bombing empty buildings. You must be willing to kill in the short term to save lives and foster peace in the long term.

This essay does not suppose that warfare is simple: "Just go out and kill 'em." Of course, incisive attacks on command networks and control capabilities, well-considered psychological operations, and humane treatment of civilians and prisoners matter profoundly, along with many other complex factors. But at a time when huckster contractors and "experts" who never served in uniform prophesize bloodless wars and sterile victories through technology, it's essential that those who actually must fight our nation's wars not succumb to the facile theories or shimmering vocabulary of those who wish to explain war to our soldiers from comfortable offices.

It is not a matter of whether attrition is good or bad. It's necessary. Only the shedding of their blood defeats resolute enemies. Especially in our struggle with God-obsessed terrorists—the most implacable enemies our nation has ever faced—there is no economical solution. Unquestionably, our long-term strategy must include a wide range of efforts to do what we, as outsiders, can to address the environmental conditions in which terrorism arises and thrives (often disappointingly little—it's a self-help world). But, for now, all we can do is to impress our enemies, our allies, and all the populations in between that we are winning and will continue to win.

The only way to do that is through killing.

The fifth edition of the *Shorter Oxford English Dictionary* defines to "attrit" as to "wear down in quality or quantity by military attrition." That sounds like the next several years, at least, of the War on Terror. The same dictionary defines "attrition" as "the gradual wearing down of an enemy's forces in sustained warfare." Indeed, that is exactly what we shall have to do against religious terrorists. There is no magic maneuver waiting to be plotted on a map. While sharp tactical movements that bring firepower to bear will bring us important successes along the way, this war is going to be a long, hard slog.

The new trenches are ideological and civilizational, involving the most fundamental differences human beings can have—those over the intentions of God and the roles of men and women. In the short term, we shall have to wear down the enemy's forces; in the longer term, we shall have to wear down the appeal of his beliefs.

Our military wars of attrition in the twenty-first century will be only one aspect of a vast metaphysical war of attrition, in which the differences between the sides are so profound they prohibit compromise.

As a result of our recent wars and lesser operations, we have the best-trained, best-led, best-equipped, and most experienced ground forces in the world in our Army and Marine Corps. Potential competitors and even most of our traditional allies have only the knowledge of the classroom and the training range, while we have experience of war and related operations unparalleled in our time. We have the most impressive military establishment, overall, in military history.

Now, if only we could steel ourselves to think clearly and speak plainly: There is no shame in calling reality by its proper name. We are fighting, and will fight, wars of attrition. And we are going to win them.

Ten Lessons from the War in Iraq

Armed Forces Journal

April 2005

Drawing rigid lessons from the military experience of the moment is foolhardy. The human capacity for mischief plays havoc with doctrinaire analysis. Yet our military establishment and, especially, its civilian leadership fell prey to a worse temptation: Clinging to a vision of war as they wished it to be, while the dimensions of conflict changed in ways that mocked their cherished plans.

We need to be wary, but we can't refuse to learn. We must do our best to harvest the enduring lessons from our recent military campaigns, while winnowing out the case-specific issues. Thereafter, we must be merciless in amending our doctrine, our procurement programs, our force structure, and above all, our mentality—if we are to lessen our risks in the grave, new world around us.

Ten lessons from Iraq seem incontestable:

1. **Technology still can't win wars by itself.** Does anyone remember "shock and awe," the farcical concept deskbound theorists sold to civilian Pentagon cadres who lacked military experience? The air campaign that was supposed to defeat Saddam Hussein's regime overnight and prove that ground forces were obsolescent (if not obsolete) was a contractor's fantasy that rapidly became a decision-maker's embarrassment.

Nothing worked as planned. Hundreds of billions of dollars' worth of hardware couldn't persuade a determined opponent to quit. An enemy whose mentality had not even been considered shrugged off our sound-and-light show.

We found that precision weaponry, for all its virtues, could be *too* precise, failing to inflict sufficient pain to create an atmosphere of catastrophic defeat. We preened about "network-centric warfare," but its proven masters aren't our service technocrats. The innovators have been the ragtag terrorists who exploited the internet, cell phones, and the global media far more effectively than we performed with extravagant, irrelevant technologies.

2. **Land warfare still demands ground troops.** The paradox of the high-tech twenty-first century is that the security problems we face are overwhelmingly of flesh and blood, arisen from a rage of souls in failing civilizations. And it still takes human beings to solve human problems—especially during conflicts in that most daunting of human creations, the city.

Soldiers and Marines, grudgingly marshaled in theater, had to win Operation Iraqi Freedom the old-fashioned way, fighting along road and river lines, through sandstorms and ambushes, and then climaxing the land campaign with bold thrusts into Baghdad. They proved, yet again, that muscle and mind still trump metal and microchips. And in counterinsurgency efforts, technology plays a useful, but distinctly secondary, role.

3. **We need those ground troops in sufficient numbers.** Mass is back. Calculating how cheaply military operations can be conducted simply makes them less likely to succeed. Numbers still matter, so if you got 'em, use 'em. Our Army and Marine Corps are too small for our inescapable global roles. Yet, Iraqi Freedom was supposed to pave the way to a cut of two to three Army divisions. Now the Office of the Secretary of Defense (OSD) is struggling to prevent a temporary (and still far from adequate) increase of 30,000 in Army end strength from becoming permanent—in order to preserve funding for Cold War legacy systems. OSD's first loyalties appear to be to the defense industry, rather than to our national defense.

4. **Speed is the dominant battlefield requirement.** In the 1980s, officers spoke of "operating inside the enemy's decision cycle." Today, our forces must "operate inside the media cycle."

The hostile global media, led by al Jazeera, won the First Battle of Fallujah. Our Marines did everything expertly and by the book. But the book called for deliberate urban operations, which gave the media time to muster world opinion against us and break the nerve of key leaders.

We won the Second Battle of Fallujah because we used overwhelming force, we didn't shirk from doing what was necessary—and we did it fast. The full-bore operation was over in less than a week.

Our armed forces will never again face a single opponent on any battleground. We will always be confronted with a third "combatant" at whom we can't return fire: the media. The only way to win is to speed the kill.

5. **The enemy must be convinced of his defeat.** Because we deployed too small a force to Iraq, the ground campaign that brought us Baghdad failed to result in a conclusive victory. The Sunni-Arab heartlands of Iraq—the source of support for Saddam Hussein's regime—never felt the agony of war. Many a Sunni-Arab town or city hardly saw an American soldier or Marine for months after we believed we had won decisively.

Our enemy didn't *feel* defeated. He felt tricked, betrayed, and shamed. Compounding our problems, we worried not only about friendly casualties, but about enemy casualties *during* combat operations—we didn't want to hurt Iraqi feelings. As a result, our technical knockout fostered the rise of a resistance.

The enemy who doesn't suffer may raise his hands above his head, but he won't surrender in his heart. Our enemies and their supporters must be broken down to a sense of utter hopelessness.

6. **The details of combat operations must be left to military professionals.** This is a lesson we just can't seem to learn. Ideology may get you into Baghdad, but it will not get you back out.

We're blessed to have an apolitical military. Attempts to use it for partisan purposes, rather than for our nation's strategic requirements, pervert the institution's essential values. Afraid that the projected costs would be so high it would be difficult to "sell" toppling the Iraqi regime to Congress and the American people, the civilian leadership in OSD refused to allow our military to prepare for a full range of contingencies. Detailed planning for an occupation of Iraq was forbidden. Everything was supposed to happen by magic.

The ideologues got their war, but the result was a great thing done very, very badly. Every American casualty that was suffered during the invasion and the subsequent occupation lies at the feet of the inexperienced civilians in OSD who refused to heed the advice of those who had dedicated their lives to uniformed service.

7. **Occupations have fundamental requirements.** Presence matters. Occupations are manpower-intensive. The defeated population must *see* their occupiers at virtually every turn. There is no such thing as occupation-lite. You must begin with a crushing weight of numbers to psychologically disarm a population shocked by the failure of their national regime. And you must impose martial law immediately.

Martial law has nothing to do with capricious brutality. Rather, it assures the population that their persons and their property will be safe, even though their world has collapsed around them. Martial law only penalizes those who seek lawless advantage or who intend to continue resistance: criminals, insurgents, and terrorists.

Everything we hope to achieve during an occupation stems from the rule of law. And while you can loosen restrictions quickly, if the situation warrants, it's almost impossible to tighten up controls after you have permitted social chaos and rampant criminality to flourish.

It's also essential to involve the local population in the reconstruction of their own country. Turning Iraq into a looting orgy for U.S. contractors was exactly the wrong thing to do: It inflated expectations beyond the possible, while failing to engage a worried, needy population.

It is *always* wise to place as much responsibility for recovery on local shoulders as possible. By immediately hiring local contractors and co-opting the local sources of power by exploiting their greed, we would have saved billions, moved faster, and put hundreds of thousands of young Iraqis to work—instead of leaving them unemployed and embittered. The repairs might have been inefficient and payrolls certainly would have been padded, but that would have worked to our advantage.

Put people to work, and keep them busy. Get the delinquents off the street corners. When complaints arise that the power isn't on or the taps remain dry, you can point to the local entrepreneurs you paid to provide for their compatriots.

Devolve onerous responsibilities as quickly as possible, while maintaining a monopoly on power. Besides, the Iraqis knew how to repair their own infrastructure. For all of our technological prowess, we didn't.

8. **Military intelligence is broken.** Despite some fine tactical improvisation, it's undeniable that our military intelligence services, as presently configured, are incapable of providing the intense, incisive, and imaginative support combat commanders require. The reason is simple: We trusted technology and slighted the human factor.

Our intelligence system remains better suited to fighting the absent-without-leave Soviet Union than it is to the ultra-human struggles in which we have found ourselves—and which will dominate our military future. Why did we place technology above people? Because the human factor is troublesome, undependable, and frustrating.

But human talent is nonetheless indispensable. Satellites can't peer into the human soul. Computers can't predict what an enemy will do impulsively. Nor will any machine do so in our lifetimes, despite the extravagant promises of the apostles of technology.

I recall visiting Fort Huachuca, Arizona, in 1984. A lieutenant colonel assured me that, by the 1990s, intelligence hands like me would be obsolete. Artificial intelligence was going to solve all of our problems. He was wrong, of course. But his promises have been replaced with other, equally foolish claims.

If we were forced to discard every technical-collection system to which we have enslaved ourselves, but could replace the hardware with more skilled analysts, agents, and interrogators, we would be far more successful. Certainly, technology can help us. But there is no substitute for talented, trained, and dedicated human minds fixed on our enemies.

9. **Language skills and cultural knowledge are vital combat multipliers.** A single officer fluent in the local language and aware

of cultural nuances can be far more valuable to our military than entire squadrons of F/A-22s.

If there is any single factor our military services neglect that could enhance our strategic and tactical performance, it's the command of foreign languages. How can we "know our enemies" if we don't know what they're saying?

Although valuable, current foreign-area-officer programs and hasty predeployment courses barely scratch the surface of our needs. Officers should be required to develop at least a rudimentary ability in one high-threat foreign language, and superior skill levels should be rewarded handsomely. This goes against our thinking about what an officer should be, but we are going to have to change our thinking as the world changes around us.

A battalion commander forced to rely on a local-hire translator is no longer the most powerful figure in his or her battalion. We will never penetrate our enemy's local codes unless we can enter his mindset, and language skills are the indispensable key.

The reply I got from one four-star general that "OPMS won't support language training for officers" was fodder for satire. If the Officer Personnel Management System isn't giving us what we need, then we need to change the system. And wartime is the one time when we can do it.

To their credit, the Marines are shaping an ambitious language-skills program. The Army must make a similar commitment. Languages are weapons.

10. **The three crucial types of operations in which our forces will engage are strategic raids, punitive expeditions, and full-scale invasions, followed by occupations.** Forget the self-imposed rule that "if you break it, you own it." Although our extended presence in both Afghanistan and Iraq makes sense, we can't reconstruct every troubled society on earth. And some (think Somalia) will be so fundamentally hostile to our values that we can only punish them and leave.

While the forms of conflict are complex, ever-mutating and never fully predictable, we can project the need for brief strategic raids that strike finite targets, then leave; longer punitive expeditions that engage a more complex enemy, reduce his capabilities, then leave; and full-scale invasions, some of which will be followed by occupations.

Such operations demand an expeditionary mentality in every service, but that's only a return to our military heritage. From the "shores of Tripoli" to the Army's campaign against the Moros, from our frontier days to clandestine special operations, we've known how to fight, win, and when appropriate, leave.

Certainly, there will be times when we wish to extend a helping hand to the opponent we knocked down. But some enemies should just be left lying there. Empires, even postmodern ones, need to be able to tell the difference.

The Shape of Wars to Come

Armed Forces Journal

May 2005

Beyond the ever-growing range of operations short of combat, there are three types of warfare that the future will force us to master: strategic raids, punitive expeditions, and general wars waged on expanded terms. No category is pure. One form may lead to or include another. Yet there are demands, purposes, and dilemmas specific to each, some peculiar to our position as the world's dominant power. We can no longer think in the theoretician's abstract terms about war but must address the specific issues that face America's armed forces.

Our military is fated to serve as an expeditionary force for an empire based not upon traditional conquests, but on values and ideas. We will take the fight to our enemies—men whose values are irreconcilable with our own and who substitute often-primitive beliefs for ideas of freedom and justice. At times, our opponents will be feudal bands equipped with postmodern technologies; on other occasions, we may confront traditional states. The core issues are who we will send to the fight, how long we will stay, and what we will hope to achieve. None of the possible answers are as clear-cut as they might appear to conventional thinkers.

STRATEGIC RAIDS

The necessity for a much-enhanced ability to conduct strategic raids goes well beyond the present struggle with terrorism. From eliminating or capturing our mortal enemies to enforcing nuclear security, the capability to dispatch a small but potent force anywhere in the world on short notice isn't a luxury or an add-on capability. This is a fundamental requirement for postmodern security. Having established a precedent for strategic preemption, we need to reassert it whenever the necessity appears.

Strategic raids may be diplomatically risky at times, but our position in the world demands that we be prepared to violate traditional concepts of sovereignty in order to prevent avoidable tragedies—or simply to stop a small threat before it becomes a great one. The crucial requirement isn't global approval, but success. We can afford occasional hard feelings, but we cannot afford to fail. The destruction of a terrorist base will be forgiven as soon as the news cycle shifts, but every "Desert One" has consequences far beyond the immediate embarrassment. Success is forgiven, but failure has lasting penalties.

Strategic raids will come in many designs, with widely varying force packages. Some may be conducted with standoff weapons alone. But we cannot afford puny, token, and ineffective strikes, such as we saw in the Clinton years. Every failure strengthens the enemy's confidence and resolve. Whether small or complex, single-service or joint, strategic raids must be decisive. Every service will have a contribution to make—if not in one raid, then in another— but all will need to revitalize their thinking and pursue practical capabilities to enable us to act with stunning swiftness and irresistible force. This has implications for everything from strategic transport and communications to body armor and ammunition weight, but above all, it requires a far more capable and appropriate intelligence capability than our current system provides.

PUNITIVE EXPEDITIONS

We may need to invent a more politically correct name, but the need to think in terms of twenty-first-century equivalents to classic punitive expeditions seems incontestable. Not every country or culture can be redeemed, reformed, and remodeled. In the age of terror and other nonstate threats, we may find it increasingly necessary to enter a territory to conduct operations more extensive and of greater duration than raids, but without the intent to remain any longer than necessary to accomplish the mission. Should we need to deploy to Somalia to destroy terrorist bases, for example, we would be foolish to imagine that a static presence thereafter would be of any benefit to us. Knowing how and when to leave is every bit as important, and often more difficult, than determining how to attack in the first place.

Tomorrow's punitive expeditions may occur in vast jungle expanses—or in the metastasizing cities of the developing world. But we must achieve greater mobility for the entire force engaged—instead of building semipermanent bases, we need to think in terms of a frontier cavalry, forever on the move and bound only to the mission, not to the terrain. Designing the force package appropriate to each effort will require far more imagination than we currently display and the annihilation of traditional concepts of each service's limited roles. Far too many of the impediments to our effectiveness are self-imposed—failures of vision, rather than a lack of physical capabilities.

Postmodern punitive expeditions won't involve burning homes and killing the cattle, but may include the destruction of an infrastructure upon which our enemy relies. Punitive expeditions have to punish. We have gotten too far away from the psychology of war, imagining that we must handle even enemies gently. But ferocity in the short term usually proves most humane in the longer term. Enemies, immediate or potential, must harbor no doubts about our resolve. This will require a major shift in our thinking, but reality will force it upon us.

POSTMODERN GENERAL WAR
Postmodern general wars may range from our recent three-week campaign in Iraq to an extended conflict with an upstart state or alliance in the out-years. They involve a vision of a more extended—sometimes enduring—commitment of forces than punitive expeditions. Yet both operations have a common requirement: To be effective, we must discard the nonsensical maxim that "if you break it, you own it." Many countries in which we may have to operate are already broken. We would be foolish to impose upon ourselves the obligation to repair them. Even if we could afford it, we often could not accomplish it.

First, the war must be fought and won, of course. We can do that, although the price will vary. The greater danger lies in our thoughtless assumption that the U.S. military must always stay until war's damage is repaired and every last bedroom repainted. At times, as in Afghanistan and Iraq, there will be sound strategic reasons for remaining on the scene or even for staging a full-scale occupation. But we must learn to tell the difference between a society or culture that can be prodded back into shape and one that is genuinely hopeless. The purpose of fighting a war is to win it, not necessarily to indulge ourselves in political and social interior decorating. Assuring an enemy that war will have no lasting penalties only makes war more likely.

THE ARMY WE NEED
Although we must beware of asymmetrical technologies and innovative thinking in the enemy's camp, the odds are that we will continue to get the machinery of war right. We have made such a deep, long-term capital investment in systems (some far more useful than others) that alarms about any country, including China, racing from behind to challenge us head-on at high noon have more to do with defense-industry marketing and service-staff fantasies than with real possibilities. The one worrisome deficit we already face—and which is unlikely to be alleviated in the future—is in our ground forces. Reviled as expensive and inefficient, land forces continue to be the fundamental requirement for warfare.

We can compensate for every other deficiency because of our redundant systems, but there is no quick and good fix for an abrupt need for more flesh and blood, trained and in uniform. Budget limitations always demand trade-offs, but the greatest single vulnerability within our armed forces is our austere troop strength. A catastrophic battlefield loss, either to weapons of mass destruction or to an innovative technology, could not be repaired using a World War II-draft model. The skills required for today's infantryman to be effective are an order of magnitude greater than those essential to the rifleman of sixty-plus years ago.

As our defense secretary notoriously (and inappropriately) remarked, "You go to war with the Army you've got." But we may not have the Army we need for future wars or the Marine Corps that global commitments will demand. The time to expand the force is now, not after additional years of Defense Department sleight of hand, deception, and self-delusion.

This is not intended to slight the contributions of either our Navy or our Air Force. Both are peerless, in every sense of the word. But those services face no significant threats and enjoy an indisputable window of superiority that will last for decades. The worst dangers, most frequent challenges, and most consuming missions face our ground forces. And the Army and Marines are just too small. The issue isn't efficiency, but effectiveness and residual capability. We must distinguish between that which we are accustomed to having and that which we truly need.

Cold War divisions of the budget pie were not written in fire by a divine finger. The exigencies of wartime have forced some temporary reallocations of funds, but we need to consider our country's genuine twenty-first-century military needs, rather than succumbing to force of habit. There is always a lobby for another weapons system, but none for the common soldier. We need to rethink our budgeting process from top to bottom, to rid ourselves of inherited prejudices in favor of innovative solutions.

Above all, we need to *think,* to stop comforting ourselves with slogans when we need creative thought about making war (in a recent, otherwise useful discussion with Air Force generals, I heard the words "air dominance" so often I thought I was listening to the chanting of Buddhist monks).

Of course, we cannot predict the contours of future wars with precision. We need to maintain a flexible force with wide-ranging capabilities. But we have downplayed the human factor for far too long. A basic rule of this high-tech century is that our security challenges are fundamentally—sometimes appallingly—human. And it still takes human beings, whether analysts, agents, or Airborne Rangers, to solve war's human problems.

In the technical services, the Navy and the Air Force, we need to examine our obsession with downsizing numbers, whether of personnel or systems, while claiming that greater efficiency makes it possible to maintain a smaller military establishment. No matter how capable a combat system may be, at some point, less is just less. Efficiency studies collapse on the battlefield, just as the notion of sending "just enough" troops proved a massive error when we occu-pied Iraq. Postmodern weapons offer us marvelous capabilities, but one is rarely as good as a hundred, no matter the qualitative differ-ence. Numbers have a power all their own—when your magazine is empty, an enemy armed with a kitchen knife can kill you.

The Navy has already begun, albeit haltingly, to discuss the pos-sible need for more, but smaller, ships. For its part, the Air Force must strive to think beyond its current dogma and ask if a mix of high-tech and mid-tech aircraft might not be more desirable than a severely shrunken fleet of planes so expensive the service dreads losing a single one.

SELF-IMPOSED RESTRICTIONS
The other great requirement for effectiveness in waging full-scale warfare in this new century is to free ourselves of self-imposed restrictions on everything from concepts of "legal" targeting to our dread of shedding even our enemy's blood. At a time when alterna-tive powers, from terrorist bands to Chinese military thinkers, are constantly broadening their definitions of warfare, we have nar-rowed our concept of war so severely that we may be astonished (as we were on September 11, 2001) by the breadth of our enemy's vision and his readiness to reject our narrow rules.

Warfare is not a moral endeavor, and unilateral restrictions will not make it one. The purpose of waging war is to win. All else is sec-ondary. The greatest "combat multiplier" we could have in this new age would be simply an unbreakable will to win, no matter the cost, on the part of our nation's leaders.

Whether we speak of strategic raids, punitive expeditions, or postmodern general wars, only victory is moral. There is no virtue in failure.

How to Defeat America

Armed Forces Journal

June 2005

Our country's leaders and opinion-makers refuse to face the realities of war in the twenty-first century. Lulled by impressive battlefield successes in Afghanistan and Iraq, where our military overmatch obscured the changing terms of conflict, we continue to restrict our definition of what is permissible in warfare while real and potential enemies broaden their visions of how the struggles of the future must be fought.

We want to wage war as cleanly as possible, to limit costs and consequences. Our enemies are prepared to fight on fronts we barely imagine and to embrace the cataclysmic nature of conflict. We seek narrow, manageable wars, but our opponents believe that defeating America demands a new form of total war waged so widely it has no modern precedent.

Our terrorist enemies of the moment are heralds of the future, even as they are throwbacks to the past. As we agonize over which targets are legal, they reject all laws of war, traditional or codified. We worry over the means; they focus on ends. Afraid to speak forthrightly about war, we allowed the ugly, but minor, abuses at the Abu Ghraib prison to become a paralyzing issue, while terrorists delighted in beheading hostages on videotape. We want to restrict our aim to enemy combatants, but our present and future enemies target social, economic, information, educational, health care, and belief systems. We attempt to limit the number of enemy casualties, while our enemies focus on inflicting as many casualties as possible on us, our allies, and civilian populations.

Our ideal war would have no penalties for anyone involved, while our enemies revel in inflicting penalties on our soldiers and on civilians. We hope to bribe our enemies into loving us, but the hard currency of war is fear. To placate critics who remain safely at home, we rush to punish combat veterans for battlefield missteps. We attempt to make war with lawyers at the commander's elbow, while our enemies turn our own delusions against us.

We are afraid to win. But neither can today's terrorists win—unless we quit. If we can avoid outright foolishness, terrorism will be defeated, if not eradicated. Yet terrorists, ragtag militias, and globo-criminals are far from the only dangers to our safety and our civilization. The minds behind the foreign militaries of the future are thinking far more creatively and ruthlessly than we allow ourselves to do.

A major war with China is unlikely, but its potential costs demand that we consider the prospect more imaginatively than we have allowed ourselves to do (and China serves as the maximal model of future opponents). For now, a war with China is little more to us than a construct deployed to justify the purchase of weapons systems conceived to fight the long-gone Soviet military. Should such a war occur, we assume it would be fought head-on, military to military.

But the Chinese (and even our potential allies, the Indians) believe that the only way to win against the United States—or to achieve a useful stalemate—is to rethink war itself. As a minimum, future opponents will refuse to play by our rules. From the terrorists of the Middle East to the general staffs of Asia, the key questions are: On how many nontraditional fronts can we engage? How can we inflict unbearable pain on American society? And even if we cannot defeat America, how can we make an American victory impossible?

In the course of a recent discussion, an Air Force general asked me what I would do if I were an enemy planning a war with the United States. My immediate answer was, "Three things: Pursue weapons of mass destruction; do whatever it takes to win the global media battle; and employ mass—military and civilian—against the numerically inferior U.S. armed forces in their technological straitjackets."

WEAPONS OF MASS DESTRUCTION

We need to get beyond the traditional, limited definition that includes only nukes, bugs, and gas. Each of those remains of great potential value to an enemy. Nuclear weapons (and imitative devices) can inflict mass casualties, destroy major weapons platforms, and play havoc with American battlefield electronics, our new and self-imposed Achilles' heel. Biological weapons have great terror value and, properly engineered, could be a catastrophic weapon of last resort for a power convinced it could trade population more readily than the United States could do. Chemical weapons, while useful in slowing battlefield activities, may be most effective as terror weapons directed against civilians.

But we need to think in more innovative terms, to consider effects as well as tools. In our super-developed society, the digital attacks of the future, conducted as part of a comprehensive effort, could do more damage than many traditional WMDs. Wouldn't a grand attack, employing cyber-sabotage and physical damage, on our all-too-vulnerable power-generation and -distribution network amount to a "strategy of mass destruction"? Wartime strikes that produced sustained power failures could lead to far more deaths than a terrorist attack with chemical or biological weapons. An energy-dependent society such as ours simply could not function if widespread power outages lasted months or even weeks.

Likewise, our overcentralized food supply is far easier to disrupt than that of an underdeveloped country. The massive processing facilities that replaced local suppliers can be brought to a standstill by introducing disease carriers or polluting key production nodes. Few might starve, but mass panic and defeatism could be even more valuable to our enemies. Similarly, strikes against our fuel processing, storage, and distribution system would have an effect an order of magnitude greater than such actions would have had in the primitive era of World War II.

Yet each of the vulnerabilities highlighted above, if examined in isolation (as the war on terrorism has conditioned us to do), makes the challenge of future total war seem less menacing than it is. No state enemy bold enough to confront the United States in future decades would content itself with one-off attacks against a single aspect of our infrastructure. The key for such an enemy would be to conduct layered, simultaneous, stand-off attacks to achieve devastating synergy. Well-designed, efficient strikes against key nodes in our power, communications, energy, and food-supply sectors could achieve far greater results than a concentration on the complete destruction of any one source of our well-being.

How to beat America? Fight holding actions against its military, inflicting as many casualties as possible, while punishing the homeland. Attack America's information systems, sabotage its crucial data banks, make it difficult to conduct everyday routines, excite competition for resources taken for granted, and above all, introduce fear. Attack the brain, rather than the body. The most effective biological weapon might not be one with a 90 percent mortality rate, but an engineered or refined disease with a 30 percent mortality rate and graphic symptoms that left survivors with enduring health problems.

PARALYZE THE SOCIETY
Just as it is often more useful to wound an enemy, rather than kill him, thus inflicting the additional systemic costs of evacuating and treating the casualty, so, too, shocking the civilian health-care system with enormous numbers of disease victims terrified of dying could be more useful than simply causing large numbers of deaths.

Preparation of the battlefield for future war would involve weakening the financial position of the United States during the buildup to war, hollowing out our industrial base and inducing reliance on foreign sources of crucial supplies that could be interdicted (sound uncomfortably familiar?). Propaganda, too, would be far more useful if developed carefully and employed for years prior to a conflict rather than if it were introduced during a fast-moving war. Future state opponents will attempt to win as much of the conflict as possible before our military engages.

Above all, the enemy of the future wins simply by not losing. WMD, defined far more broadly than we do today, will be a part of any wise enemy's war plan. We need to escape the narrow vision we have of WMD by incorporating new categories, from tomorrow's behavior-control weapons to advanced digital attacks.

WIN THE GLOBAL MEDIA BATTLE
The first purpose of this is to align world opinion against the United States and to cause America's active allies to withdraw from

the conflict, denying us legitimacy, bases, numbers, resources, and moral support. The media struggle would also aim to add another level of paralysis to our war-making efforts by inspiring a series of disparate regional crises that dissipated American power and complicated Washington's decisionmaking processes. The ultimate goal would be to interact with other asymmetric assaults to convince Americans that the price of continuing the war is too great to bear.

Although it certainly would be foolish for an opponent to underestimate American courage and resolve (as the terrorists did on 9/11), we also must avoid relying on false historical analogies. Yes, the Germans and Japanese continued to resist, despite extensive bombing campaigns that produced mass civilian casualties. And I'm not suggesting that Americans would rush to surrender (although a weak administration might negotiate for peace). But we do need to assess the enormous distance developed societies have traveled since the 1940s, when Germany's agriculture was horse-powered, Japan's food supplies were local, access to data was limited, and the world still walked to work. The societies of World War II were sustainable under bombardment. Could ours endure multiple catastrophic disruptions, even in the absence of casualties?

Complexity equals fragility. The American character may remain robust, but our infrastructure is more vulnerable than it ever has been. By layering cataclysms atop one another, while exploiting the power of the global media to publicize events, could a twenty-first-century enemy persuade us to seek a disadvantageous peace? The ultimate mission of the enemy's media fight is to convince Americans to quit.

EMPLOY MASS

In order to defeat the United States in a future war, an enemy will need to calculate ruthlessly when it comes to accepting—or actively pursuing—high numbers of casualties on his own side. Whether unleashing biological weapons or forcing nuclear exchanges, the side that believes it has a clear demographic advantage is the side that will raise the stakes with less hesitation. Whether the goal is to inflict a catastrophic defeat upon the United States or only to gain a specific strategic advantage, an enemy who does not fear his own losses, military or civilian, has a tremendous psychological edge.

On a lesser scale, terrorists have been willing to inflict civilian casualties on their host societies when they found it tactically advantageous or, even better, if they could shift the blame onto American shoulders (with the media's help). In a general war, civilian casualties that could be blamed, however questionably, on American forces would support the global media struggle. Our enemies will seek to win with blood—as much of their own as necessary. This does not mean that we should hesitate to act, only that we must be prepared to endure the second- and third-order effects.

When fighting against America's superior technology, deploy superior numbers of human beings. Force Americans to kill and to keep on killing. Shock the Americans with your willingness to suffer casualties. Create images of massacre. Give the Americans no respite. Force the Americans to appear as murderous bullies.

Human beings aren't the only tools available to "swarm" American efforts. If there is one obvious vulnerability to America's techno-services—our Air Force and Navy—it lies in the ever-diminishing numbers of combat systems they can deploy. Our pursuit of hyper-capable, devastatingly expensive aircraft and ships means that we have ever fewer of them. One grows sick of hearing how less is really more. At some point, less is just less.

When the risk of losing an aircraft or ship becomes a dominant consideration in shaping a war plan, we have crippled ourselves before the shooting starts. The Navy is terrified of losing an aircraft carrier (let alone several). Conditioned to peace, the Air Force dreads risking a single B-2—and the F/A-22, should we buy more of those grotesquely useless aircraft, is unlikely to be employed boldly, even if a mission could be found for it.

No matter the hyperbolic promises of defense contractors, a single system can only address a finite number of threats. Instead of attempting to compete with the U.S. military technologically, the obvious counter is to field overwhelming numbers of midtech systems—enough to sacrifice nine aircraft for the tenth to down a weapons-depleted American fighter. Attack American ships with volleys and short-interval waves of cruise missiles and alternative weapons, as well as with weapons of mass destruction.

Shock the overrefined American system by introducing multiple threats that U.S. collection systems may well be able to identify, but which the limited number of available American combat systems will not be able to defeat. Use mass and speed against the United States Navy and Air Force. Use human attrition against the Army and Marines. If you cannot defeat the United States in a traditional sense, make the cost of sustaining the conflict unbearable.

As we try to make of war a sterile thing, with minimal pain and embarrassment, with slight bloodshed and little damage, our enemies of the moment and our potential future opponents calculate how to make war as destructive and painful as possible. We design weapons to produce ever smaller, more precise effects, to minimize collateral damage. For our enemies, the collateral damage is increasingly the point. We have deluded ourselves as to the nature of war by falling for surreal theories concocted by think tanks and listening to the divorced-from-reality promises of contractors for whom war is a matter of profit and abstractions.

Instead of attempting to narrow war down to a "cakewalk" without penalties—a polite affair we can win on technical points—we need to expand our definition of warfare as widely as our enemies are doing. This does not mean that we will imitate all of their behaviors, only that we need to be ready to counter them.

We have entered a new age of comprehensive war. The old rules are finished. We need to learn the new ones, to the extent that rules still exist.

The Ultimate Weapon

Armed Forces Journal

August 2005

For decades our military has fielded weapons that deliver unprecedented capabilities. Commanders control tools that their predecessors could hardly have imagined. If wars were won on technical specifications, it would be impossible for us to lose.

But wars are won by human beings, not machines. Technological wonders may assist us, but they cannot substitute for courage and strength of will. Indeed, the centerpiece precision weapons that theorists insisted had "changed the nature of war" proved to be self-defeating and morally corrosive when far too much was expected of them. We began to plan our wars around our weapons, rather than fielding weapons to suit our wars. A tactical enabler, technology turned out to be a strategic tyrant.

The price of precision has been dangerously shrunken arsenals, fantasies of bloodless war, and combat without the graphic destruction and casualties essential to convince an enemy of his defeat. Without precise intelligence—which we rarely possess—precision weapons make very expensive holes in the wrong walls and only encourage further enemy resistance.

Despite claims of revolutionary effects, precision weapons are simply linear extrapolations of weapons of the past. The roots of precision-strike capabilities lie in the massive numbers of bombs, aircraft, and lives it took to destroy targets in Nazi Germany. Naturally, we wanted to do what we had to do more cheaply in terms of lives and aircraft. But the critical distinction weapons developers failed to make—as they fell in love with technology for its own sake—is that precision weapons are about efficiency, while warfare demands effectiveness.

A single aircraft with a single bomb may destroy a bridge or bunker that would have required repeated missions and cost dozens of aircraft even a generation ago. But in our quest for tidy solutions to the bloody dilemmas of war we forgot that, while reducing our own pain is desirable, reducing our enemy's suffering is not.

Precision weapons are splendid for striking a terrorist hideout, if you can find one, but they have only collateral value in winning wars. That value turns negative rapidly, if unrealistic expectations are raised. Promising too much—as the advocates of techno-war invariably do—results in a popular sense of failure even when we perform well above historical norms.

BREAKTHROUGH WEAPON

But the worst sin of the precision-weapons advocates has been their neglect of the enemy's psychology. A determined opponent must suffer, often terribly. If he does not, he has no incentive to surrender. We are trying to fistfight with feathers.

We analyze war as engineers and attempt to wage it as diplomats. Our enemies, present and potential, think about war as strategists and fight like savages. The asymmetry is not in our favor.

For all of our undeniable, sometimes-valuable technological triumphs, it took our impoverished enemies to develop that breakthrough weapon of our time, the suicide bomber. Cheap, disposable, bloodcurdling, and dauntingly precise, the suicide bomber's perfect guidance system and practical utility negates our expensive advantages at the tactical level—with strategic effect. Explosives, an old car, one willing martyr, and good human intelligence (an outlay of a few hundred dollars, if you steal the car) amount to a weapon that's effective *and* efficient. Terrifying, too.

The suicide bomber is impossible to deter and difficult to interdict. Our expensive aircraft burn fuel above Iraq as generals huddle with lawyers and politicians refuse to accept war's reality. Meanwhile, our enemy is teaching us what warfare means when the nonsense is stripped away: It is about imposing your will on the enemy, any way you can and without hesitation or scruples.

We approach war in terror of lawsuits and criminal charges. Our enemies are enthusiastic killers. Who has the psychological advantage?

Among the many sound reasons for opposing the F/A-22 fighter or the Virginia-class submarine is the fact that such systems, for all their technical qualities, are linear developments of the last century's weapons. Buying them locks us into obsolescent modalities of warfare. We become prisoners of our very expensive purchases.

Advertisements may claim that this or that platform is "revolutionary," but it's difficult to find a single system under development for any service that breaks with inherited concepts of how we should equip, organize, and fight.

The closest thing we have to a revolutionary system at present is the unmanned aerial vehicle (UAV). In the long term, UAV technology may help us achieve remarkable successes in specific forms of conflict, such as combating terrorism, though UAVs will not win general wars.

The most useful UAV capabilities for the peculiar forms of militarized police work our age demands would be "bloodhound" technologies that target a single individual—a high-value target—or a series of individuals who fit a hostile profile, whether terrorists or enemy soldiers. Tomorrow's UAVs should do the work of bounty hunters. We cannot predict with confidence which line of research might prove the most effective in developing tomorrow's hunter-killer UAVs, but various recognition technologies will take us far beyond current limitations.

Future UAVs will be able to loiter, go to ground, hide indefinitely, calculate, and patiently hunt their quarry. Target identifiers may be any combination of visual recognition, scent identification, behavioral profiling, association patterns, or hypercomplex programs that still lie beyond the horizon. The UAV that "fox hunts" is inevitable, and it will be a great aid when it comes.

But the war-winning technology of this century will be far more comprehensive in its effects and vastly more terrifying in its capabilities than the most lethal UAV. The bad news is that our enemies are apt to develop that wonder-weapon first, since it contradicts every illusion we have come to cherish about war.

The military equipment we currently own shackles our imaginations. We can't see beyond our trillions of dollars of hardware. Unencumbered by our wealth of possessions, our enemies are free to dream.

IDEAL WEAPON

The twenty-first-century weapon of genius will be far darker than nuclear bombs or even engineered viruses. It will cut to the soul of warfare, focusing on war's fundamental purpose. Potential state enemies, such as China, are far more likely to pursue it than we are. And none of the weapons we have under development will have the least effect against it.

What is the purpose of going to war? To convince the enemy to submit to your will. What would the ideal weapon do? Reach past every physical defense to control the enemy's behavior.

The weapons of tomorrow will be behavior-control technologies that penetrate titanium and bone to target the human brain and nervous system. And they're closer than anyone thinks.

Certainly, a well-aimed bullet, or even a spear, makes a very effective behavior-control weapon under the right circumstances. *All* weapons aim at convincing the enemy to surrender. But imagine a weapon that could reach into the sky and, instead of shooting down an aircraft, fatally disorient the pilot or even take control of his decisionmaking ability. Imagine a weapon that could persuade a targeted individual of an attacker's good intentions, render a squad unable to think, paralyze an aircraft carrier's entire crew or strip the will to fight from a field army—or a nation.

We wrack our brains about how to build more effective aircraft, more survivable ships, and safer personnel carriers. But our present and potential enemies know they cannot compete within such conventional parameters. Even now, terrorists concentrate on reaching past the military metal to the consciousness of the masses: They already view the media as a behavior-shaping weapon. Tomorrow's grander enemies may focus on directly disabling the human brains serving the "unsinkable" ship and on crippling the minds that move combat vehicles forward.

We have become so enchanted with technology that we have lost sight of the purpose of any war. Possessing less, our enemies must think harder. Terrorists and developing-world colonels alike understand that war is a contest of wills in which any rule may be broken, while we fight as if afraid of committing a foul. Despite our recent experiences, we suffer from an imagination deficit when it comes to warfare.

Behavior-control weapons aren't even a new concept. The Soviets were interested in them before their empire's collapse. The extent to which the Russians continue to pursue such technologies today remains unclear, but it would be surprising if the Chinese (or even the Indians) were not deeply interested in developing capabilities that allowed them to leap past our physical superiority.

Given our research-and-development infrastructure, we would have the best chance of developing a suite of behavior-control technologies, but remain the least likely to investigate such revolutionary capabilities. The reasons range from our mammoth investment (sunk costs) in equipping our forces for war through the defense industry's fear that such weapons might derail profitable programs to ethical concerns.

We are suffocating under the weight of the force we currently have and suffering from a mind-set that demands ever-better versions of the weapons with which we're comfortable. We need to pause and consider that, should an enemy develop behavior-control weapons, the only reliable deterrent would be even more capable weapons of our own. If we find ourselves defenseless, we may, literally, never know what hit us. We could possess the finest traditional military in history, yet find ourselves enslaved.

DRUGS AND MUSIC

There are so many potential approaches to behavior-control weapons that it's impossible to forecast which type will appear first, but the advent of such tools is a question of when, not if. These will be the ultimate weapons of war, able to pierce the chaos and cost of battle to literally change an enemy's mind.

In one of the hideous paradoxes of which history is so fond, we may see our dream of bloodless war come true at last—but in place of gore we could see thousands (or millions) of human beings with permanently impaired mental faculties. The irreparable destruction of decisionmaking powers or even consciousness could result in the casualties of the future being veterans with severely diminished mental capacities—perhaps unable to perform routine functions—or even large segments of the population reduced to a status of "living dead." At best, we might hope for Orwellian weapons that would merely make us do our master's bidding without a thought.

Imagine a battlefield on which, in the space of moments, we were confronted with thousands of American troops reduced to an infantile state from which there would be no possibility of recovery. What if an enemy then threatened to turn such a weapon on our civilian population?

Were we even to consider developing such weapons ourselves, our line of research would pursue the ability to inflict temporary effects that created windows of opportunity, while avoiding permanent "inhumane" damage. Our enemies would not have such scruples. From the perspective of a power facing war with the United States, the more terrifying the results of a weapon's use, the likelier it would be to collapse the will of our government and population. In the language of an earlier age of danger, we would pursue "low-yield" solutions, while our enemies would strive for the largest yields attainable.

Strategic behavior-control weapons may be generations away; however, given the pace and nonlinearity of technological change, we simply cannot know. But the initial tactical systems probably will be difficult to calibrate for "nonscarring" impacts. More sophisticated, better-focused behavior-control weapons might appear eventually, but the first such weapons fielded may be indiscriminate and devastating to the victims—again, better suited to the temperament of our enemies than to our own.

There is also a possibility that the first power to possess a strategic behavior-control capability will achieve such global control that there would be no need to further develop the weapon. Far from seeing universal democracy in the future, behavior-control weapons in the wrong hands could result in universal slavery.

If this sounds like the stuff of science fiction, consider a few developments that point toward behavior-control weapons.

Last spring, a scientific study concluded that a compound derived from studying the brain could inspire unwarranted trust in the person who inhaled it, disarming innate suspicions. Corporate America doubtless leapt to attention, dreaming of how such a formula might be employed against the American consumer, but the military implication was obvious and, presumably, ignored. What if an aerosol deployed on the battlefield could erase an enemy's hostility and create friendly feelings toward the opponent? What if the new chemical warfare transformed a combatant's attitude from "Kill 'em all!" to "Hey, peace, dude!"? What if such a weapon could be applied to an entire city? By an enemy bent on savagery, not on taking prisoners?

In truth, behavior-control weapons have existed for generations, although the military exploits them halfheartedly. Packaged-content broadcast and communications means, from radio through television to the internet, all successfully alter human behavior, persuading us to watch this, read that, and above all, buy the advertised product. What is a good television commercial if not an exercise in behavior control? Internet offers modify our behavior. And you're likelier to get a speeding ticket while listening to a heavy metal radio station than while tuning in to a Chopin nocturne.

Broadcast sound, then sound and image compounded, have proved to be such extraordinarily successful behavior-modification tools that businesses around the world spend billions of dollars on advertising each year. If commercials didn't work, they would have disappeared. But we *do* buy what we are told to buy.

What if a future broadcast weapon could exploit tomorrow's research into the finest nuances of brain function and compact a lifetime's worth of persuasive sensory effects into a burst transmission "shot" at a bomber's crew? What if we could move beyond the need for pictures and noise to excite associative responses to work directly upon the electrical or chemical reactions within the brain?

We've known since the interwar years that sonic effects can shape the behavior of crowds. At Nazi rallies, subsonic bass tones were used to unsettle the audience and prepare it for a frenzied response to Hitler. Music has been a part of war and politics for centuries. Sonic weapons that combine extreme intensity with the artful manipulation of cognition may achieve far more than rap music blared at today's terrorist prisoners can do. The light shows of 1960s San Francisco may prove to be the grandparents of tomorrow's sensory manipulation systems, while the CIA's prehippie-era experimentation with LSD may simply have been too far ahead of its time.

How do you induce euphoric passivity in a tank crew? "Better living through chemistry," as a pop phrase of the 1960s had it. As we worry over the last century's weapons of mass destruction, are we about to enter a new age of chemical warfare?

THE WILL TO WIN

Whether the initial wave of behavior-control weapons involves sonic tools, chemicals, microwaves, hyperbroadcasts, or means still hiding beyond research horizons, we would be foolish not to consider the potential for such asymmetrical means to wreak havoc upon our approach to warfare—and even upon our homeland.

The possibilities sketched here are superficial and perhaps wrong in detail. But behavior-control weapons are so obviously the logical culmination of warfare that blithe disregard for an entire field of research guarantees disaster.

As this series of columns has stressed, we must regain a visceral grasp of what war means. It isn't merely about target sets, or arriving on the objective, or about exit strategies. War is about persuading the enemy to obey you, to do what you want him to do, even though it may be anathema to all his values.

For now, though, warfare remains about killing the enemy and smashing his environment with sufficient force and resolve to make further resistance psychologically and physically impossible. There may be small wars, but there are no soft wars. Nothing matters more than the will to win.

In the future we may see a true revolution in military affairs whose effects dwarf the overhyped gimmicks of our time. We or our enemies may achieve bloodless war, after all. But if anyone does so, the result is apt to be more horrible—more inhumane on the most fundamental level—than anything military planners now imagine.

Warfare is about changing the enemy's mind. The weapons of tomorrow will do it directly.

Occupation 101

Armed Forces Journal

September 2005

Few matters in military affairs lend themselves to checklists. One is preventive maintenance. Another is preflight checks. A third is the occupation of a defeated state.

Had we planned to botch the occupation of Iraq, we hardly could have done worse than the administration did without a plan. Despite inadequate support and abysmal civilian leadership, our troops saved us from disaster.

Now the Iraqis are beginning to pull some of the weight. But had the Office of the Secretary of Defense (OSD) adhered to common sense and tasked the military to develop a full-scale occupation plan, we would have saved many American and Iraqi lives, the situation in postwar Iraq would have been far more tractable, and international terrorists would not have gained momentum.

The civilians atop the Pentagon were ideologues determined to have their war. Nothing was going to stop them. Some were true believers, convinced that Saddam Hussein's overthrow would lead to the Age of Aquarius in Baghdad, but the critical realization that forbade serious occupation planning was that the projected costs in troops, resources, and funding would have caused Congress to think twice.

The situation was worsened by the conviction among civilian appointees who never had served in the military that they understood twenty-first-century warfare better than the generals. For the ideologues in OSD, military officers were second-raters, at best, and our troops were merely the janitors of policy. No senior official had a family member at risk. War had no visceral reality for them. It was simply a continuation of policy through other means—a loathsome European dictum that never applied to America.

Ridding Iraq and the world of Saddam was a noble thing. But the willful ineptitude with which OSD did it remains inexcusable.

Done is done, as the ideologues realized all along. We *are* in Iraq, winning is vital, and it's too late to correct the mistakes that didn't have to be made. We'll be compensating until the day the last American soldier leaves Mesopotamia. But we'll need to do better next time.

And there will be a next time.

Our military doesn't want the occupation mission. But no one else can do it. No other organization has the resources, skills, or sense of responsibility. From the Philippines through Germany and Japan, the Army in particular conducted successful occupations. And the Army will need to do it in the future, assisted by the other services.

If the Army doesn't emerge from its experience in Iraq with a sound doctrine for future occupations, the blame won't fall on civilians next time, but on the generals who ducked their responsibilities to our soldiers and our nation. We cannot pretend we will never do this again—any more than we can wish away war itself.

THE RULES

1. **Plan and prepare for the worst case.** This is the iron rule of military planning. If you go in loaded for bear, you can handle the squirrels. Plan for every contingency imaginable, then plan for the unimaginable. This is the sort of common sense taught at every staff college. Good intentions and crossed fingers are no substitute. As former Army Chief of Staff Gen. Gordon Sullivan put it, "Hope is not a method." Any senior commander prevented from doing detailed planning should resign. Publicly. Otherwise, the blood of his soldiers and the shame of the nation will be on his head and hands.

2. **Impose the rule of law immediately.** This means martial law in the first hours, days, and weeks of an occupation, although we

may employ less menacing terminology. The rigorous enforcement of basic laws is every bit as much to the benefit of the subject population as it is to us. When the political order collapses, hurling the economy and society into crisis, the defeated crave certainty and security. Rhetoric about democracy can come later. In the awful confusion of war's aftermath, the average citizen needs to be reassured that his family, his home, and the streets are safe—that criminals or renegades will not be allowed to prey upon him or his loved ones.

Psychologically, the defeated population is reduced to a childish state. They don't want unregulated freedom. They need clear, parental rules. They need to know that crime will be punished and good behavior rewarded. The situation is identical to that faced by a teacher on the first day of class: If order isn't established from the opening bell, it's hard to impose it later in the term.

When U.S. forces arrive in a given country, they're granted a period when the population is disoriented, malleable, and responsive. Squandering that window is a tragic error, and the occupation may never fully recover.

When our troops arrived in Baghdad without orders to impose the rule of law, we lost our credibility with many Iraqis. Some expected punishment, but few expected us to tolerate a looting and arson spree by criminal elements. By allowing looters free rein, we alienated law-abiding citizens. *And* we embarrassed ourselves in the eyes of the world.

The rule of law is essential for all else we hope to achieve. Without it, you not only will not have order in the streets, but you will never establish a true market economy where corruption is under control. You certainly cannot build a just democracy. We like to speak in stirring terms about our noble intentions, but men and women need to feel safe when they walk the streets or shut their doors at night. Attempting to put "freedom and democracy" before the rule of law is a prescription for anarchy and violence.

There's no way in which we could have made every Iraqi love us. But had we brought the rule of law from the first hours of occupation, most would have respected us.

3. **Send enough troops from the start.** There is no such thing as "occupation-lite." Presence matters. The defeated population

needs to see our troops on every corner. Visible troops create an image of power that declarations from headquarters cannot rival. The people need to feel overwhelmed, to sense the occupier's omnipresence and, by extension, omnipotence. Out of sight is out of mind.

If troops are deployed in sufficient numbers at the start of an occupation, it may be possible to draw them down in a matter of months. But stingy deployments that attempt to hold down the political costs at home guarantee that the enemy will not experience an enduring sense of defeat. A lack of occupation troops inspires resistance—and we find ourselves deploying additional forces to support a troubled effort.

Numbers matter. In an occupation, no technology, ideology, or amount of financial generosity can substitute for adequate troop strength. In a thoroughly broken society, such as Iraq, only large numbers of occupation troops provide a sound foundation for the rebirth of civil order. Wherever we cannot be, latent enemies emerge. The primary tool of a successful occupation is the *visible* soldier.

4. **Don't turn an occupation into a looting orgy for American contractors.** Lavishing inappropriate contracts on American firms to "rebuild" Iraq not only squandered tens of billions of taxpayer dollars, but actually worked against us on the ground. We created false expectations for Iraqis, making promises we couldn't begin to keep. Again and again, civilian contractors failed to complete their missions. Some fled. The administration's ideological obsession with outsourcing impeded military operations as well. While the policy's defenders may point to local successes, the overall effort remains an expensive shambles.

We didn't send in American firms to rebuild Germany and Japan. We made the locals do the work themselves. They knew their countries better than we could know them. In Iraq, we tried to impose American standards and practices, and more often than not we found ourselves in a stalemate in which the old systems stopped running and the made-in-America systems couldn't be brought on line. Even our most successful projects will need American support for years to come.

The focus should have been on enabling Iraqis to help themselves, to fix the systems they had (no matter how decayed).

They knew how to do that much. If we wished to be more generous, we needed to take our time and do a thorough, on-the-ground assessment. Instead, we created a wish-list and stuck the American taxpayer with the bill.

How do you do it right? It isn't hard, if you don't treat war as an opportunity to enrich well-entrenched firms. Operating under emergency wartime provisions, military contracting officers should trail the leading brigades, empowered to write agreements and disburse funds to local authority figures to undertake needed repairs. Even if the locals are barely competent, this is the only strategy that advances our overall goals.

Consider what you achieve when you hire Sheikh Ali to fix the water system. First, he's going to pad the payroll with everyone in his tribe. That's just what we want the sheikh to do.

For any occupation to succeed, you must get young men off the streets. Unemployed young men form the pool in which the resistance fishes. Corruption must be battled in every other instance, but when a local contractor hires five young men to do the job of one, it's a good investment—just make sure those five men show up, stay at work, and get paid, that the money isn't pocketed. Not only do you employ the most dangerous demographic, men with jobs can take care of their families and keep their pride. Humiliate a man through unemployment and you make an enemy.

The other crucial aspect of this approach is that it gives influential locals a stake in the occupation. Never underestimate the power of greed. If opinion-makers profit from your presence, they are far more likely to support (or at least tolerate) your programs.

5. **Devolve responsibility, retain authority.** This relates to the previous rule. If you hire Haji Mustapha's construction firm to unclog the neighborhood drains, you have an out when the people complain that the work is unsatisfactory. Just open your books and direct them to the haji (then threaten to kick the haji off the gravy train). Maintain a monopoly of power, but put responsibility for the infrastructure on local shoulders.

This applies at the national level, as well. As soon as possible, give natives real responsibility for nonessential portfolios. When feasible, allow them the illusion of power over key departments. If they perform to reasonable standards, you can increase their authority. But it's crucial to get Uncle Sam off as many blame-lines as possible. Lay down rigorous guidelines, but put indigenous politicians and bureaucrats to work.

Does any veteran of Fortress Baghdad believe that Iraqis could have done any worse than the young, utterly inexperienced and incompetent political hacks the administration sent to the Green Zone to rebuild a major state and its economy?

6. **You can't govern from a distance or without risk.** Under the Coalition Provisional Authority, the Green Zone might as well have been in Lincoln, Nebraska. By governing from a hermetic fortress, you never gain a tactile feel for the local reality (even if you think you do). Every bit as bad, you create the impression that you're afraid. And frightened occupiers are rarely successful occupiers.

You must be willing to take judicious risks, and you must smell the country's dust every single day. This is one more reason why the military, with its ability to defend itself and its discipline, has to control an occupation's decisive initial phases. Any deployed government civilians must be willing to bear a measure of risk. During my stay in Iraq last year—strictly among Iraqis—the Green Zone was regarded as a laughingstock and an impediment to progress.

7. **When it's time to fight, fight ruthlessly.** You cannot begin an occupation gently. As badly as you may want to be loved, it's essential to be feared. At the first sign of an insurgency, terrorist activity or violent criminality, you must respond with a ferocity that shocks your would-be opponents, their sympathizers, and yes, the media. Bad press in the short term comes to nothing, if you succeed in the longer term. But calibrating an occupation to please the media guarantees a higher toll in bloodshed down the road. Crush resistance immediately, without restraint or compromise. The toll in casualties and human rights will be far lower in the end than if you try to win over implacable enemies.

Our occupation of Iraq—which wasn't supposed to be an occupation—will stand as a textbook case of how to squander opportunities, lives, and taxpayer dollars. Although Iraq may prove a reasonable success, the cost did not have to be so painfully high.

A crucial lesson is that amateurs should not interfere with the practical details of military planning. Although civilian authorities will always decide where and when we go to war, the how should be left to those who have devoted their lives to uniformed service. When that rule is broken, our troops are forced to redeem failed policies with their blood.

No Silver Bullets: Fighting the Insurgency in Iraq

Armed Forces Journal

January 2006

Along with impatience, a great American weakness is our belief that every problem has a straightforward solution, if only we can figure it out. Especially in complex foreign endeavors, such as counterinsurgency warfare or the struggle with religious terrorism, this search for a silver bullet hampers our efforts: We demand clear-cut results in a fractured, tormented world in which the best possible outcomes are always flawed and usually slow in coming.

Which approach is better? The fist? Or the warm embrace? Should we smash down doors to demonstrate our power, or build cooperative relationships with local leaders? Are our goals best served by a strategy of securing key population nodes and expanding our control outward? Or by aggressively seeking our enemies and attacking them? Should we strike enemy strongholds fiercely, as in Fallujah, or methodically, as in Tal Afar?

The answer is all of the above. The veiled argument among generals over whether one division's approach was too heavy-handed compared with another's dexterous touch misses the fundamental truth that the right response to the layered problems we've faced in Iraq depends on multiple factors, from the atmosphere of the moment to the location and scope of the specific challenge.

No single set of tactical or operational rules leads to comprehensive success. The technique that prevailed in City X in 2004 may be counterproductive if employed in Town Y in early 2006. Local cultures may vary from village to village (and certainly from country to country). The situation, military and political, shifts unexpectedly. Resources dictate what can or cannot be done at a given time. There is no single "right" approach to counterinsurgency or stability operations. Although some deficiencies and errors—such as cultural ignorance, poor intelligence work, hitting the wrong target, or weak media management—invariably harm our efforts, there is no cheat-sheet formula that leads to an early redeployment back to peacetime garrisons. Commanders at all levels need to master a wide repertoire of "plays" and to develop the tactile sense to call the right ones in sequence under murky, dynamic circumstances. Then the game changes.

Nor does every tactical or operational situation have one ideal solution. Some challenges can be handled in a variety of ways, while others have no good solution at all. At times, one deft touch defuses a potential explosion. At other times, you can only improvise bloodily until you hit on means that work halfway. The clarity of the classroom is singularly lacking in real counterinsurgency operations. Some local problems have no just solutions—or no real solutions at all. We want firm results, but fighting insurgents is sometimes a matter of buying time, not of achieving decisive, final victory. Counterinsurgency warfare is the realm of the officer who can think beyond the textbook, who thrives in the absence of rules.

To date, the progress made in Iraq has been achieved solely by the commitment and the quality of our troops and their uniformed leadership. They did it by dealing with on-the-ground complexities that staff colleges cannot teach, that politicians cannot accept, and that theorists cannot grasp.

Insurgencies are so complex and different from one another that one of the worst things that can happen to a force is to have achieved a recent success that is then carried along as a template for operations in a profoundly different culture. After much preening about its experience in counterinsurgency operations in northern Ireland and self-satisfied observations about American clumsiness, the British military in Iraq, operating in a relatively benign environment, employed the "light touch" it had learned.

The result was to hand Basra and the south to Shi'a militants. The British limited their own casualties and "kept the peace," but fostered the rise of fanatic parallel power structures that, to put it kindly, are not democracy-friendly. Whether or not the British "won" southern Iraq for Iran, they certainly delivered it unto the most reactionary and intolerant of Iraq's Shi'as. If Iraq still exists as a state ten years from now, the most backward and truculent provinces will be those that enjoyed a British occupation.

What worked in Belfast didn't work in Basra.

LESSONS OF HISTORY

Historical examples can deepen our understanding of the problems we face, but they rarely offer appropriate solutions. It's been fascinating to listen to the phenomenal amount of nonsense offered up as the "lessons of history" about insurgencies by those who have no serious knowledge of the past, still less of the Middle East, and none whatsoever of our military.

We have been warned that it's virtually impossible to defeat insurgencies, which is simply wrong. Down the centuries, few insurgencies succeeded. Those that did triumph generally opposed a decayed state from within or a troubled empire on its vulnerable frontiers. With the sympathy of a minority of the population, an insurgency can cause infernal trouble, but it cannot win against a steadfast power. The key variable is commitment—or, simply put, time (which takes us back to American impatience, exacerbated by the poisonous and irresponsible media). Fighting a robust power, the only hope an insurgency possesses is to outlast its opponent, to win an eventual political victory in place of the military victory it has no hope of achieving. That is what the insurgents—and terrorists—in Iraq intend to do.

Our enemies aren't wizards of cultural understanding. They've gotten much wrong about America, especially by underestimating the courage and skill of our troops. But they cling to one big, promising idea that may yet pay off for them: To our enemies, the crucial lesson of Vietnam is that America gets tired. Media-wise and internet-savvy, both insurgents and terrorists are very much aware of the political bickering in the United States and the (overhyped) antiwar movement. Their strategy comes down to attriting our forces and staying in the headlines, to win through the media what they cannot win with bombs.

Our own weak grasp of history plays into their hands as commentators insist—forever citing Vietnam—that insurgencies always win. Yet the United States has been fighting insurgencies and winning since before we were a nation, on the Indian frontier, in a great civil war, against the Ku Klux Klan (a struggle waged on and off for over a century), against the Muslim-fundamentalist Moros and later the Huks in the Philippines, and in Central America. Our track record has been very good. Even in Vietnam, we defeated the insurgency. North Vietnam had to send in its regulars—and still only won after our troops were recalled and aid to South Vietnam was cut off. Saigon fell to a massive invasion, not to an insurgency.

But facts don't matter. The struggle on our domestic front (where Iraq may well be lost) is all about emotion, resentment, and scoring political points. History has often been prostituted, but rarely with such shamelessness. The one historical truth that administration opponents refuse to accept is that defeating insurgencies takes time—about a decade, on average. For purely partisan purposes, an influential segment of our population is in a rush to declare defeat. The insurgency's most potent weapon is our media, and the struggle's center of gravity is in the U.S. Senate, not in Iraq.

Even those in the military or hovering around it suffer from a selective study of history, endlessly citing T. E. Lawrence out of context—yet, that flamboyant self-promoter's "revolt in the desert" would have come to nothing without the advance of the British Empire's conventional forces. Lawrence was colorful. Allenby was effective. Lawrence understood the Bedu. More important, his British masters understood Lawrence and used him as an effective auxiliary—but an auxiliary, nonetheless. Although reading *Seven Pillars of Wisdom* offers enduring insights into Arab behavior and motivations, it doesn't offer a formula for winning our present war.

Others cite Trinquier and the French in Algeria, proposing an "ink-blot" or "oil-spot" strategy that pacifies a key node, occupies it, and expands outward from it, creating zones of security for the population: stability operations instead of aggressive hunting. Apart from the facts that the French lost and that the interim effectiveness of their strategy depended on having a half-million troops on the ground, there is certainly some merit in using such a technique as part of a larger strategy. But if adopted as a sole solution, it relinquishes the initiative to the insurgents (who already have an inherent advantage in that regard); requires a heavy and immobilized troop presence; and effectively hands sovereignty beyond the wire over to the enemy. To be effective, an ink-blot strategy requires local cooperation, dependable native troops and police in large numbers—and relentless offensive actions to keep the enemy on the defensive while the pacified population centers develop and expand.

You can't just circle the wagons—especially given our national impatience. And you can't allow the enemy to fortify "liberated" zones while you concentrate on cities X and Y. You have to hold firmly and attack aggressively at the same time. That requires numbers that our forces in Iraq were never allowed.

The point isn't to attack one worthy approach, but to stress the importance of flexibility, of refusing to limit ourselves to a single formula, of using every play in the playbook and never ceasing to develop new combinations for use against an adaptive enemy.

To study the history of insurgencies seriously, we would have to begin at least twenty-five centuries ago and march forward. The twin lessons would be that, while insurgencies generally fail, there is no easy formula for suppressing them—other than ruthlessness at a level we cannot presently permit ourselves.

SO WHAT DO WE DO?

Given the many restrictions under which our forces have had to operate in Iraq, they've performed magnificently. The mission is very, very hard, and it was exacerbated by inadequate troop strength, incompetence among civilian leaders, and the "lost year" of 2004, when the administration did its best to avoid decisive combat, casualties, and images of destruction until after the presidential election (the timing of the Second Battle of Fallujah was far more cynical than any claims about weapons of mass destruction). With more troops and more presidential will, the political renovation of Iraq would have come much farther by now. With iron resolve at the top of our government, even a smaller, special-operations-heavy postwar effort—backed by sufficient political will—might have worked better than our too-small-for-this, too-big-for-that force could do. It's a tribute to our military that we've done as well as we have, given that the National Command Authority got virtually every postwar detail wrong.

From NCOs to division commanders, we've seen a praiseworthy ability to figure things out on the ground, to fight effectively under widely varied circumstances, and to cope with extreme cultural obstacles. Although the insurgents and terrorists can keep on killing indefinitely, they cannot win—unless we quit, defeated by the media.

The media have been a factor in warfare since the religious wars of the sixteenth and seventeenth centuries, and the press in Imperial Britain and the United States always had plenty to say about the way professional armies dealt with distant insurgencies. Between the world wars, the British media condemned as inhumane the use of aircraft against rebellious tribesmen on the Northwest Frontier, and the U.S. Army's long but successful campaign to defeat the Moros had plenty of domestic critics who worried about the rights of deadly fanatics a century ago.

Yet the hyperintensity of today's 24/7 news cycle, the immediacy of reporting, and the cutthroat competition for sensation to bolster ratings now combine to make the media not just an observer, but a party to every conflict—and often an enemy at which our troops cannot return fire.

The military appears as naïve about the culture of the media as it long has been about foreign cultures (try thinking about reporters as a tribe of talented cannibals). Just as the need for officers to speak foreign languages was relegated to the don't-bother-me-now-I'm-on-the-gunnery-range category, so media management tends to be relegated to an unread annex in the operations plan. Yet the media now possess the power to turn an American victory into a defeat—or at least a mixed result.

Think of any image from Iraq. When you read those words, did a photo from Abu Ghraib come to mind? Although impermissible and shameful, the mistreatment of prisoners at Abu Ghraib was hardly a strategic matter—until the media made it one. After a brilliant performance by our troops in Second Fallujah, which image was impressed upon the world? A Marine shooting a wounded prisoner, presented out of context as an ambitious reporter grabbed his moment in the spotlight. What is the No. 1 photo request lodged with the government and the courts by the media? To shoot flag-draped coffins returning from Iraq.

Certainly there are honorable journalists. But they, too, can be infected by the madness of the herd—reporters complain that they want new stories but flock to cover the same story as their peers. "Press freedom" is their constant cry, but we rarely hear of media responsibility. If there is any self-important, self-indulgent, and self-serving major institution running amok in our country today, it's the media, which long since has sunk from healthy skepticism to smug cynicism. A free press is a safeguard of democracy, but irresponsible media are democracy's enemy within.

The pertinent points are, first, that the media now can have a decisive influence in overturning the verdict of the battlefield, transforming American victories into defeats through biased reporting, and, second, that the complexity of dealing with the media is yet another aspect of counterinsurgency warfare that has no silver-bullet answer.

What do we do in Iraq? Whatever works. We're better at learning as we go than we are at adhering to frozen-in-time doctrine. Although it would have been better had the Army, especially, gone into Iraq with more serious recent thinking about counterinsurgency warfare, we should all be surprised that an undertaking of such magnitude and difficulty has gone as well as it has. Day-by-day, we see the problems—amplified by the media. But when you stand back, the performance of our forces has been extraordinary.

It's up to those back home to let our troops win. The surest way to lose an insurgency isn't by military or cultural blunders. It's by quitting.

INEVITABLE DOCTRINE

No matter how our efforts end in Iraq, new counterinsurgency doctrine will emerge. It is essential that it be written by recent veterans, not by contractors relying on second-hand accounts. And that doctrine must avoid the temptation to impose a uniform, limited set of rules on a complex form of conflict in which every insurgency has unique qualities. We certainly should stress the criticality of better intelligence work and the role of cultural knowledge as a combat multiplier (or preempter of combat), but it's hard to be hopeful about the present Army leadership (the Marines are different) doing anything much about intelligence, language skills for officers, and cultural studies beyond mouthing platitudes, and then heading back to the same old rodeo. Still, if only the next iteration of our counterinsurgency doctrine started off, "There are no easy answers or uniform solutions to insurgencies," we would have made enormous progress.

Fighting insurgencies demands imagination and determination, empathy and patience, power and restraint, boldness and caution, adaptability and unwavering moral strength. The seeming contradictions are nearly endless. The one certainty is that there is no certainty that applies to all insurgencies. If there is anything like a key to dealing with a given insurgency, it's understanding the insurgents so well that specific knowledge shapes your strategy, operations, and tactics. Ultimately, no doctrine can prescribe how we fight all insurgents or terrorists everywhere. The best doctrine written in garrison will be a bare beginning in the field. But if we take the pains to understand our enemy, the enemy will tell us what to do.

And then it will change again.

Freedom Fighters

New York Post

November 11, 2003

They looked so old. That was the thing that struck me. Men in their late thirties, they looked at least ten—sometimes twenty—years older. And they were the survivors.

I was a lieutenant when I reported in to the 1st Battalion of the 46th Infantry. As an enlisted man in the bitter peace of the 1970s, I had already seen the wreckage of Vietnam, the noncommissioned officers so badly shot up that they could no longer serve in the infantry but had to be posted to easier jobs in support units to "make their twenty."

I had seen them limping and scarred, with rebuilt jaws and reconstructed limbs—still serving as best they could, hanging on to their pride as younger men like me, untried by war, left them behind in a short march to the parade ground.

I had seen them, but never quite the way I did as a new officer in an Infantry outfit. *These* NCOs had been healed of their wounds sufficiently to return to the work they loved hopelessly and complained about endlessly. Their faces had been burned by the sun in jungle clearings and cut by winter sleet. Awful chow had ruined their guts and—in those days—far too many cigarettes, along with an irrational devotion to doing freedom's toughest job, had ravaged them. They'd spent hard years away from the healing comfort of loved ones. They looked old and worn and battered.

They were *proud* men. The best of them were master teachers,
rigorous but fair with the young soldiers entrusted to their care and
determined to make "their" lieutenant the finest in the battalion.
They cursed and mocked and worked miracles.

None of us fully appreciated them, of course. We said we did
and meant well. But we were officers. We would serve our troop-
time and then move on to staff jobs and schools, returning to tactical units now and then to punch our tickets.

We made a great display of waiting until the enlisted men were
fed before we ate, of being fitter and fleeter than the NCOs, of leading by example. We shared their hardships, sleeping in the snow or
rain, competing to show how tough we were. But as we moved on to
further our careers, "old sarge" remained behind, shifting from one
Infantry battalion to another, perhaps drawing the odd staff job he
hated automatically because a good NCO despised "staff weenies."

We meant to treat them fairly, but the truth is that we didn't.
We relied on them, but they could never fully rely on us. We were
only passing through. The battalion—some battalion—would always
be their home. They welcomed us as tourists.

After Vietnam, those men faced constant complaints from civilians about the generosity of military pensions. Half-pay after only
twenty years? It was an outrageous waste, according to those who
avoided serving their country. Yet far too many of the NCOs I
knew were unlikely to live to collect their Social Security. They
did the work the Harvard grads would never have dreamed of
doing and gave us the best of their lives. And got half-pay in a bro-
ken-health retirement.

Grocery chains campaigned against the military commissaries
that allowed soldiers to feed their families more cheaply. The system was "unfair competition," according to the business execs
whose families never had to stretch the chili-mac.

Military medicine (much improved now) was a shambles. Military housing (still inadequate) was often so bad that a civilian landlord offering the equivalent would have been sued as a slumlord.

One sergeant first class I remember, a Vietnam vet just short of
retirement, died of a heart attack during a physical training run.
Friends watched a young NCO drown in a few inches of ditch water
after his tracked vehicle flipped over during training. The vehicle

was so heavy that nothing could be done. They watched him struggle to free himself, then go limp. Another NCO died of a broken heart, I think, after his dream of being a first sergeant was unjustly frustrated.

All this was in peacetime. Today, we are at war again. The pay's better, as is the medical care. The commissary system survives but remains a target of corporate grocers and bureaucrats for whom outsourcing is a secular religion.

And the NCO is *still* my candidate for the most underpaid professional in any walk of life.

Oh, the enlisted soldier always has politicians ready to pat him—or her—on the back and pose for a photo op. The rhetoric gushed over our troops would make an advertising copywriter blush. As elections loom, no congressman rations the attaboys.

But there's little substance behind the ringing words. The truth is that soldiers have few friends on Capitol Hill. They aren't big campaign contributors or powerful lobbyists. When it comes down to the crunch, the money-men win and the veterans make do.

Elected officials lavish praise on our troops, but lavish money on their revolving-door pals in the defense industry. Indeed, Operation Iraqi Freedom was supposed to prove that the old-fashioned soldier isn't even a major player on today's battlefields, that technology trumps all.

Yet the road to Baghdad was opened by soldiers and Marines fighting in close-quarters combat. And the dangerous work of building peace doesn't lend itself to technological solutions. Conflict is, above all, a human problem—and human problems require human solutions.

The thanks of a grateful nation? A proposal to add a mere 10,000 troops to our overstretched Army died a rapid death. Instead, we're buying nearly useless F-22 fighters at one hundred and fifty million dollars *each*. While our soldiers in Iraq don't have enough body armor. There isn't much profit in equipping infantrymen, you see.

Veterans Day, which we hardly honor anymore, began as Armistice Day, memorializing those who fell in the "war to end all wars." But the only thing that always ends is peace. And then we turn, again, to those in uniform.

Think about them today.

Saving the U.S. Air Force

New York Post

February 11, 2005

We need to save the United States Air Force—from itself. This critical component of our national security has become corrupt, wasteful, and increasingly irrelevant. The problem doesn't lie with the front-line pilots or ground crews. The cancer is at the top, in the Department of the Air Force and on the Air Force Staff.

Consider just a few recent problems:

- Former Air Force Secretary James G. Roche, who resigned last month to evade a corruption investigation, has just been cited for ethics violations in dealing with the defense industry.

- The service's top acquisition official, Darleen Druyun, is in prison for her role in a corrupt tanker-leasing deal. The scam had been a top priority under Roche.

- The Air Force's top lawyer got the boot for sexual shenanigans with subordinates.

- The service continues to demand the nearly useless, three-hundred-million-dollar-per-copy F/A-22 fighter, a Cold-War legacy system wildly out of sync with our security needs.

- The Air Force's "shock and awe" effort that opened Operation Iraqi Freedom was a complete bust. The sound-and-light show over Baghdad was supposed to prove that we no longer needed ground troops to win wars. The reverse proved true.

- In our current operations in Iraq, the Air Force's procurement choices have left it searching for missions to prove its relevance. Recently, one Army division commander shook his head and told me, "I had aircraft stacked up, begging for missions so the pilots could get combat credit. But I just couldn't use them."

America needs a strong Air Force, but we have the wrong Air Force. The service's leadership, military and civilian, displays greater loyalty to the defense industry than to our national defense (the contractors who supply the Air Force teem with retired generals). Today's Air Force clings to a fight-the-Soviets (or at least the Chinese) model with greater passion than yesteryear's Army clung to the horse cavalry.

And Air Force leaders lie. Last year, in war games with the Indian air force, our blue-suiters suffered embarrassing defeats. Our guys were arrogant and failed to think innovatively. We also had crucial high-tech gear turned off. The Indians used imaginative tactics—and overwhelmed us with numbers.

Our Air Force's response? To insist the humiliation "proved" the need for the F/A-22. Yet purchasing that gold-plated piece of junk means that we could afford still fewer aircraft in the future— we could be swarmed by other countries with lower-tech, affordable planes, just as the Indians did it.

Numbers matter. The Air Force doesn't need fewer, "more capable" aircraft. It needs more metal. But not the junk the contractors want to foist on the taxpayer and that ethically challenged senior officers want to buy. We need:

• **A revitalized transport fleet:** We rely on the workhorse C-130 for tactical lift, but the design is nearly a half-century old. The Army and Marines are told to make tomorrow's combat vehicles fit into the C-130's tight hold. That's backward. Next-generation combat vehicles will be so systems-rich that no amount of miniaturization will let them fit in a C-130. We need to design the fighting systems we need, and then build planes to lift them.

• **An affordable replacement for the great, but aging B-52 bomber:** Those magnificent craft continue to outperform later, platinum-priced bombers, such as the Rube-Goldberg B-1 and the fragile B-2. We need a new, cost-efficient, and robust bomber to replace B-52s nearly twice as old as their crews.

• **A no-nonsense ground-attack aircraft** to replace that splendid killing machine, the A-10. Ground-attack operations—especially in urban environments—are the wave of the future. The Air Force needs to stop dreaming of the missions it wants and face the missions we've got.

• **A multirole-fighter fleet that rejects Cold-War-era designs** and starts afresh. Billions already spent are no reason to waste billions more on yesterday's concepts. Don't throw good money after bad. Our Air Force needs fresh thinking, adequate funding, and an increase in the numbers of airplanes we can launch. Instead, we get old thinking, massive waste, and a shrinking fleet.

The Air Force has been Defense Secretary Donald Rumsfeld's darling. The Army and Marines were supposed to shrivel to free up more funding for Air Force whistles and bells. Rumsfeld was so happy with the state of affairs in our disintegrating Air Force that he actually tried to move arch-scoundrel Roche over to become Secretary of the Army. Fortunately, Senator John McCain put a stop to that.

Now Rumsfeld is fighting to prevent desperately needed permanent increases in the size of our ground forces, while struggling to preserve disgraceful Air Force legacy buys. It's time for the Senate to call him on the carpet.

The Air Force badly needs reform. Our men and women in uniform deserve it. For a start, the service needs a secretary chosen from the ranks of retired Marine or Army four-stars, a man with joint experience who can do what a series of corporate-America secretaries could not: Hold the Air Force's renegade generals to account.

Second, the senior Air Force generals need to be purged. Instead of intellectual relics with fighter or bomber backgrounds, Air Force special-operations commanders—men who know what postmodern warfare means—should be given the service's top jobs. With the mission of making the Air Force relevant to the twenty-first century.

The Sleeping Service

Armed Forces Journal

December 2005

If any service is out of sight and out of mind in our present wars, it's the Navy. Even our Air Force, which has made almost every wrong decision it could, is more visible in our military endeavors. Meanwhile, the Navy refuses to strip for action and continues to add an ever more elaborate superstructure to its twentieth-century approach to warfare: "Net-centric warfare" appears to be far more net than war.

Given its intellectual crisis and time on the warfighting bench, the Navy is apt to suffer far deeper cuts than our security needs can bear. Despite the misdirection provided by our current land wars, the United States remains primarily a maritime power. And the globalization of trade—an ancient phenomenon accelerating madly in our time—makes control of the sea more important than ever.

Unlike the Marines, with their relentless combat catechism, our Navy suffers from a selective memory and the sort of wishful thinking that characterized the Army in the 1990s. But the fundamental future requirement of our Navy has already been described—by Fleet Admiral Chester W. Nimitz on the day of his 1948 departure from his position as Chief of Naval Operations.

Quoting Sir Walter Raleigh, Nimitz observed that "whoever commands the sea, commands the trade; whosoever commands the trade of the world commands the riches of the world, and consequently the world itself."

Our nation and economy are more dependent on international trade than ever before. The only saving grace is that our greatest potential enemy, China, is even more reliant on vulnerable shipping than we are—and far less able to secure the sea lanes vital to the Beijing government's economic survival and prolonged war-making capability.

The Chinese realize it. Their activity on the Indian Ocean's littoral, from Burma to eastern Africa, focuses on securing supplies of oil and other raw materials, and on denying the U.S. Navy port facilities in a crisis through diplomatic art and bonds of reciprocity. The Greater Indian Ocean's shipping lanes are China's strategic lifeline. By preparing the theater now, Beijing believes it can limit the U.S. Navy's operating capabilities in what is, for the United States, the most distant, politically complex, and strategically challenging maritime region.

The Chinese are not determined to fight us, but they are determined to be prepared for any future war that may occur. Beijing is thinking much further ahead than Washington seems able to do. They have the vision, but thankfully, not yet the means.

THE FOOLS' WAR

A war between the United States and China would be terribly costly to both parties, and such a war is utterly unnecessary. But with sufficient stupidity on both sides—a quality never lacking in governments—we might find ourselves fighting that war in a future decade. Were such hostilities to open, their contours probably would be far different than those we now project.

As a former Army officer and a recent convert to the belief in the primacy of naval power, it appears to me that our Navy will have three overarching requirements in the future, only one of which has much appeal to sea-service officers. In order of importance, those demands are:

1. The ability to protect our maritime trade while interdicting that of an enemy; policing the sea lanes under the conditions of peace or lesser crises and dominating them through unrestrained power and strategic blockades in wartime.

2. The ability to promptly destroy or otherwise neutralize the naval capabilities of any enemy power or combination of hostile powers.

3. The ability to influence land warfare through massive fire-power delivered anywhere on the globe, no matter the distance of the target from the sea.

At present, our Navy remains fully serious only about the second requirement, while the strategic issues of the moment make the third particularly appealing to those outside the Navy and to those within the service who are anxious, above all, to preserve funding. Yet the decisive capability in a future great war would be the first requirement, with the second mission most useful in support of the broader control of the seas and the third an adjunct (if a critical one) to the operations of the other services.

While stressing again that a war with China is neither inevitable nor desirable, consider alternative historical analogies for how such a war might be waged and, ultimately, won.

First, the grand fleet action so appealing to those who command warships would be unlikely to resemble Midway or even the final naval battles fought as our forces neared Japan. A naval exchange with China, fought in strategic proximity to the Chinese mainland, would probably result in a second Jutland, a far more lethal and more dispersed exchange in which the Chinese, after inflicting more damage on our Navy than we allow in our war games, would nonetheless realize that the cost of doing so was prohibitive to its own force. The remaining Chinese fleet-in-being would become a fleet-in-hiding, bottled up and wary of further encounters.

The crucial naval activity in defeating China would be a rigorous, globe-spanning blockade that swept aside peacetime civilities and prevented China from receiving any resupply of raw materials, especially oil and gas. (A crucial indicator that the Chinese anticipated a war would be an attempt to accumulate massive, dispersed stockpiles of vital resources.) As China's appetite increases, it will become ever easier to bring its economy to its knees by closing the sea lanes (and freezing its global accounts and investments, by any means necessary). Pipelines, no matter how ambitiously constructed, not only could not provide adequate supplies, but—as U.S. forces learned to their dismay in Iraq—are easy to interdict.

A war with China would be a long war (even with resort to weapons of mass destruction), involving the sort of blockade that starved Germany in the First World War, combined with a strategic pummelling of China's vulnerable industrial base and its military. Just as Iraq is a boots-on-the-ground war, a war with Beijing would be a destruction-from-a-distance war, waged in the hope that internal rivalries in China would lead to the profound sort of regime change we saw in St. Petersburg, Russia, in 1917. (Internally, China is becoming more unstable, not less so). Our grand strategy in such a conflict would be to turn the conflict inward, making it a Chinese versus Chinese struggle.

On the high seas, the role model for our naval captains would be less Bull Halsey and more Raphael Semmes—the skipper of the *CSS Alabama*, the greatest commerce raider of the Civil War. Although it is hard today to imagine our vessels taking hundreds of merchantmen into custody—or sinking them—the issue of maritime trade will shape our naval future. In a globe-spanning war, shipping can only proceed at our sufferance. Faced with a war about our continued preeminence and even survival—enduring asymmetric Chinese attacks on our homeland—we will do what needs to be done, without regard for the niceties of international law or custom.

To remain with the First World War as a precedent a moment longer, recall that Britain's grand battle fleet served only a negative purpose and experienced a largely passive war (as our own grand fleet might do after Jutland II, the Pacific Version). Despite the German U-boat campaign, Britain's naval power (and its no-nonsense employment) enabled the movement of troops and supplies between theaters. Without the command of the seas, the resources of the empire would have been meaningless and the intervention by the United States would have been far more costly and protracted. Britain's command of the seas did not make its victory on the Western Front inevitable, but it made a German victory impossible. Even in the Second World War, the inability of the Japanese fleet to penetrate and command the enduringly vital Indian Ocean allowed the British Empire a crucial lifeline between its surviving possessions. Our own offensive action in the Pacific meant that the Japanese Navy was running out of fuel by the war's end.

Too often ignored by strategists in the nuclear age, the command of the seas remains the fundamental basis for American military power and our national security.

DECADES OF CONFLICT

In this age of distinctly unpeaceful peace, our Navy is apt to find itself tasked to behave far more intrusively with foreign shipping and local maritime craft than would presently be comfortable to our National Command Authority, Congress, or the Navy itself. Practical requirements, forced upon us by hostile actors, will dictate policy (despite 9/11, we still are not remotely serious about warfare). Policing the high seas is going to demand a Navy with more, if often smaller, vessels as the service reluctantly assumes the role of civilization's global coast guard.

A worrisome trend in our Navy is the elevation of technology above personnel to a degree never seen before. It appears to an outside observer that the desire to reduce crew size to a minimum on the next generation of vessels may prove to be a prescription for sharply reduced capabilities, if not occasional disasters. Despite the notion that a warship might seal itself against an assault, a crew so small that it cannot defend itself will, sooner or later, find itself in a position where it cannot defend itself. Postmodern manning initiatives appear to allow for no vital redundancy. Yet management theories and personnel cost savings that sound awfully good at budget time in the Navy Annex simply replicate the false savings the Army garnered by reducing manning so severely that deploying units had to be augmented by raiding the personnel rosters of like units (or the Reserve component).

Warfare remains an endeavor of the people, by the people, and for the people. The machines are means, not ends. Although there is an obvious cultural divide between the Navy and Air Force, in which people support systems, and the Army and Marines, in which systems support people, the Navy must overcome its utterly false belief that all problems have technological solutions. *People matter.*

Although we may be able to reduce the size of aircraft carrier crews without diminishing our capabilities, if we try to man tomorrow's über-tech frigates or destroyers with skeletal crews we limit our ability to perform many of the missions the future will demand in war and peace. Until robotics advances to the point where machines suffice for boarding parties and landing parties, we had best have crews of sufficient size to have a look for themselves.

This is merely a return to our naval traditions—if to traditions the big-war Navy slights. If the domination of commerce in wartime and its protection short of war is an essential requirement—which it is indisuptably—it would appear that we need far more vessels designed for independent operations (whether in the manner of the *CSS Alabama* or the British patrol vessels that interrupted the slave trade—the latter offering a sound and rigorous model for dealing with terrorists at sea). And those vessels need crew members in adequate numbers and sufficiently trained to function as naval infantry when required. Not every postmodern ship will have room for a Marine detachment, but designated sailors on every vessel should be trained for boarding duties and limited security actions ashore.

Meanwhile, the "grand fleet" will need to serve dual roles: first, that of defeating or containing the enemy's navy and, second, delivering massive firepower to targets deep inland—the importance of putting steel on target in large volumes will only increase as the Air Force insists on putting ever smaller payloads on ever fewer aircraft. The myopic killing of the arsenal ship proposed in the 1990s was as much about naval wishful thinking as the Air Force's self-destructive obsession with the F/A-22. Although even the arsenal ship would not have approached the required level of redundant firepower, it would have been a beginning. It is essential for naval planners to address this issue, since our Air Force is on a path to quantitative incompetence to fight a war with a power such as China.

A crucial issue with strategic nonnuclear firepower is, of course, cost. The most desirable breakthrough for which we might hope would be the development of a means to deliver country-ravaging, yet accurate firepower on a grand scale—and affordably. One of the painful lessons of our otherwise-impressive march to Baghdad during Operation Iraqi Freedom was that, even in a minor war, our stocks of hyperexpensive precision weapons are rapidly depleted. This need for an affordability breakthrough should cause us to mourn the essential demise of the arsenal system, since private defense contractors have little incentive to discover ways to do cheaply what can be done far more expensively and at greater profit.

The Mission: control of the seas and dominance of the global commerce that depends more on sea lanes with each passing day; the destruction or neutralization of opposing fleets; and the global delivery of overwhelming firepower. Obviously, each requirement relates to the others; yet, in the shorter term, they will appear to be in conflict, posing different demands. The Navy is in a position similar to that of the Army, which longs to return to a limited range of missions, but will be unable to do so in our lifetimes. Fulfilling the requirements future crises will impose upon the Navy requires no-holds-barred, imagine-the-unimaginable thinking today. At present, an outsider senses a great deal of intellectual activity in the Navy—but directed toward renovation, not revolution. (As history has instructed us again and again, military technologies in and of themselves are not revolutionary—it's their incisive employment that makes all the difference).

Yet a true revolution in naval affairs—a series of revolutions—is essential, in fields as diverse as reimagining the law of the seas and designing affordable ships that address the missions our Navy actually will have, rather than those it wishes to embrace. The future is the Navy's to seize. One sees no sign of the Navy reaching out to grab it.

THE FINEST NAVY

For all the criticism offered here, our Navy today is the finest that ever rode blue water. No fleet commanded by Nelson, or even Nimitz, could come close. Yet, our great Navy does not appear ready to recognize that the world is changing far more swiftly than our cumbersome efforts at military thought have been able or willing to address. The best reply one could wish to this article would be a response from a naval officer that tore the arguments presented here to shreds—then offered better ones.

Meanwhile, the figure of Captain Alfred Thayer Mahan is reemerging from the mists at sea. In a recent book, I argued that, while Clausewitz certainly remains worth studying, Mahan's vision is far more relevant to the future of the United States. We don't rely on coaling stations, of course, and major fleet actions will be few and far between. Many of Mahan's details are dated—but he understood our enduring strategic requirement: The command of the seas. Mahan saw with all-American clarity that the United States can enjoy neither lasting peace nor prosperity without the control of the world's sea lanes.

It is up to our Navy to secure our strategic future.

Simplification and Slaughter

Future Armies, Future Challenges

Edited by Michael Euzus, Alan Ryan, and Russell Parkin, 2004

When traditions crack and social orders struggle, men and nations yearn for reassurance. Those that feel the weight of change most painfully do not want to know why they have failed; rather, they want to know who they might blame. No man desires to face his own inadequacy, nor do civilizations blame themselves for their own collapse. Once, men blamed the gods. Now, in the Middle East, they blame America and the West. The difference is hardly one of substance.

The threat of intercivilizational violence that we face today arises from the massive dimensions of much of humankind's unwillingness—or inability—to accept responsibility for failures wrought at home. This flight into excuses is an ancient phenomenon, but modernity has intensified its effect and dramatically broadened its scale. Now the advent of the postmodern, techno-industrial juggernaut of Western civilization is pushing the matter toward a culmination. We are witnessing the globalization, not of democracy, but of blame and self-exonerating simplifications insisting that centuries of bad choices do not count in human failure so much as that distant, satanic America of liberty, justice—and opportunity—for all.

Freedom terrifies the failed, whether we speak of individuals or of entire civilizations. Men cling to what they know, despite the flood of evidence that what they know will only drag them under, and the more traditional the society, the more desperately those

71

myriad hands clutch at the myth of a golden, unmolested past. We have entered the age of global mass delusion, of global accusation, of civilizational rage that cannot bear the burden of its shame. Our times will not be bloodless.

This human aching for simplification and bogeymen to blame has always come to the fore when social organization proved inadequate, whether it had to do with plague-ridden Greeks who raced to appease their deities, or with plague-ridden Europeans slaughtering Jews to drive out the Black Death. The greatest crisis of the Western order in the past thousand years (and the catalyst of the West's rise), the Protestant Reformation spawned no end of cults as prescriptive as those of today's Islamists. Yet even then the West had begun to feel its vitality and the cults were soon driven, bloodily, to the periphery. The next greatest crisis, the Industrial Revolution, with its social and geographical dislocations, drove men with traditional skills and yearnings to despair. The simultaneous emergence of utopian political theories sought to make the world at once intelligible and manageable. However, like all theories, these ideologies only sought to simplify contemporary understanding of change. No matter how complex any theory may appear, mankind is infinitely more inventive, more inspired, and more mischievous than any theoretical approach can accommodate. Marxism and Socialism, then Fascism, National Socialism, Stalinism, and the Japanese imperial religion that responded to modernity with fury—all of these were efforts to simplify an ever more complex world. Seduced and deluded by rhetoric, we misunderstood each of these counterrevolutions: None was about the future. Every single ideology inflicted upon the world, whether nominally of the right or the left, was conservative in its unwillingness to accept the sprawling diversity of human possibilities. Beyond the anglophone world and much of Western civilization, the purpose of many political thinkers has always been to limit human possibility and to force humankind into a mold congenial to the disaffected intellect.

Even the English-speaking world was not entirely immune to the reductive disease of theory and ideology, although our adaptive structures and our head start on human liberty bred a population that always viewed the bookbound "revolutionary" with suspicion. Our culture argument inoculated us against demagogues—a circumstance of great historical fortune. Nonetheless, a minority of the anglophone population, alarmed at the dislocations of their times, turned to a series of fundamentalist "religious awakenings," from the latter half of the eighteenth century, each revival of rigorous faith synchronized with only the slightest delay behind waves of disorienting progress. Blessedly, most of these turns to religion were benign, and some were even beneficial to development, emphasizing sobriety and duty. Elsewhere, ideology, with its delicious absolutions and its ready-to-hand villains, swept the most developed states. Imagine how dreadful the twentieth century would have been—how much worse—had French intellectuals had the courage of their "leftist" totalitarian convictions.

In the twentieth century, the human passion for simplification—in the degenerate forms of theory and ideology—led to massive slaughters, and it is no accident that the adaptive anglophone states, with their allergy to prescriptive ideologies, were the ultimate victors. The struggle often seemed a near-run thing—and that struggle was spawned by the discontent of states that were, with the exception of Russia, largely historical successes that had been tripped up in their forward march; these states were, even at their lowest points, not without hope. Their sense of failure was trivial compared with that in the Islamic world today. Now we face a phenomenon without historical precedent: An entire civilization of global reach has failed before our eyes. Certainly, regional cultures and civilizations have failed in the past, and some have disappeared but for scattered ruins. Humankind has never before had to contend with the stubborn noncompetitiveness of a billion like-thinking people. As already indicated, conservative Islamism is profoundly prescriptive. Islamists are drawn together by a utopian belief that the "Golden Age" of Islam can be resurrected, but only by abandoning secular forms of government and institutions in favor of theocracy. That which traditional, conservative Muslims cherish in the matter of social organization—from the subjugation of women to the behavioral strictures of faith—guarantees economic, cultural, and military failure in the modern (to say nothing of the postmodern) era. Given human nature and the failure's inchoate rage, it is no wonder that we are confronted with merciless acts of terror. The miracle is that we have seen so little terrorism to date.

If we list the cardinal factors (out of a complex of thousands, large and small) that enabled the most-developed states, led by the robust, meritocratic civilizations of anglophone nations, to succeed beyond the dreams of even our own parents, we find that each enabling characteristic is anathema to most states with majority Islamic populations—and nowhere more so than in the old Muslim heartlands. We thrive and we compound our successes because of the degree to which we have broken down barriers of privilege, gender, race, and religion. Our societies cherish the freedom of information and have developed, over centuries, an innate sense of what is true and false. We are scrupulous bookkeepers (and the recent Enron scandal in the United States demonstrated what happens to those who cheat). We minimize corruption throughout our societies and enjoy the mechanisms for pulling even the mighty down when their misbehavior becomes evident. We do not rely on bloodlines for protection and have broken the tyranny of the extended family (one of the greatest impediments to human progress). We have learned an astonishing degree of tolerance (excepting British football hooligans). We value education and have struck a functional balance between extending its benefits equitably and ensuring that the most talented are not stymied. We view work as a virtue in itself, and last but not least, we have learned the painful art of self criticism: When things go wrong we sometimes lose our tempers, but soon enough we ask ourselves what went wrong, and then we apply sophisticated skills to fixing the problem.

If you turn each of these points into its negative, you have described Saudi Arabia, Pakistan, Egypt, Sudan, and many another state that is little more than a cultural prison. And here we must state firmly: Every one of these failures is homegrown. The Crusades are a worse excuse for nonperformance than "The dog ate my homework." Islam's blows against Europe were far harsher, enduring into the nineteenth century in the Balkans and on the marches of the Russian Empire. Islam's failure is in no sense the fault of the West. The development of Muslim societies is crippled by their core values, by the lies they tell to each other and to themselves, and by the cruelty with which they have organized their societies.

Of course, it would be better for all of us were the Islamic world to evolve, swiftly, into a success story in which prosperity, tolerance, and the rule of law enabled us all to interact to our collective benefit. However, the core Muslim states are not going to develop successfully in our lifetime—and likely not thereafter. We will have to contend with the consequences of failure in a civilization that, by functional Western standards, is increasingly unbalanced psychologically. This is not good news.

For some states, there may, indeed, be hope. Iran may surprise us, as it slowly flushes extremism from its system. This country's tragedy was that it got what it wanted, and now that what it wanted does not work, it may find a chance to set a healthier direction. Iran may be able to climb back up—although success is far from guaranteed. It is, at least, a country whose culture is older, richer, more robust, and much more promising than that of the Arab world. The next decade or so may well see Iran and the United States become strategic partners once again, with both allied with India, Israel, and Turkey (where ethnicity trumps religion and history differs) in a disciplinary alliance against the murderous impulses of the region's many failures.

The jury remains out on Malaysia and Indonesia, and the factors involved are so complex and case-specific that they cannot be addressed here even in summary. In the past, Indonesia has made the classic error made by other Muslim states, such as Egypt and Pakistan. Attempts to appease extremists by avoiding extensive crackdowns and by looking the other way in the hope that the problem will remain tolerable have not worked elsewhere—the cancer that is fundamentalist terrorism does not simply go away. In the wake of the Bali bombings, Indonesia has been forced to confront the terrorists in its midst. The future of Islam is up for grabs in Indonesia and Malaysia. We can only hope that the trend continues toward political secularism, not toward religious extremism. However, these possible exceptions only prove the rule. We do not so much face Samuel Huntington's "clash of civil civilizations" as bear witness to the crash of one civilization. This is no equal struggle, and we are going to win. Increasingly, however, the peoples of the old Muslim heartland display a virulent turn of mind: *après nous, le déluge*—with, quite literally, a vengeance.

When people turn to ideologies, the secular movements take on religious overtones and transcendental rhetoric, while reactionary religious "rivals" focus on secular behaviors and physical destruction. Nazism and Stalinism both evolved into religions with mortal gods (as did, explicitly, the Japanese Greater East Asia Co-Prosperity Sphere). Now, fundamentalist Islam focuses not on spiritual content, but on overt behaviors mandated by God—rendering the deity no more than a brutal headmaster—and on earthly retaliation for imagined wrongs. Indeed, what a visitor to any Islamic country comes away with is a haunting sense of how cruelly the local elite has exploited their coreligionists. The blame for this exploitation is often deflected onto the CIA, or onto Hollywood, or onto Zionism—that indispensable enemy of failed, corrupt, and degenerate regimes.

Invariably, such ideologically driven movements, religious or secular, turn apocalyptic in their desperation. In the twentieth century, such movements have butchered *kulaks* by the millions, imprisoned tens of millions of the "enemies of the people" in camps, and gassed perceived enemies in death factories. Raping and slaughtering their way through the cities of lesser races, they have not been content until they had caused destruction of millenarian proportions, bringing down the walls of Berlin around themselves or the walls of the World Trade Center Towers around us. The impulse is always toward extravagant forms of death, and every ideological movement approaching its zenith adorns itself with macabre rituals. Our petty theories do not explain this deeply human impulse, and many of us refuse to accept this ingrained taste for darkness—despite the evidence served up by the twentieth century. Now we see before our eyes clear evidence of a civilizational death wish among the more extreme Islamists—but suicidal visions require a great deal of foreign company for grand immolation. It may be wise for us to pay attention.

Elsewhere, I have written of the differences between practical and apocalyptic terrorists. On September 11, 2001, we were shocked so deeply because we had long since grown accustomed to dealing with practical terrorists, those whose goals are political and of this earth (if sometimes grandiose). Such terrorists hijack planes and hold the passengers captive as bargaining chips. We were unprepared to deal with apocalyptic terrorists, whose vision is, ultimately, not of this earth, and whose deepest urge is toward nihilistic destruction—no matter the passing rhetoric about earthly injustice.

Apocalyptic terrorists, who cannot be appeased or ever sated, hijack airliners with a very different intent, as America learned so painfully on September 11, 2001.

Across the past few decades, we have seen a fundamental shift in the tenor of terrorism. The liberation and separatist movements of the 1960s and 1970s that sought to change local orders through violence are still with us. However, they have increasingly yielded pride of place to men possessed by visions of a blood-soaked divinity, men who claim that the finger of god has chosen them for vengeance, men whose rewards are finally not of this earth. The practical terrorist may be willing to sacrifice his life for his cause, but he would rather live to see his dreams made real. The apocalyptic terrorist, in his purest form, yearns for death, for annihilation and cosmic resolution. He is the unhappiest of men, incapable of finding contentment on this earth. Usually, he cannot find a satisfactory relationship with society, no matter his level of privilege—and, with remarkable consistency, he lives in terror of female sexuality. He aches for clear rules amid the chaos of change. Despite his willingness to sacrifice himself (in his case, a selfish impulse), he is finally a man afraid. He longs for a mythic past that he has conjured as a golden age when men such as he were accorded their full due, and when those of less rigor were punished appropriately. The apocalyptic terrorist would always rather destroy than build, rather kill than redeem, and no matter his calls for justice, he could not build a workable regime upon this earth, since humanity would ever disappoint him.

Certainly, the vigor of the apocalyptic terrorist's commitment varies—not all are anxious for martyrdom. But enervated societies and rotten regimes can be upended by even a small number of men desperate to die "for god." Such men hope to kick start Armageddon and to bring on the end of days, to borrow from Christian parlance, since apocalyptic terrorism, historically, has produced plenty of Christian killers, and Jewish and Hindu ones as well. It seems that Islam has simply come up for its turn, although the scale of the problem has no precedent, thanks to the raw numbers of the disaffected and the dualistic nature of modern technologies. Contrary to the media, the problem is not the Muslim masses, but the critical mass of madmen within the huge reactor of society—and that molten core is growing.

No matter how successful and sustained our war against terrorism, we still will suffer more blows. We can, however, reduce the frequency and scale of those attacks dramatically, and that is what we are doing as I write. Still, this is a struggle that will endure beyond our lifetimes, fought in fits and starts. I do not doubt our ultimate success, but we must prepare ourselves for some unpleasant surprises along the way. We must not hesitate to terrorize the terrorists. Only ferocity works against such men. All measures short of resolute and uncompromising violence directed against them amount to slow surrender.

Fortunately—in a perverse sense—we may rely on these apocalyptic terrorists themselves to help us maintain the resolve to exterminate them wherever we find them. Their weakness always lies in their success: They inevitably overreach, exciting outrage and allowing us to discard the superstructures of nonsense that peace imposes on our policies and our militaries. The viciousness of these terrorists reminds us that we must be feared by all those who wish us ill. The attacks of September 11, 2001, provide a classic example: Had the terrorists only struck the Pentagon, much of the world would have cheered, and even some of America's nominal allies would have snickered behind closed doors. However, the graphic monstrosity of the attacks on the World Trade Center Towers brought home to every civilized state the necessity of fighting back with vigor. Without the terrorists' success, America would likely not have mustered the backing for its subsequent successes against them. Even the late-2002 terrorist attack on India's parliament serves as an illustration: Savagery in Kashmir was one thing, but attacks against the government in New Delhi quite another, and Pakistan was lucky, indeed, that the United States had a momentary interest in keeping the local peace.

In Peshawar madrassas, Hamburg apartments, or Afghani mountain caves, terrorists talk themselves into a fantasy world of greater power than they wield in practice, imagining that their attacks will bring down states, empires, and civilizations. But the ambition—the madness—of the apocalyptic terrorist always outstrips practical possibilities in the end. Such men are impatient for death and God, and certainly impatient with the world. Small successes encourage them to great follies. This fact may be small comfort for their victims, but it guarantees that their tactical successes ultimately lead to strategic defeats.

This chapter strikes a pessimistic tone, but only because it has discussed the failing civilization of Islam. Yet even Islam sheds some rays of hope, if fewer than we might desire. There will be, at last, a liberal reformation in Islam, perhaps beginning in this very decade (although the process will take longer to mature). That reformation is, however, not going to come in the desolate, bitter Islamic heartlands. It is likeliest to begin in North America and the anglophone world, where the successes of our societies, economies, and culture will seduce the children and grandchildren of Muslim immigrants, inspiring them to repair their faith and fit it to modernity, as those of other religions have done before them. The positive pressures exerted by our societies, the vivid examples abounding, and the possibilities that open up to open minds are far likelier to drive humane reforms in the Islamic faith than the delicious resentments and indispensable hatreds of those states where Islam chokes the future to death.

No matter what the situation is in the Muslim world, the West and its allies will do just fine. We are only at the beginning of a century that promises tremendous expansions of our wealth, power, and possibility. In this age of multiple, intermingled revolutions—in gender, racial, and religious relations in our societies, in technologies, to citizen empowerment, in military reach, in economic vigor and the power of information—we possess the skills to reinforce success, while discarding things that fail along the away. We of the West are creatures of change, while our antagonists resist the very changes that could begin to liberate them. But, then, liberation is really a Western concept, after all; adapted as a slogan by nonWesterners, it rarely led to freedom and opportunity (except for local elites, who stole with unbelievable panache, from Africa to the Middle East to Asia). Freedom, democracy, equitable laws well enforced—we grew these in our backyard gardens, and we cannot yet know how well they will transplant to other cultures. The coming century will decide. That century will belong to those men and women unafraid of change.

The Counterrevolution in Military Affairs

The Weekly Standard

February 6, 2006

Revolutions notoriously imprison their most committed supporters. Intellectually, influential elements within our military are locked inside the cells of the revolution in military affairs, where hi-tech bars obscure warfare's realities. Our current conflicts have freed the Army and Marines from at least some of the nonsensical theories of techno-war, but the Air Force and Navy remain captivated by the notion that machines can replace human beings on the battlefield. Chained to their twentieth-century successes, they cannot face the new reality confronting us: Wars of flesh, faith, and cities. Meanwhile, our enemies, immediate and potential, appear to grasp the contours of future war far better than we do.

While we squabble over funding for yesterday's weapon designs, the counterrevolution in military affairs is well under way, from Iraq's Sunni Triangle to Chinese military staffs. We are seduced by what we *can* do; our enemies focus on what they *must* do. They cannot outspend us, but they threaten to outthink us.

We have fallen so deeply in love with the means we have devised for waging conceptual wars that we are blind to their marginal relevance in actual conflicts. We continue to buy ever more expensive systems that bedazzle us but fail to deter our enemies. Terrorists, for one lethal example, do not fear "network-centric warfare" because they have already mastered it for a tiny fraction of one cent on the dollar, achieving greater relative effects with the internet, cell phones, cheap airline tickets, and cheaper explosives than all of our military technologies have delivered. Our prime weapon in our struggles with terrorists, insurgents, and warriors of every patchwork sort remains the soldier or Marine, yet confronted with reality's bloody evidence, we simply pretend that other, future, magical wars will justify the systems we adore—purchased at the expense of the assets we need. Meanwhile, a single news cameraman on the scene can limit or even prevent the use of our most extravagant weapons—the media play a potent role in the counterrevolution in military affairs, as well as in the reaction against the unsettling social and economic changes exemplified by the United States.

Stubbornly, we continue to fantasize that a wondrous enemy will appear who will fight us on our own terms, as a masked knight might have materialized at a stately tournament in a novel by Sir Walter Scott. Yet, not even China—the threat beloved of major defense contractors and their advocates—would play by our rules if folly ignited war. Against terrorists, we have found technology alone incompetent to master men of soaring will—only our own flesh and blood provides an effective counter. At the other extreme, a war with China, which our war games blithely assume would be brief, would reveal the quantitative incompetence of our forces as our assault on a continent-spanning power swiftly drained our stocks of precision weapons, ready pilots, and aircraft. We have been buying Ferraris, when we need a big fleet of pickup trucks.

Quality, no matter how great, is not a reliable substitute for a robust force in being and deep reserves that can be mobilized rapidly. In the Second World War, the Germans fielded the finest tanks, but we overwhelmed their limited numbers of Tigers and King Tigers with vast swarms of just-good-enough M-4 Shermans. In a conflict between Washington and Beijing, the situation would be reversed. We would stun our opponents—for the strategic equivalent of fifteen minutes. Thereafter, our weapon stocks would be exhausted and we would struggle to hold the line.

There is not a single enemy in existence or on the horizon willing to play the victim to the military we continue to build at crippling expense. Our revolution in military affairs was always oversold. Now, faced with men of iron belief wielding bombs built in sheds and basements, it appears more an indulgence than an investment.

In the end, our enemies will not outfight us. We'll muster the will to do what must be done—after paying a needlessly high price in the lives of our troops and damage to our domestic infrastructure. We will not be beaten, but we may be shamed and embarrassed on a needlessly long road to victory.

Free of the burden of our intellectually corrupt procurement system, our enemies continue to outthink us. We are under the spell of the wicked witch of gimmicks.

WEAPON OF GENIUS

After spending trillions of dollars over decades on super-tech weapons and the lavish systems that support them, not a single item in our arsenal reflects the genius of the suicide bomber—the breakthrough weapon of our time. Our intelligence systems cannot locate him, our arsenal cannot deter him, and, all too often, our soldiers cannot stop him until it is too late. A man (only occasionally a woman) of invincible conviction—call it delusion, if you will—armed with explosives stolen or purchased for a handful of soiled bills can have a strategic impact that staggers governments. Abetted by the global media, the suicide bomber is the wonder weapon of the age.

The suicide bomber's willingness to discard civilization's cherished, impractical rules for warfare gives him enormous strength. In the Cain-and-Abel conflicts of the twenty-first century, ruthlessness trumps technology. The moral force of the man willing to walk into an elementary school or women's clinic and detonate himself has a greater impact than any of the sterilized weapons in our arsenal.

We refuse to comprehend the suicide bomber's soul—even though today's wars are contests of souls and belief is our enemy's ultimate order of battle. We write off the suicide bomber as a criminal, a wanton butcher, a terrorist. Yet within his spiritual universe, he's more heroic than the American soldier who throws himself atop a grenade to spare his comrades: He isn't merely protecting other men, but defending his god. The suicide bomber can justify any level of carnage because he's doing his god's will. Any crime of violence is permissible, if it furthers the cause of faith. We agonize over a prisoner's slapped face, while our enemies kill innocent masses (even of fellow believers) and are lauded as heroes for doing so. We continue to narrow our view of warfare's acceptable parameters even as our enemies amplify the concept of total war.

Islamist terrorists, to cite the immediate example, would do anything to win. Would we? Our enemies act on ecstatic revelations from their god. We act on the advice of lawyers. Who exhibits the greater strength of character: the individual willing to do whatever he finds necessary to fulfill an all-consuming mission, or a vast military waiting for permission to arrest a looter? It is astonishing that we have managed to hold the line as well as we have.

The ultimate precision weapon, the suicide bomber simultaneously redefines the scope of "legitimate" targets. Delighted to kill our troops, this implacable enemy who regards death as a promotion is equally ready to slaughter men, women, and children of unknown identity who have done him no slightest harm. His strength of will towers over our own. He cannot win wars on the traditional battlefields we cherish, but his commitment and actions transcend such tidy limits. In the moment of his deed, the suicide bomber is truly larger than life. The world's a stage, and every suicide bomber is, at least briefly, a star.

We will develop the means to defeat the majority of, if not all, improvised explosive devices (IEDs). But the suicide bomber—the living, thinking assassin determined to die—may prove impossible to stop. Even if we discover a means to identify him at a distance from our troops, he has only to turn to alternate, easier targets. Virtually anything the suicide bomber attacks brings value to his cause—destruction of any variety is a victory. The paradox is that his act of self-destruction is also an undeniable assertion that "I am," as he becomes the voice from below that the mighty cannot ignore. We are trained to think in terms of cause and effect—but the suicide bomber merges the two. The gesture and the result are inseparable from and integral to his message. Self-destruction and murder join to become the ultimate act of self-assertion.

And his deed is heralded, while even our most virtuous acts are condemned around the world. Even in the days before mass media, assassins terrorized civilizations. Today their deeds are amplified by a toxic, breathtakingly irresponsible communications culture that spans the globe (and remains immune to our feeble RMA). Photogenic violence is no longer a local affair—if a terrorist gives the media picturesque devastation, he reaches the entire planet. We cannot measure the psychological magnification, although we grasp it vaguely. And the media's liturgical repetition of the suicide bomber's act creates an atmosphere of sacrament. On a primal level, the suicide bomber impresses even his enemies with his conviction. We hasten to dismiss his deed as a perversion, yet it resounds as a vivid act of faith. Within his own cultural context, people may hate what the suicide bomber does, yet revere his sacrifice (and, too often, they do not hate what he does).

We may refuse to accept it, but suicide bombing operates powerfully on practical, emotional, and spiritual levels—and it generates brilliant, dirt-cheap propaganda. To the Muslim world, the suicide bomber's act is a proof of faith that ensnares the mind with a suspicion of his righteousness. He is a nearly irresistible champion of the powerless, the Middle East's longed-for superhero, the next best thing to the Mahdi or the Twelfth Imam.

We praise Nathan Hale's willingness to die for his cause. Now imagine thousands of men anxious to die for theirs. The suicide bomber may be savage, brutal, callous, heartless, naive, psychotic, and, to us, despicable, but within his cultural milieu he is also heroic.

The hallmark of our age is the failure of belief systems and a subsequent flight back to primitive fundamentalism—and the phenomenon isn't limited to the Middle East. Faith revived is running roughshod over science and civilization. Secular societies appear increasingly fragmented, if not fragile. The angry gods are back. And they will not be defeated with cruise missiles or computer codes.

A paradox of our time is that the overwhelmingly secular global media—a collection of natural-born religion-haters—have become the crucial accomplices of the suicide bomber fueled by rabid faith. Mass murderers are lionized as freedom fighters, while our own troops are attacked by the press they protect for the least waywardness or error. One begins to wonder if the bomber's suicidal impulse isn't matched by a deep death wish affecting the West's cultural froth

(What if Darwin was right conceptually, but failed to grasp that homo sapiens' most powerful evolutionary strategy is faith?). Both the suicide bomber and the "world intellectual" with his reflexive hatred of America exist in emotional realms that our rational models of analysis cannot explain. The modern age's methods for interpreting humanity are played out.

We live in the new age of superstition and bloodthirsty gods, of collective madness. Its icons are the suicide bomber, the veil, and the video camera.

ASYMMETRICAL MINDS

One of the most consistently disheartening experiences an adult can have today is to listen to the endless attempts by our native intellectuals and even intelligence professionals to explain religious terrorism in clinical terms, assigning rational motives to men who have moved irrevocably beyond reason. We suffer under layers of intellectual asymmetries that hinder us from an intuitive recognition of our enemies. Our rear-guard rationalists range from those convinced that every security problem has a technological solution, if only it can be found, to those who insist that members of al Qa'eda and its affiliates are motivated by finite, comprehensible, and logical ambitions, which, if satisfied, would make our problems disappear.

Living in unprecedented safety within our borders and lacking firsthand knowledge of the decay beyond our shores, honorable men and women have convinced themselves that Osama bin Laden's professed goals of driving the United States from the Middle East and removing corrupt regional governments truly are what global terror is all about. They gloss over his stated ambition of reestablishing the caliphate and his calls for the destruction of Israel as rhetorical effects—when they address them at all. Yet Islamist fanatics are more deeply committed to their maximalist goals than to their lesser ones—and their unspoken ambitions soar beyond logic's realm. Religious terrorists are committed to an apocalypse they sense within striking distance. Their longing for union with god is inseparable from their impulse toward comprehensive annihilation. They seek their god in carnage and will go on slaughtering until he appears to pat them on the back.

Before staking too much upon the explicit statements of an enemy such as bin Laden, consider how badly our predecessors were taken in when they trusted Adolf Hitler's claims of limited ambitions (the enthusiasm for assigning virtues to monstrous enemies is a uniquely Western phenomenon, as helpful to Stalin as to Saddam Hussein). At first we were assured that Hitler only wanted to "reclaim" the Rhineland, which had been "unjustly" occupied by the allies. Then he only meant to protect the ethnic Germans living in the Sudetenland in Czechoslovakia. Hitler never stated publicly that he intended to exterminate Europe's Jews. Few enemies publish detailed programs of their every goal (we're becoming an exception, as our national leaders make extravagant claims about all they intend to accomplish—only to renege on their pronouncements).

A dangerous asymmetry exists in the type of minds working the problem of Islamist terrorism in our government and society. On average, the "experts" to whom we are conditioned to listen have a secular mentality (even if they go to church or synagogue from habit). And it is a very rare secular mind that can comprehend religious passion—it's like asking a blind man to describe the colors of fire. One suspects that our own fiercest believers are best equipped to penetrate the mentality—the souls—of our Islamist enemies, although those believers may not be as articulate as the secular intellectuals who anxiously dismiss all possibilities that lie outside of their theoretical constructs.

Those who feel no vital faith cannot comprehend faith's power. A man or woman who has never been intoxicated by belief will default to mirror-imaging when asked to describe terror's roots. He who has never experienced a soul-shaking glimpse of the divine inevitably explains religion-driven suicide bombers in terms of a lack of economic opportunity or social humiliation. But the enemies we face are burning with belief, on fire with their vision of an imminent, angry god. Our intelligentsia is less equipped to understand such men than our satellites are to find them.

All of our technologies and comforting theories are confounded by the strength of the soul ablaze with faith. Our struggle with Islamist terror (other religious terrors may haunt our descendants) has almost nothing to do with our actions in the Middle East. It's about a failing civilization's embrace of a furious god.

WARS OF FAITH

We are not (yet) at war with Islam, but the extreme believers within Islam are convinced that they are soldiers in a religious war against us. Despite their rhetoric, *they* are the crusaders. Even our conceptions of the struggle are asymmetrical. Despite the horrors we have witnessed, we have yet to take religious terrorists seriously on their own self-evident terms. We invaded a succession of their tormented countries but haven't come close to penetrating their souls. The hermetic universe of the Islamist terrorist is immune to our reality (if not to our bullets), but our intellectuals appear equally incapable of accepting the religious extremist's reality.

We have no tools of persuasion effective against a millenarian belief. What logic can we wield against the soul fortified by faith and barricaded beyond argument? Even if we understood every nuance of our enemy's culture, the suicide bomber's intense faith and the terror chieftain's visions have burned through native cultural restraints. We are told, rather smugly, that the Koran forbids suicide. But our enemies are not concerned with how we read their faith. Religions are living things, and ultraextremists are improvising a new and savage cult within Islam—even as they proclaim their return to a purified faith.

Security-wise, we have placed our faith in things, in bright (and expensive) material objects. But the counterrevolution in military affairs is based on the brilliant intuition that our military might can be sidestepped often enough to challenge its potency. Certainly, we inflict casualties on our enemies—and gain real advantages from doing so—but we not only face an enemy who, as observed above, views death as a promotion, but one who believes he has won even when he loses. If the suicide bomber completes his mission, he has won. But even if he is killed or dies short of his target, he has conquered a place in paradise. Which well-intentioned information operations of ours can compete with the conviction that a martyr's death leads to eternal joy?

Again, our intelligentsia falls woefully short. The most secularized element of our society, educated to avoid faith (or, at the very least, to shun enthusiastic, vigorous, proud, and public faith), our professional thinkers have lost any sense of a literal paradise beyond the grave. But our enemies enjoy a faith as vivid as did our medieval ancestors, for whom devils lurked in the undergrowth and paradise was an idealized representation of that which mortals knew. We are taught that we should never underestimate our enemies—yet we underestimate the power of his faith, his most potent weapon.

Nor should we assume that Islamist extremists will remain the only god-haunted terrorists attacking established orders. This century may prove to be one of multisided struggles over the interpretation of god's will, between believers and unbelievers, between the varieties of the faithful, between monotheists and polytheists, between master faiths and secessionist movements, between the hollow worshippers of science and those swollen with the ecstasy of belief.

Naturally, we view the cardinal struggle as between the West and extremists within the Islamic world, yet the bloodiest religious warfare of the coming decades may be between Sunni and Shi'a Muslims or between African Muslims and the new, sub-Saharan Church Militant. Hindu extremists gnaw inward from the epidermis of Indian society, while even Buddhist monks have engaged in organized violence in favor of their ostensibly peaceable faith. In a bewildering world where every traditional society is under assault from the forces of global change, only religion seems to provide a reliable refuge. And each god seems increasingly a jealous god.

Faith is the great strategic factor that unbelieving faculties and bureaucracies ignore. It may be the crucial issue of this century. And we cannot even speak about it honestly.

Give me a warrior drunk with faith, and I will show you a weapon beyond the dreams of any laboratory. Our guided bombs may kill individual terrorists, but the terrorist knows that our weapons can't kill his god.

THE COUNTERREVOLUTION'S OTHER EXTREME

Even in preparing for "big wars," we refuse to take the enemy into account. Increasingly, our military is designed for breathtaking sprints, yet a war with China—were one forced upon us by events—

would be a miserable long march. We may face other conventional conflicts, but none would be so demanding as a war with China; for all the rhetoric expended and the innumerable war games played, the best metaphor for a serious struggle with Beijing—perhaps of Homeric length—comes from that inexhaustible little book, Joseph Conrad's novella, *Heart of Darkness*, with its pathetic image of a Western gunboat lobbing shells uselessly into a continent.

Given the comprehensive commitment and devastation required to defeat strategically and structurally weaker enemies, such as Japan and Germany, how on earth dare we pretend that we could drive China to sue for peace by fighting a well-mannered war with a small military whose shallow stocks of ammunition would be drained swiftly and could not be replaced in meaningful quantities? Would we try "shock and awe, part II," over Beijing, hoping to convince China's leaders to surrender at the sight of our special effects? Or would our quantitative incompetence soon force us onto the defensive?

We must be realistic about the military requirements of a war with China, but we also need to grasp that, for such an enemy, the military sphere would be only one field of warfare—and not the decisive one. What would it take to create an atmosphere of defeat in a sprawling nation of over one billion people? A ruthless economic blockade, on the seas, in the air, and on land, would be an essential component of any serious war plan, but the Chinese capability for sheer endurance might surprise us. Could we win against China without inflicting extensive devastation on Chinese cities? Would even that be enough? Without mirror-imaging again, can we identify any incentive China's leaders would have to surrender?

The Chinese version of the Counter-RMA puts less stress on a head-to-head military confrontation (although that matters, of course) and more on defeating the nation behind our military. Despite the importance Beijing attaches to a strong military, China won't fall into the trap that snared the Soviets—the attempt to compete with our military expenditures. Why fight battles you'll lose, when you can wage war directly against the American population by attacking its digital and physical infrastructure, its confidence and morale? In a war of mutual suffering, which population would be better equipped, practically and psychologically, to endure massive power outages, food-chain disruptions, the obliteration of databases, and even epidemic disease?

Plenty of Americans are tougher than we're credited with being, but what about the now-decisive intelligentsia? What about those conditioned to levels of comfort unimaginable to the generation that fought World War II (or even Vietnam)? Would twenty-first-century suburban Americans accept rationing without protests? Could China win by focusing its efforts to wreak havoc on urban professionals, soccer moms, and the media, while ignoring "red-state" America? It only takes a few hundred men and women in Washington to decide that a war is lost.

Regarding the media's prejudices and power, whenever I encounter Chinese abroad I am astonished by their chauvinism. Their confidence is reminiscent of Americans half a century ago. Should we pretend that Chinese opinion-makers, such as they are, would feel inclined to attack their government as our journalists attack Washington? A war with China would be a massive contest of wills. And China might need to break the will of only a tiny fraction of our population as our governing elite continues to lose touch with heartland America.

As for our overhyped military technologies, how, exactly, would an F/A-22 destroy the Chinese will to endure and prevail? How would it counteract a hostile media? Assuming we had any of those aircraft left after the first few years of war?

If we should worry about any strategic differences with China, they are the greater simplicity and robustness of China's less-developed (hence, less fragile) infrastructure and a greater will to win in Beijing. No matter how well our military might perform, sufficient pain inflicted on the American people could lead a weak national leadership to a capitulation thinly disguised as a compromise. Addicted to trade with China, many in America's business community would push for a rapid end to any conflict, no matter the cost to our nation as a whole (when Chinese fighters forced down a U.S. reconnaissance aircraft on Hainan Island several years ago, American-business lobbyists rushed to Capitol Hill to plead for patience with China—they had no interest in our aircrew or our national good).

The Chinese know they cannot defeat our military. So they intend to circumvent it, as surely as Islamist terrorists seek to do, if in more complex ways. For example, China's navy cannot guarantee its merchant vessels access to sea lanes in the Indian Ocean—routes which carry the oil on which modern China runs. So Beijing is working to build a web of formal and informal client relationships in the region that would deny the U.S. Navy port facilities, challenge the United States in global and regional forums, and secure alternate routes and sources of supply. China's next great strategic initiative is going to be an attempt to woo India, the region's key power, away from a closer relationship with the United States. Beijing may fail, but its strategists are thinking in terms of the out-years, while our horizon barely reaches from one Quadrennial Defense Review to the next.

Even in Latin America, China labors to develop capabilities to frustrate American purposes, weaken hemispheric ties, and divert our strategic resources during a Sino-American crisis. We dream of knockout blows, while Beijing prepares the death of a thousand cuts. The Chinese are the ultimate heirs of Liddell-Hart and his indirect approach: They would have difficulty conquering Taiwan militarily but believe they could push us into an asymmetrical defeat through economic, diplomatic, and media campaigns in the Middle East, Africa, Europe, and Latin America—while crippling the lifestyle of America's citizens at home.

It's become another cliché to observe how much of our manufacturing capability has moved to China while we tolerate, at our own business community's behest, Beijing's cynical undervaluation of its currency. If you don't think this matters, try to go a single week without buying or using a product made in China. A conflict with Beijing might be lost on the empty shelves of Wal-Mart. Indeed, Beijing's most effective international allies are American corporations.

In the Second World War we famously converted our consumer industries into producers of wartime materiel. Will a future president find himself trapped by our defense industry's inability to produce consumer goods in wartime?

If you want to ponder a war with China, think beyond mere military capabilities. It would be a total war, waged in spheres where our military is legally forbidden to engage, from data banks to shopping malls. How many readers of this journal have participated in a war game that addressed crippling consumer shortages as a conflict with China dragged on for years? Instead, we obsess about the fate of a pair of aircraft carriers. For that matter, how about a scenario that realistically portrayed the global media as siding overwhelmingly with China? The metastasizing power of the media is a true strategic revolution of our time—one to which our narrow RMA has no reply.

Oh, by the way: Could we win a war with China without killing hundreds of millions of Chinese?

IF NOT PARADISE, UTOPIA

Many of us have struggled to grasp the unreasonable, even fanatical anti-Americanism in the global media—including the hostility in many news outlets and entertainment forums here at home. How can educated men and women, whether they speak Arabic, Spanish, French, or English, condemn America's every move, while glossing over the abuses of dictators and the savagery of terrorists? Why is America blamed even when American involvement is minimal or even nonexistent? How has the most beneficial great power in history been transformed by the international media into a villain of relentless malevolence?

There's a straightforward answer: In their secular way, the world's media elites are as unable to accept the reality confronting them as are Islamist fundamentalists. They hate the world in which they are forced to live, and America has shaped that world.

It isn't that the American-wrought world is so very bad for the global intelligentsia: The freedom they exploit to condemn the United States has been won, preserved, and expanded by American sacrifices and America's example. The problem is that they wanted a different world, the utopia promised by socialist and Marxist theorists, an impossible heaven on earth that captured their imagination as surely as visions of paradise enrapture suicide bombers.

The global media may skew secular, but that doesn't protect them against alternative forms of faith. Europeans, for example, have discarded a belief in God as beneath their intelligence— yet they still need a Satan to explain their own failures, just as their ancestors required devils to explain why the milk soured or the herd sickened. Today, America has replaced the horned, cloven-footed Lucifer of Europe's past; behind their smug assumption of superiority, contemporary Europeans are as superstitious and irrational as any of their ancestors: They simply believe in other demons.

The absence of religion in their lives is a crucial source of their discontents. European intellectuals and their American imitators substituted Marx and Mao for the Judeo-Christian god their pride discarded. But the socialist utopia never arrived; instead, those crass, workaholic, uncultured, naively religious Americans created a hyper-power society in which native talent and hard work counted for more than pedigrees of birth or education. America destroyed the dream of the dictatorship of the intellectuals, the secret fantasy of the most fervent Marxists.

One of the most perverse aspects of anti-Americanism in the global media and among the international intelligentsia is that it's presented as a progressive, liberal movement, when it's bitterly reactionary, a spiteful, elitist counterrevolution directed against the empowerment of the common man and woman (the core ethos of the United States). This counterrevolution is extremely powerful and galvanizing, since our social and economic revolutions threaten traditional privileges and structures even more profoundly than our RMA threatens the conventional forces of would-be competitors.

Ever wrong, the global intelligentsia has gotten things precisely backward: We, the American people, are the true revolutionaries, in every sphere. Our enemies are the forces of reaction, of the *ancien régime*. Despite their outward differences, intellectuals are the logical allies of Islamist extremists—who are equally opposed to social progress and mass freedom. Of course, the terrorists have the comfort of religious faith, while the global intelligentsia, faced with the death of Marxism and the triumph of capitalism, has only its rage.

Human beings are hardwired for faith. Deprived of a god, they seek an alternative creed. For a time, nationalism, socialism, Marxism, and a number of other -isms appeared to have a chance of working—as long as secular intellectuals rejected the evidence of Stalin's crimes or Mao's savagery (much as they overlook the brutalities of Islamist terrorists today). The intellectuals who staff the global media experienced the American-made destruction of their secular belief systems, slowly during the Cold War, and then, jarringly, from 1989 to 1991. The experience has been as disorienting and as infuriating to them as if we incontrovertibly proved to Muslim fanatics that their god does not exist.

In the absence of a new faith, the impulse to react against America and its fabulous successes filled the void—a devil to blame turned out to be more immediately necessary than a god to worship. Islamist condemnations of "godless America" are psychologically identical to European complaints about the "inhumanity" of the American economic system (an old joke has the French president admitting that France created no new jobs, but observing that, had France created any jobs, they would have been better ones than those created in America . . .).

America's triumph shames the Middle East and Europe alike, and has long dented the pride of Latin America. But the brotherhood of Islamist terrorists and the tribe of global intellectuals who dominate the media are the two groups who feel the most fury toward America. The terrorists dream of a paradise beyond the grave; intellectuals fantasized about utopias on earth. Neither can stomach the practical success of the American way of life, with its insistence on individual performance and its resistance to unearned privilege. For the Islamists, America's power threatens the promises of their faith. For world-intellectuals, America is the murderer of their most precious fantasies.

Is it any wonder that these two superficially different groups have drifted into collusion?

WHY IT MATTERS

The suicide bomber may be the weapon of genius of our time, but the crucial new strategic factor is the rise of a global information culture that pretends to reflect reality, but in fact creates it. Iraq is only the most flagrant example of the disconnect between empirical reality and the redesigned, politically inflected alternative reality delivered by the media. This phenomenon matters far more than the profiteers of the RMA can accept—the global information sphere is now a decisive battleground. Image and idea trump the finest military technologies.

We have reached the point (as evidenced by the First Battle of Fallujah) when the global media can overturn the verdict of the battlefield. We will not be defeated by suicide bombers in Iraq, but a chance remains that the international media may defeat us. Engaged with enemies to our front, we try to ignore the enemies at our back—enemies at whom we cannot return fire. Indeed, if anything must be profoundly reevaluated it's our handling of the media in wartime. We have no obligation to open our accounts to proven enemies, yet we allow ourselves to be paralyzed by platitudes.

This doesn't mean that all of the media are evil or dishonest. It means we need to have the common sense and courage to discriminate between media outlets that attempt to report fairly (and don't compromise wartime secrets) and those whose track records demonstrate their hostility to our national purposes or their outright support for terrorists.

We got it right in World War II, but today we cannot count on patriotism among journalists, let alone their acceptance of censorship boards. Our own reporters pretend to be "citizens of the world" with "higher responsibilities," and many view patriotism as decidedly down-market. Obsessed with defending their privileges, they refuse to accept that they also have responsibilities as citizens. But after journalistic irresponsibility kills a sufficient number of Americans, reality will force us to question the media's claim that "the public has a right to know" every secret our government holds in wartime.

The media may constitute the decisive element in the global counterrevolution in military affairs, and the video camera—that insatiable accomplice of the terrorist—the cheap negation of our military technology (and beware the growing capability of digital technology to create "American" atrocities from scratch). We are proud of our ability to put steel precisely on target anywhere in the world, but guided bombs don't work against faith or an unchallenged flood of lies. We have fallen in love with wind-up dolls and forgotten the preeminence of the soul.

We need to break the mental chains that bind us to a technology-*ueber-alles* dream of warfare—a fantasy as absurd and dated as the Marxist dreams of Europe's intellectuals. Certainly, military technologies have their place and can provide our troops with useful tools. But technologies are not paramount. In warfare, flesh and blood are still the supreme currency. And strength of will remains the ultimate weapon.

Welcome to the counterrevolution.

PART II

Scouts Out

Our True Enemies

New York Post

August 11, 2003

Our immediate missions in the War Against Terror aren't enough to win a decisive victory.

Yes, those missions—preventing as many attacks as we can, killing or capturing terrorists, destroying terrorist organizations—are essential goals, but they focus on surface tumors while ignoring the cancer beneath.

The security environment will improve as Saddam, Osama, and their most virulent supporters are killed. Eliminating terrorist operatives, masterminds, and supportive dictators brings vital results. But we will never reduce Islamic terrorism to nuisance level unless we address the greater evil behind the deadly strikes.

One cannot have much sympathy with Osama bin Laden, whose vision of a vengeful god thirsty for infidel blood is utter blasphemy. Nor could any decent human being excuse the acts of terror committed by his followers, or by Palestinian suicide bombers, or by any of the morally crippled youths who murder in the name of their religion.

But it *is* possible to recognize that the majority of the lower-rank terrorists whose lives their overlords throw away so callously have been set up psychologically by the corruption and hopelessness of their societies. And those societies have been wrecked by

Arabs and other Muslims to whom we cling as partners and whom we even imagine to be our friends.

From North Africa through Arabia's sands to Kashmir, those with whom we do business, upon whom we rely for advice and assurances of stability, with whom we have dinner and play golf—these are the very creatures who have stolen everything they could steal from their own people, who have ravaged educational systems, looted treasuries, corrupted institutions, tortured and murdered populist opponents, and turned once-promising states into financial and moral basket cases.

Corruption and hypocrisy may be elements of the human condition, but Arab elites have developed them to a superhuman extreme. If they could, they would steal the air itself and charge the poor for breathing.

The little guy hasn't got a chance in the Middle East, and America should always be on the side of the little guy. Instead, we've given Arab fat cats a license to kill, steal—and betray us.

Even the Saudi delight in funding anti-Western murderers, and the regional habit of allowing terrorists to slip through phony dragnets amount to symptoms, not the disease itself.

Yes, we want that twenty-year-old terrorist dead or imprisoned. But we are naive and self-defeating if we simply continue to pick off terrorists in ones and twos, or even in hundreds, without recognizing that the very people whom we have embraced in Middle Eastern societies have created the environment in which terror thrives. And those same pals of ours have done their best to deflect all blame onto us.

We have looked away as the few destroyed the chances of the many, as the greedy ground the impoverished into the dirt. Now we are paying a price not for what we have done to Muslims, but for what we have failed to do.

Until the recent war against Saddam's regime, we never stood up for freedom in the Arab world.

We have *consistently* tolerated or supported those who said the right things to us, who signed the oil contracts, who promised to keep things quiet—and who made a mockery of every value our nation professes.

Our reward? Terror. But the truth is that we should be astonished that there is so *little* anti-American terrorism, given how long, how dishonestly, and how virulently our supposed friends preached their theology of blame to local audiences.

As our political and business partners bankrupted their countries and created stagnant societies careless of human wastage, they accused us. They stole and said we did it.

They bought mansions in the south of France, in London and Aspen, and then told their people that Egyptians and Palestinians lived in hovels because America had stolen the wealth due to them—with the help of Zionist conspirators.

Our willingness to trust those who smile and pick up the dinner tab in Riyadh or Washington has been a bipartisan sin—and a national disgrace. Hillary Clinton embraced Madame Arafat and Pakistan's peerlessly corrupt Benazir Bhutto. Both Presidents Bush refused—and continue to refuse—to acknowledge the vicious strategic agenda of the Saudi royal family.

Administrations from both parties bribed Hosni Mubarak with billions of dollars in aid while his cronies robbed Egypt into destitution. From the Straits of Gibraltar to the Himalayas, we have sold our nation's soul to second-rate devils for small change.

Future historians will regard our groveling at the feet of Saudi bigots and whoremongers as the equivalent of down-market strippers dancing for drunkards' tips.

The present administration has done an admirable job of waging the immediate, tactical fight against terrorism. But we will never achieve an enduring strategic victory until we recognize how cheaply Democrats, Republicans, and corporate America have sold out to those who damn us from their pulpits behind our backs, insisting that the only hope for Islam is to destroy Israel and America.

Why isn't there a serious bipartisan outcry to expose Saudi misdeeds? Why do we get nothing but pro forma, made-for-the-microphone complaints from both sides of the aisle? Because both political parties are horrified at the thought of the Saudis revealing what they know about us, about the sweetheart deals, the retainers-for-nothing, the inflated contracts, and the appalling shabbiness of politicians, businessmen, and lobbyists willing to look away from human suffering, injustice, and the deepest roots of terror in exchange for a game of tennis with Prince Bandar.

We have unleashed a great wave of change in the Middle East. But we will never make decisive progress against terror until we address the underlying causes—and stop supporting the smiling thieves who rob their own people then ask us out to lunch.

For all the blood on his hands, Osama has higher ethical standards than our Arab "friends."

No Final Victory

New York Post

September 11, 2003

Two years after the 9/11 attacks marked the true beginning of the twenty-first century, the United States has altered the global strategic landscape. We have taken the fight to our enemies, and now those enemies must fear us far more than we need fear them.

In the War Against Terror, no other power or organization can defeat America. But America remains dangerously capable of defeating itself.

Our strength is without precedent in the social, cultural, economic, military, and moral spheres. But, when faced with determined enemies whose capabilities are no more than the smallest fraction of our own, we reveal two dangerous weaknesses: Impatience, and the profoundly mistaken notion that the absence of a clear-cut victory means that we have been defeated.

There are few flawless victories. Even the Second World War, while incontestably an American and Allied triumph, left Eastern Europe in thrall to the Soviet Union, our Chinese Nationalist allies nearing collapse, and Europe's colonial empires in deadly tumult.

Does any of this mean that World War II wasn't worth fighting? Or that we lost?

The imperfect results of our own Civil War still awaited resolution a century later, in the 1960s. Does that suggest that a Union defeat, leaving slavery intact and our nation permanently divided, would have been a more desirable outcome?

If the men and women of the nineteenth century committed the sin of romanticizing war, then we twenty-first-century Americans are in danger of embracing a new sin, that of rejecting war's complex realities in favor of a reality-TV approach to combat and its aftermath. We seem, at times, to expect war to conform not only to election requirements, but to television broadcasting schedules.

And we'd like a nicely wrapped-up Hollywood ending, thanks. When the battle doesn't end at the top of the hour, or war's aftermath conflicts with the kickoff of the NFL season, our pundits and politicians tell us our efforts have been in vain, our sacrifices misguided.

This intellectual frivolity poses a serious danger. It discounts war's many-layered consequences, while imposing naive and impossible measures of success. The truth is that many aspects of a war's outcome remain obscure for years. Instant judgments of failure—or claims of enduring success—are no more than long-shot bets in the casino of history.

Wars do not necessarily conform to the victor's desires. Outcomes surprise. Results can never be fully anticipated—and imperfect results are the norm. If the winning side achieves most of its goals, it often must compromise on others.

The Second World War in Europe began in defense of Poland's freedom against Nazi tyranny. It ended in a tremendous Allied victory, but left Poland subject to an alternate despotism.

Aims change even in the course of war, as well as in war's aftermath. No one can fully foresee which conditions will prevail at the conclusion of general combat. War is risk—not only the risk faced by the soldier, but the risk of unintended consequences. If every outcome could be foreseen, one side or the other would simply surrender at the outset. Or neither would go to war.

The impatience and unreasonable expectations of our "opinion-makers" are exacerbated by our "Gotcha!" culture, in which no critic or candidate admits that vast gray areas exist between the extremes of unconditional victory and abject defeat. Indeed, although the Iraqi people had the good fortune to be freed from the Ba'athist regime by American troops, they now suffer the misfortune of liberation in the run-up to a U.S. presidential election.

At present, election politics, both Democratic and Republican, pose a greater danger to a long-term favorable outcome in Iraq than do regime die-hards or international terrorists.

We are in danger of talking ourselves into politically expedient actions, artificial deadlines, and an unmerited sense of failure—when we have, in fact, achieved a notable triumph, the immediate results of which are overwhelmingly positive and whose ultimate results, though still undetermined, could have the most positive influence on the Middle East of any events in the last several centuries.

Democratic presidential aspirants insist that our success is really failure, clinging perversely to each bit of bad news and belittling all signs of progress. The Republican administration, too, has begun to appear more concerned about the coming election than about Iraq's real needs, anxious to achieve the appearance of success and of costs contained, even if the penalty is to undercut the progress we have thus far achieved.

If Democrats and Republicans alike fail to recognize the stakes in Iraq, we may, indeed, maneuver ourselves into failure. If our problems, at home and abroad, seem larger and larger, it's merely an optical illusion created because our political leaders, on both sides of the aisle, have grown smaller and smaller.

We need to return to our bipartisan tradition of supporting the president's foreign policy initiatives in wartime. And make no mistake: We are, and will remain, at war. Our enemies are not Democrats or Republicans, but terrorists and butchers. It would serve us well were our political leaders to remember that.

Iraq is only one campaign in the greater War Against Terror—although it is, indeed, an important stage in that war. Those who insist on seeing Islamic terrorism as a limited problem to be dealt with in detail, rather than as the most dangerous contemporary threat in a long struggle between freedom and oppression, are engaged in wishful thinking.

9/11 wasn't so much a matter of Osama bin Laden's success as of the failure of Middle Eastern civilization.

Islamic terrorism isn't a problem that can be isolated from its welcoming environment. By default, we have become the wardens of a strategic madhouse, the decayed domains of Middle Eastern Islam. The terror that we face isn't merely the product of a few misguided souls, but of a miscreant civilization. Of course, our enemies insist, as madmen will, that we, not they, are criminally insane.

If that dying civilization cannot heal itself—with or without our help—there will be no end to terror. In the meantime, we have no choice but to deal with the terrorists confronting us. In Iraq. Or wherever else we may find them.

With the overreported rush of events in Iraq, a substantial but vocal minority of Americans have lost their perspective, focusing on tactical problems, rather than on our strategic advances. But the challenges that seem so great in Iraq today are transient in nature, requiring only strength of will and adequate resources to be overcome.

The overarching War Against Terror is another matter. Far greater dangers lie ahead than a few car bombs in Baghdad.

Although we will win on many battlefields, we shall never see a final victory over terror in our lifetimes. It isn't in the nature of this war.

No matter how effectively we fight terror, a few terrorists will slip through to harm Americans. Inevitably, there will be additional terrorist attacks on American soil. When those attacks occur, we will be told that the War Against Terror has failed—as we are now told that the war in Iraq has failed.

Such claims will be nonsense. If our government stops 499 terrorists, but number 500 gets through, it doesn't mean there was no value in stopping all the others. In this fight, we will win the overwhelming majority of victories, large and small. But the enemy will manage, sooner or later, to get in a few more blows of his own.

The War Against Terror is much closer in nature to fighting crime, if on an unprecedented scale, than to traditional wars—although such wars will continue to be necessary to eliminate terrorist havens and sources of support.

No reader expects crime to be eliminated entirely—our goal is and always has been to reduce crime to a minimum. Terrorism—the ultimate criminal endeavor—will never be fully vanquished, either. Our purpose must be to limit its impact on our freedom and well-being to the greatest degree possible.

And as with criminals, it is always better to fight the terrorists on their home ground, rather than in law-abiding neighborhoods. The terrorist attacks we face in Iraq today are preferable to attacks in Manhattan or Miami. We have not created new enemies, but only drawn out those whose existence had been hidden from us.

Far from a provocation, the presence of our troops in the Middle East is an indispensable manifestation of our strength and resolve—as well as our most effective tool for killing terrorists. Instead of imposing artificial time limits on ourselves, we need to recognize the timeless nature of our enemies.

On this second anniversary of 9/11, we should set aside our partisan bickering, our personal resentments and prejudices, and recognize that our government has done a remarkable job since that tragic day. We have been kept safe, despite the fury of the terrorists at the damage we have, repeatedly, inflicted upon them.

Every day without a terrorist attack on our country or its citizens is a triumph, but the struggle must be renewed each day, one second after midnight. If we insist on setting unrealistic goals, we will defeat ourselves. You cannot fight terrorism with a stopwatch, and you can't fight it on the cheap.

Iraq will never become Iowa—our goal should be a better, if still imperfect, Iraq. Afghanistan will always remain Afghanistan. It is enough if it is a somewhat-improved country, less dangerous to us and less oppressive to its citizens. By such rational measures, we already have achieved notable victories.

Despair is the preferred narcotic of the intellectual classes. The rest of us must stand up for what we know in our hearts and souls to be right and true. Our cause *is* just. Our efforts in this great, global war have been admirably successful. Our soldiers have kept us safe and made us proud. We owe them unity, not divisiveness.

No power on this earth can defeat us, unless we defeat ourselves.

The Longest Struggle

New York Post

October 19, 2003

Better armed and better trained, a Western army "liberates" Arab territory. Divided among themselves, some Arabs cut deals with the invader, while hardliners resist the occupation. Assassins from a terrorist organization haunt—and hunt—local leaders.

Sunnis and Shi'as compete for advantage. Long-suffering minorities wonder whether to welcome their liberators or distrust them. Divided between new powers and old, the Westerners squabble over issues of international law, political authority, and trading privileges. Favored parties win economic concessions from the victors.

Having failed to block the advance of the invading army, the Turks meddle in Arab affairs. And a portion of the soldiers in the conquering army feel they've done what they came to do and want to come home.

Iraq, 2003?

No. The Middle East at the close of the eleventh century, in the wake of the First Crusade.

The point is not to play clever games with history, but to stress that the dilemmas of our own day are not exceptional or new. On the contrary, our worthy destruction of Saddam's regime can be seen as part of history's longest war: the battle for hegemony between Middle Eastern and Western civilizations.

We don't have to like the idea of such an endless conflict before admitting its existence. Well-meant denials help no one, while hindering understanding. The historical record shows that the conflict between Islam and the (Judeo-) Christian West began in the middle of the seventh century, as Muslim armies burst from the Arabian peninsula, energized by a new vision, destroying or sub-jugating the Christian and Jewish populations of the eastern Mediterranean.

The war never really stopped.

When Arabs complain of their victimization by the West, inevitably citing the interlude of the Crusades, they neglect to men-tion that, within a century of the birth of Islam, Muslim armies had swept across North Africa, through Spain, and deep into France. In the process, Christian communities that had shaped the faith were devoured.

To the north, the Arabs relentlessly pushed back the Orthodox Christian empire of the Byzantines. Turkic tribes thrust westward, across the Russian steppes and through the Balkans, establishing Islam's frontiers in today's Hungary and Romania.

The combat hardly paused. And the tide slowly turned. Long weakened by the West's internal rivalries, Byzantium fell in the mid-dle of the fifteenth century. But by the end of that century, the Moors had been expelled from Spain. After a thousand years of defeats, the West's march to dominance began.

Even so, a Turkish army besieged Vienna as late as 1683—until defeated by the valor of a Polish king. Russia fought fanatical Islamic warriors throughout the nineteenth century—as Russia does again today. And the Balkan wars that finally expelled the Turks in the early twentieth century were vastly more horrific than those of our own time.

The struggle did not stop. It only moved. With the age of Euro-pean imperialism, the conquests shifted in the other direction. The Islamic world of the greater Middle East, proud of its tradition of conquest, found its methods and values could not compete with modern, mechanized, liberal societies. The Mahdi's horsemen fell to Maxim guns.

The new debate in the Muslim world, begun two hundred years ago and still under way, is between those who seek to emulate the processes of the West and those who advocate a return to religious rigor. Tragically, the fanatics appear to be winning the tactical debate, which leads, inevitably, to strategic defeat and further humiliation.

Now we face something unique in history: the collapse, before our eyes, of the competitiveness and competence of a vast civilization, that of Middle Eastern Islam. None of its cherished values— the subjugation of women, religious intolerance, economic organization based on blood ties—works anymore. The people of the Middle East simply can't compete on their own terms. And the Arab world appears close to hitting bottom.

A decade ago, that rarest of creatures, a courageous academic—Samuel P. Huntington—advanced his theory of a "clash of civilizations." His honesty met outrage from those for whom emotion and prejudice trump facts. Yet all that Huntington really did was to note that the emperor of political correctness wore no clothes.

Still, even Huntington fell short by suggesting that this clash of civilizations was something new. Clashing is what civilizations *do*. Especially monotheist civilizations, with their one-God, one-path-to-the-truth, our-way-is-best convictions.

We should not be surprised at the current clash of civilizations. It would be far more surprising if it were *not* occurring. Such conflict is the rule, not the exception.

Of course, we would be fools to celebrate this clash, despite our own triumphs. It would be better for all if the Middle East could regain its moral and economic health. Cooperation *is* better than warfare. Peace *should* be our ultimate goal. But not peace at any price. And cooperation doesn't work unilaterally.

Our soldiers in Iraq aren't engaged in a religious crusade. But ours is, undeniably, a *cultural* crusade, based upon our belief that the values of our civilization, from human rights to popular sovereignty, are superior to archaic forms of oppression. It's an old, old struggle, fought on postmodern terms.

Today's Middle East has become a citadel of tyranny. And tyranny must be fought without compromise. If that's a crusade, there's no reason to deny it.

The Persuasion Myth

New York Post

November 3, 2003

Suppose the Saudi government launched an "information campaign" intended to convince Americans to adopt a strict Islamic lifestyle and that democracy, women's emancipation, open government, human rights, and freedom are not in our best interests.

One doubts that the Saudis would change American minds.

In essence, that's the challenge faced by our own efforts at "public diplomacy"—at changing stubborn minds in the Middle East. We persuade the already persuaded but don't make a dent in the Arab street's perception.

All men and women cling to their cherished values. It isn't a matter of right and wrong, but of what's familiar, comfortable, and reassuring. It's a foolish error to imagine that, if we only find the right combination of reasoned arguments, we might convince the populations of the Middle East to love us and embrace our national values.

Words never alter deeply rooted beliefs—although words can enliven drowsing hatreds.

If you want to change the mindset of another culture, your only hope is to "lead by example," as our military puts it—to demonstrate the incontestable superiority of your approach until it sinks in. The cliché is invincibly true: Deeds speak louder than words.

This doesn't mean that our efforts to provide accurate information to Middle Eastern audiences are completely wasted—only that we must have realistic expectations about their impact.

The prejudice of the campus bleeding heart or the diplomatic dilettante in favor of "reasoned argument" is utter nonsense. When you hear calls for "constructive dialogue," grab your flack jacket, because the end result will always be greater violence.

You can't win a debate with Osama bin Laden. You can't persuade God's self-appointed avengers to channel their madness into an academic conference. You can't even talk the man in the street into believing that your way of tying shoelaces is better than his own.

Yes, freedom and human rights are objectively superior to oppression and torture. Yes, the cultures of the Middle East are decayed, dysfunctional, and unable to compete in the modern world. But the Muslim populations of Eurasia don't want our logical explanations for their failures. They want revenge for self-created disasters. They want excuses for the inadequacy of their social, political, and economic regimes. Arab civilization, especially, has backed itself into a historical corner where it deteriorates by the day. It's humiliating to them.

The downtrodden don't want sober analysis. They want someone to blame. And the United States (along with Israel) fits the bill perfectly—facts be damned.

The failures of the Middle East are no more attributable to the wickedness of the West than the triumph of the West is due to the weakness of the Middle East. But comforting lies are humanity's favorite narcotic.

The cultures of the Middle East are so crippled that they can't even limp along without the psychological crutch of blaming all their ills on foreign devils. No amount of well-intentioned information disseminated by the United States will persuade the Arab masses that we're innocent of the cruelties their own leaders and social systems have inflicted upon them. Men and women everywhere believe their own kind first.

The *only* hope we have of eventually convincing the populations of the Middle East that our intentions are sound and that our interests lie in their success, not in their continued failure, is to take a long-term view and demonstrate our purpose on the ground.

Still, even if we spend decades doing good in the Middle East, the most embittered Muslims will be unwilling to accept our advocacy of human rights and freedom. We have entered an age of fiery reaction, of ecstatic, irrational rage, of *global* fundamentalist rejection of the demands of modernity.

Our enemies everywhere praise their God but prefer a powerful Satan they can blame for their disappointments. We are, and will remain, their indispensable bogeyman.

Our only hope of building a constructive, long-term relationship with the people of the Middle East is to focus on what Americans do best: work. Starting in Iraq.

Leave the bilious rhetoric to the demagogues. *Work* to bring positive change. Let our deeds proclaim themselves. Prove our accusers wrong. *Prove* that our values breed success.

It's an approach that requires enormous patience and fortitude. But it's the only approach that has a chance to succeed. It's easy to dismiss a government pronouncement. It's harder to deny practical results.

Unappreciated Americans

New York Post

November 27, 2003

As suicide bombers terrorize much of the planet, America has been remarkably free of such attacks since 9/11. Much of the credit goes to our law-enforcement establishment, as well as to our government's determination to take the War on Terror to our enemies.

But we also owe a debt to our Muslim immigrant communities, as well as to all Americans with family ties to the Middle East. They've been unreceptive to terrorists and want no part of violent extremism. Overwhelmingly, America's newest Muslims are determined to be good citizens.

Yes, a tiny minority of American Muslims *do* have some sympathy with our enemies. A fraction of that minority has made headlines through half-baked jihadist plots, schemes to aid captive terrorists, or donations to suspect "charities." But the excessive attention paid to the few who turn against America distorts the overall picture.

Viewing all American residents with Middle Eastern backgrounds as potential threats to our security does a disservice both to our fellow citizens and to America itself.

Will some Muslim immigrants find themselves disenchanted with the United States? Sure. It occurs in every immigrant community. But 99 percent and more have the same dreams for themselves and their children as did our own immigrant ancestors. They, too, will become loyal, responsible citizens, indistinguishable from any others.

First-generation immigrants of any background feel conflicting cultural loyalties and suffer a great deal of psychological tension. It takes time to master our country's complexities. But America is wonderfully seductive. And freedom really is magic.

Of course, for anyone who reads history, the prejudice expressed toward American Muslims is an old story. Current bigotry echoes that directed toward earlier immigrants. The sky was always falling, the foreigners were always too foreign.

When Irish immigrants, fleeing poverty and oppression, poured into our harbors, Americans insisted they could never become good citizens. Their religion supposedly prevented them from giving their first loyalty to our country. Culturally, they were too different, too backward. They crowded together for protection, suspicious of outsiders and the authorities. They were involved in sinister, violent plots.

Sound familiar?

Thousands of Irish-Americans *were* involved in sedition and riot within our borders, during our Civil War and afterward. Yet who seems more American now than Irish-Americans? American jihadists? How about the German-Americans who went back to the *Vaterland* to fight for Hitler? And just by the way—the greatest terrorist organization in our history was the Anglo-Saxon Ku Klux Klan.

Thus far, Muslim-Americans look remarkably good in comparison to the historical record of many a group now accepted as all-American.

Every ethnic and religious group that has come to these shores has enriched us with good citizens. It takes time, but America always wins. After the Irish began to overcome the prejudice against them, cookie-cutter bigotry was directed against Italians, Slavs, Jews, Chinese, Hispanics, and others. Yet, history *always* proves the bigots wrong.

Why do we have so little faith in the transformative power of America?

This column has been bluntly critical of the failing cultures of the Middle East, of the dictatorships and the regional disregard of human rights, of the oppression of women and the paralyzing corruption. But Arab or Iranian or Pakistani immigrants came here to *escape* from those realms of failure, not to import them to Detroit or Washington, D.C. They have the same practical ambitions everyone else's immigrant ancestors had: to build better lives for themselves and those they love.

Doubtless, many new Americans from the Middle East quietly cooperate with our law-enforcement authorities, while others work to keep their communities in good order. American Muslims fear a repeat of 9/11 more than the rest of us do—they worry about the blanket prejudice that would spread over their families. They each want to achieve their American dream, not to live in a nightmare.

Meanwhile, the rest of us overlook the tremendous good American Muslims are likely to do not only for our country, but for the entire Muslim world. We've all heard the complaint that Islam's problem is that it "never had a Reformation." In fact, Islam had more reformations than Christianity, but they were all reactionary reformations (as Martin Luther's back-to-the-Bible movement was meant to be, until it spun out of control).

The overdue liberalizing reformation is coming to Islam. And it's likeliest to start in North America. Just as the decency and openness of our society continue to transform Christianity and Judaism, so, too, this country will inspire Muslims to reexamine the man-made chains that encumber their great faith.

The theologians of the Middle East look backward to an over-imagined past, but the Muslim thinkers who emerge in America will look forward to a better future. The great schism in the Islamic world in coming years may well develop between modernizing reformists in North America and arch-conservatives abroad.

That ought to sound familiar, too.

Suicide bombing will come to our streets eventually. It's too cheap and effective a technique not to be employed against us by our enemies. But we should be very encouraged that, to date, the masterminds of terror have not been able to persuade young American Muslims to blow themselves up. When the young have hope, they do not rush to die.

America makes people want to *live*.

In the long term, our citizens with Middle Eastern roots may turn out to be our most powerful advantage in the War on Terror. Meanwhile, they're busy being Americans.

Making Democracy Work

New York Post

December 5, 2003

Building democracy in Iraq is the biggest challenge facing the Iraqi people and the American-led coalition. Attacks on our troops by guerrillas and terrorists make headlines, but the real test will come with national elections.

Eliminating Saddam's last thugs is ultimately a tactical problem, if an ugly one. Our *strategic* mission is helping Iraqis construct a system of government "with justice for all, and malice toward none."

The odds of success aren't great. But rolling the dice of liberty is worth the painful cost. Even if the Iraqis fail themselves and waste their one great chance, this will *still* have been a noble, far-sighted endeavor.

The Middle East desperately needs a success story that doesn't involve dictatorships, corrupt oil sheikhs, or suicide bombings. Even a 51 percent solution in Iraq would offer a galvanizing example to tens of millions treading historical water, from Iran and Syria to Egypt and Saudi Arabia.

We're fighting for the future, while our enemies defend the past.

But Iraqi democracy faces enormous hurdles. Democracy doesn't work magically on it own. It must be learned and earned. Each trial has its errors. And the debate continues as to whether

117

democracy is culturally specific—a hothouse flower rather than a tough and beautiful weed.

Historically, democracy has worked well in two types of environment. First, it works in homogeneous nations, such as Sweden, where there are no serious ethnic or religious differences and the citizen allocates his or her vote based upon individual concerns.

The second situation in which democracy works well is a state—such as the United States—whose populace is so diverse in ethnic origin, religion, and race that no single group can dominate all the others at the national level. Parties must build complex, shifting coalitions and can't permanently exclude anyone.

Both forms of democracy work well, although the more complex U.S. version generates greater social and cultural dynamism—more forward motion—while the European model plays it safe, elevating group welfare over individual opportunity.

The form of democracy that has *not* worked is the model in which one tribe composes an outright majority or a large plurality of the population and uses its power as a voting block to dictate the rules to the smaller tribe or tribes. When democracy is imposed upon an artificially created state with dysfunctional borders and a fiercely divided population, such as Rwanda, Burundi, Zimbabwe, Nigeria—or Iraq—it tends to devolve rapidly into a winner-take-all spoils system.

In Iraq—where the Shi'a Arabs compose about sixty percent of the population, and the Kurds and Sunni Arabs each have around twenty percent, with some much smaller minorities on the fringes—a strong, centralized democratic state cannot and will not work. Although the wisest course of action would be to break up this Frankenstein's monster of a country and allow the major population groups smaller states of their own, we are, for now, committed to a unified Iraq.

The *only* hope an undivided Iraq has is to form a loose confederation in which the major groups each enjoy maximum autonomy in their home regions. For the Kurds, of course, this is the only possible justice. The Kurds have earned their freedom and security, and the United States must acknowledge and defend their rights, even at the cost of the dissolution of the central state.

But the Sunni Arabs, too, need maximum autonomy—even though they are the current source of anti-Coalition violence and will remain the most troublesome segment of the population.

The Sunni Arabs enjoyed the most benefits from the old regime, and no one anywhere likes to lose their power and wealth. At best, it will be many years before they resign themselves to their reduced status.

Despite Sunni-Arab misbehavior, we need to take a strategic view. That means that each group must be safeguarded against the dominance of any other group or coalition of groups. In the long term, Iraq's Sunni Arabs must enjoy the same legal rights and protections in a new state as everyone else—even if they never forgive us for toppling Saddam.

Thus far, the Shi'as have behaved remarkably well. In part, it's because they're glad the old regime's gone. But it's also because their leaders realize that, in a centralized democracy, Shi'a numbers at the polls mean Shi'a dominance. That's why the Grand Ayatollah Ali Sistani, among others, has demanded early national elections. But national elections can't be held before safeguards are in place to defend the rights of Iraq's minorities. We must stand on that principle, no matter the short-term cost.

Because of our own fortunate experience, we see democracy in terms of raw numbers. But the key element in any successful democracy—after the rule of law—is a spirit of compromise. Even in a polarized political environment, the winner can never take all.

For a unified Iraqi state to exist under democratic conditions, a "bill of minority rights," including a right of secession, needs to *precede* both elections and a constitution. Neither the Shi'as nor anyone else should be able to take Iraq's unity for granted. The national government must have an incentive to honor the rights of every Iraqi citizen.

If its minorities are not protected, Iraq will dissolve anyway—in blood.

A Tyrant Humbled

New York Post

December 15, 2003

"Ladies and gentlemen, we got him!" Those words may go down as the most memorable line of Iraq's liberation. The outburst of cheers and applause that followed Paul Bremer's remarks echoed around the world.

And a myth as old as humankind collapsed.

Despite the intense media coverage of Saddam's capture that greeted us as we woke on Sunday morning, Americans can't quite grasp the psychological power this event holds for Iraq, for the Middle East—and for the world. We take our freedom for granted.

Much of the world has had to take oppression for granted. For thousands of years. Now America and her allies have changed the rules.

Even after Saddam's statues tumbled, even after his monstrous sons were killed, and despite the presence of Coalition troops in their midst, fear lurked in the minds of every Iraqi: Like a creature of legend impossible to slay, the tyrant who had ravaged their lives for decades might return.

The myth of Saddam wasn't only about the strength of one man. He drew his power not only from the gun and the noose, but from the long tradition of cruel sultans and dictators, of rulers so strong that common men and women could do nothing. Defeatism and apathy have haunted the Middle East for countless centuries.

Now, with the capture of an unwashed old man in a hole in a shabby farmyard, the myth of the mortal god on a throne that prevailed since the days of Nebuchadnezzar has been revealed as a lie no one need believe.

Saddam, who admired Stalin and emulated Hitler, did not go down in a violent blaze of glory. He didn't fire the pistol he carried or even make a fist. He cowered below the earth until our soldiers dragged him out.

Even as dismayed pundits struggled to find a dark lining in this enormous silver cloud, the people of Iraq erupted in cheers. To the horror of their European colleagues, Arab journalists could not stop shouting, "Death to Saddam!" as the monitors in Baghdad showed a broken prisoner having his scalp inspected for lice.

The capture of Saddam marks the real birth of the new Iraq. But thousands of miles from Baghdad, hundreds of millions of other human beings instinctively understood the importance of the event, even if they could not articulate all they felt. The myth of the invincible dictator ended in a farmyard.

Bashir Assad, Kim Jong-Il, Robert Mugabe, the old mullahs in Teheran, the Saudi royal family, the already cowering Moammar Khadafy—and that would-be caliph of all Muslims, Osama bin Laden . . . all of the dictators, authoritarian rulers, and terrorists-who-would-be-king saw their own faces in the place of Saddam's.

We put fear into the hearts of the men who thrived by striking fear into helpless millions.

Media coverage will focus on short-term events. If there is a spurt of attacks on Coalition forces as psychologically castrated hardliners struggle to prove that they remain capable and determined, we'll hear no end of analysis suggesting that Saddam's capture, while dramatic, wasn't so important, after all.

But it *was* important. Vitally important, in ways too great to quantify or fully describe. The effects will reverberate for decades, if not far longer.

Stand back and consider anew the greatness of what America and her partners have done. For the first time, the forces of freedom refused to wait for a dictator to strike again, whether against us or against his own people. Defying former allies comfortable with the old pattern of embracing cooperative tyrants, we changed the global rules.

And freedom won.

Yet even this huge milestone is only a beginning. The hardest of the hard-core militants, the Ba'athist thugs who've lost everything, will continue to annoy us for months to come—although their strength will dwindle. Terrorists will continue to try to turn back the clock.

But the people of Iraq now know that they truly *are* free, that their future is *theirs* to decide. And other degraded populations in the Middle East now see that they, too, *can* be free.

As the image of a humbled Saddam flashed on millions of screens, thousands of years of the armed few tyrannizing the suffering masses came to a symbolic end. And America stood taller than it has since the spring of 1945.

Now we must go forward without hesitating.

President Bush's historic speech of November 6 acknowledged that, in the distorted strategic environment of the Cold War, the United States made grave errors by supporting dictators and authoritarian regimes, imagining that such men and their acolytes guaranteed stability. Instead, the strongmen brought only misery to their people and crises to the rest of us.

One dictator who received a measure of American support was Saddam. Our president faced up to that responsibility, and now we have paid our debt to the people of Iraq. But in the months to come, we'll face another challenge as the Iraqi people bring Saddam to trial.

We need to live up to our president's own words, to show the world further proof that America has forever moved beyond her brief tolerance for tyrants, that our actions in Iraq were neither selfish nor an exception. When Saddam raises—as he will—the support Americans once provided to him, we should go him one better and make every record available to the court.

We Americans must always have the courage to stand up and admit it when we've made mistakes. We must resist the temptation to classify the details of this long-ago visit by special envoy X or that covert aid during the Iran-Iraq War. Just tell the truth. The short-term discomfort will be minor compared to the enduring force of our example.

Let those Europeans who assured Saddam that they'd save him stand beside him in the court of world opinion. Let *every* detail come out. Hide nothing. Create such shame that even the French will think twice before coddling another dictator.

The capture of Saddam was a far greater matter than any image can capture or any words can suggest. This was a turning point in human history.

Comforting the Enemy

New York Post

March 25, 2004

Democracy is, by far, the greatest system of government yet created by human genius. The problem is the elections.

In a routine presidential contest, the thundering emptiness of the rhetoric from both sides does little lasting harm. Our system is robust. Collectively, the American people are remarkably sensible.

But this isn't a normal election year. We are at war. Although many domestic issues deserve debate, the War on Terror demands unity of purpose from both parties. It is *essential* that our enemies understand that we're united in fighting terrorism.

That's not the message we're sending.

This week's "9/11 hearings" on Capitol Hill are useful to a degree, but they're poorly timed. Both parties hope for political gain, but our paramount goal should be protecting our country.

The worst election-year sin is the focus on past errors, real or purported, and the lust to assign blame. What's done is done. We need to concentrate—hard—on the future.

Unfortunately, serious thinking about the threat is on hold until November. We need the best that both parties have to offer. Instead, we get the worst. Winning elections trumps defending our citizens.

We shall hear no end of claims from both sides that the other party is leading—or would lead—America to disaster. But the terrorist threat will force similar responses from whichever party occupies the White House. Any administration would rapidly (if perhaps painfully) learn the need to fight relentlessly, remorselessly, and globally against our terrorist enemies. The War on Terror is not a matter of choice.

Danger will dictate our actions. The future won't conform to the wishful thinking of either the left or right. Our tragedy is that, until November, our energies will be devoted to exhuming political corpses, rather than protecting American lives. Both sides will lie. America will suffer.

Consider a few implacable—if unpalatable—truths:

• There is *nothing* we can do to satisfy religion-inspired terrorists. If we do not kill them, they will kill us.

• The War on Terror cannot be won decisively and will endure beyond our lifetimes. You can no more eliminate terror than you can wipe out crime or drug abuse. But—as with drug abuse and crime—you can't just ignore it, either. The goal is to reduce terrorism to a bearable level. The lack of a final victory doesn't mean the effort is useless or a failure.

• We must think, plan, and act in terms of decades, not months. Even as we fight today's battles, we must think about challenges a generation ahead.

• This *is* a war, not law enforcement. The struggle requires every tool in our national arsenal, from commandos to cops, from diplomacy to technology, from economic sanctions to preemptive war. At different times, in different locations, the instruments of choice will vary. There is no magic solution—or even a set of rules.

• The best defense *is* a strong offense. We cannot wait at home for terrorists to strike. We must not waver from the current policy of taking the war to our enemies. The moment we falter, our enemies will bring the war back to us.

• Nothing will make us invulnerable. Our goal is to reduce our vulnerability to the lowest practical level—while balancing wisely between security and freedom.

• A terrorist attack on the United States is not a victory for either of our political parties or for any school of thought. It's a defeat for all of us. When the next attack occurs—as one eventually will—we must blame our enemies, not each other.

- Allies are valuable, but they are not indispensable. In the end, we must always do what is necessary, whether or not it is popular abroad.

- The Islamic world's problems are not our fault, and we are not to blame for terrorism. We cannot force other cultures to be successful, nor can we avoid their jealousy.

- There is only one measure of success that matters in the end: Can terrorists harm the United States and its citizens? Although some future strikes are inevitable, the inability of terrorists to strike our homeland since 9/11 is indisputable proof that, however imperfect, our approach to the War on Terror has been working.

- Our will must always be stronger than that of our enemies. Otherwise, they'll win, despite our countless advantages. If we cannot maintain the courage for the fight, the terrorists will fill the courage vacuum. The War on Terror *is* a zero-sum game.

The hearings in Washington are history lessons, at best. But America is about the *future*—about turning our backs on the past and avoiding the old world's obsession with ancient injuries. Instead of savaging one another over what we failed to do yesterday, we must ask what we can do better today and tomorrow.

Election-year recriminations over the tragic events of our time serve no one but political hacks and the terrorists themselves. The message our bickering sends to al Qa'eda and its sympathizers is that Americans are divided and can be defeated.

The terrorists are drawing the—incorrect—lesson that a Democratic victory this November would allow them to regain the global initiative. Although every new administration inevitably makes some mistakes, a Kerry presidency would have to face up to the need to combat terrorism as vigorously as the Bush administration has done. The man in the Oval Office doesn't get a choice on this one.

But the terrorists read things otherwise, thanks to our public venom. They'll attempt to strike here, as they did in Spain, to influence our elections. If they succeed, *both* of our political parties, with their craven bickering, will be guilty of inciting our enemies.

We Americans may disagree about many issues, but we cannot afford disunity in the face of fanatical killers. Nor are we remotely as divided as our enemies are led to believe. The problem is the politicians, not the people.

Where the Fighting Isn't

New York Post

April 8, 2004

Suleimaniye, Iraq—As violence in Iraq dominates the news, imagine a Middle Eastern country in which the government works in simple offices and spends its money on education, a state in which the prime minister still lives in his parents' home and builds libraries instead of palaces.

How about a Middle East in which young men and women study together at a university where no political party rules the campus, freedom of speech is encouraged, and internet access is unrestricted.

Try, if you can, to imagine a Middle Eastern population that regards America with respect and gratitude.

It isn't a dream. It's a reality.

Welcome to free Kurdistan.

As my former comrades in the military struggled against terror and violent rebellion in central and southern Iraq, I was embarrassingly safe in the same country. While mortar rounds were landing in Baghdad and our military displayed its power and resolve in Fallujah, I was sweating in a traffic jam.

It was a *great* traffic jam. In this case, it was a sign of the economic progress the Kurds have been making. And the only "terrorist" is the occasional lousy driver.

People walk the streets and live their lives without fear. And women aren't attacked for dressing as they choose.

The Kurdish capital city of Suleimaniye can seem like a giant construction site. But in place of the corruption that plagues development elsewhere in the region, much of the work is done under rigorous government-private sector partnerships. The Kurds are even implementing zoning codes and thinking about the environment.

Anyone who has ever been to the Middle East knows that this is just short of a miracle. The prime minister, Dr. Barham Salih, doesn't fit the pattern either. Instead of fearing him or hating him, the people love him—he's the closest thing Kurdistan has to a matinee idol. And instead of using his popularity to enrich himself or establish a ruling dynasty, he's encouraging democracy. (He's even had a kebab shop named after him. I'm still waiting for Bush Burgers in D.C.)

The University of Suleimaniye, devastated by Saddam, has been rebuilt and now has over 7,000 students. And they're a lively bunch—serious, hardworking, and most important, full of probing questions. Female students can choose for themselves whether or not to wear headscarves. Most choose not to—but everyone respects everyone else—and they all sit and study together. American parents of college-age sons and daughters could only envy the intensity and hunger with which these young people pursue education.

Go to that university and, instead of hearing anti-American protests, you'll hear how the 101st Airborne Division got their Dell computers through to them, red tape be damned. On how many campuses in the world do the students regard an American general (in this case, Major General Dave Petraeus) as a hero?

The United Nations stole the money the Kurds should have received under Saddam. Now, the United States has redirected the remaining Oil-for-Food funds and the Kurds are using them with an efficiency never before seen in the region. Astonishingly, the money is really going to the people. Instead of the U.N.'s outdated, overpriced medicine, the Kurds can now bargain hard in the marketplace for the goods the people desperately need.

Most importantly, instead of succumbing to the culture of blame that plagues the Middle East, the Kurds have gone to work to build a better future.

Their country is still very poor. But it's free. And freedom really does work.

Business is encouraged, the government stresses the future, not the past, and the leaders are trying their best to work constructively with old enemies. Despite horrific suffering in the recent past, the leaders are hopeful, not vengeful. They know that a unified Iraq may not work—but they're determined that the failure will not be their fault. And they cherish freedom.

Isn't this what we claim we want in the Middle East?

At a time when elements within both Sunni Arab and Shi'a Arab Iraqi society are trying to kill the Americans who liberated their country and when there is no sense of gratitude for our sacrifices, how can the Bush administration fail to grasp that the future of the region lies in what the Kurds have done successfully, not in the Arab cult of failure?

The Kurds are far from perfect. So are we. We're all human. But this small people deserves our respect and support—no matter what else happens in Iraq. If we truly want to help spread freedom, we have to start by backing those who have made freedom work—against tremendous odds.

Almost a hundred years ago, Lincoln Steffens, an American charlatan, returned from the brand-new Soviet Union. Disembarking from his ship on a New York City pier, he told a great lie. A radical socialist, he said, "I have seen the future, and it works." I hope I'm more honest than Steffens was, but I'll paraphrase his words and say, "I've seen what the future of the Middle East could be. And we should all hope to God that it works."

The Iraqi Passion

New York Post

April 11, 2004

Halabja, Iraq—In Iraq on Good Friday, I thought of the film *The Passion of Christ*. I am a Christian. The film brought me close to tears. But not for quite the reason Mel Gibson intended.

Watching the grotesque suffering on the screen, my thoughts were less of Christ than of what human beings do to one another. I didn't really see the Jerusalem of two thousand years ago. I saw Auschwitz, Rwanda, Cambodia, the Gulag . . .

And I saw Halabja.

On a morning in early spring almost twenty years ago, with the grass just turning green in the meadows and snow still on the mountains of northern Iraq, Saddam's forces slipped into position in the hills above the Kurdish town of Halabja.

There were no *peshmerga*—freedom fighters—in the town. Only families.

At twenty minutes to noon, a massive bombardment began—with conventional artillery rounds, with napalm, and with chemical weapons delivered by aircraft. The Iraqi forces used both mustard gas, which scorches human flesh, and sarin, a nerve agent that kills swiftly and provides no chance of survival.

Saddam's men knew what they were doing: The combination of munitions was the deadliest possible mix.

Five thousand men, women, and children died in the time it takes a busy man to eat lunch. The survivors outside the veil of nerve gas—some horribly burned—fled across the mountains into Iran. Halabja became a dead city.

And then it was resurrected. After Saddam's forces were driven south by American might in the aftermath of Desert Storm, the survivors began to return.

Today, Halabja's thriving again. Poor, but vivid with life, it's a monument to the human will to survive.

Much has been written about Halabja over the years. But that town wasn't an exceptional atrocity in the campaign of Ba'athist cruelty. It became famous only because an Iranian news crew happened to be in the city as Saddam's killers approached. Equipped with gas masks, they were able to film the bombardment and the chemical plague that littered the streets with corpses.

Humanity owes those journalists a debt. The small, haunting museum in Halabja is filled with still images from their video. And even the goriest Hollywood epic doesn't come close to the impact of those photographs. Concocted films never quite capture the eternal clumsiness of the dead, their odd embarrassment, or random placement. Make-up artists can't quite get the subtle discoloration of a child's face or her look of astonishment at the moment of death.

The gore of *The Passion* pales beside the open eyes of a child surprised by nerve gas.

All those who take delight in telling the world that our liberation of Iraq was unjustified because we didn't find weapons of mass destruction should go to Halabja. If I could, I would march them there.

But Halabja was oddly blessed—at least its suffering lives on in those photographs. Tens of thousands of other Kurds died unreported in Saddam's offensives.

On the day before I visited Halabja, I went into the mountains with veterans of the struggle against the Ba'athist regime. The journey, through a land of stunning beauty, was haunted by countless ghosts. In one remote village, Saddam's chemical attacks killed 154 people. In the next valley, hundreds more died. There were no cameras. The great world never heard about their fate.

And, frankly, the world didn't care.

The land of the Kurds is as beautiful as its history is tragic. Today, the people live in peace and safety—for the first time in centuries. But there will always be another Halabja somewhere in the world. And another Srebrenica, a Lidice, a Babi Yar . . .

The maddened debate about the film *The Passion* centered on the antique question, "Who killed Christ?" My fellow Americans, Christian, Jew, Muslim, or of any other faith, I'll tell you who killed Jesus. It was mankind.

And we never stopped killing Him.

Holy Turf Wars

New York Post

April 20, 2004

Whenever I visit history-haunted Istanbul, my first stop is the cathedral of Saint Sophia. The greatest monument of Christianity's first millenium is now a museum run by the Turkish government.

It never occurred to me to demand it back.

History moves on, and we must move with it. Those who cling to the shipwreck of the past drown their future. Apart from our ability to love, the most impressive human talent is our ability to rise up from our failures and start again.

The ultimate symptom of the collapse of Arab civilization isn't terrorism or abusive regimes, nor is it the persecution of minorities or even the baffling lack of creativity. Rather, it's the narcotic Arab embrace of past glories—always gilded, sometimes forged.

Those who live in yesterday cannot build tomorrow.

Even after last month's Madrid bombings, few Westerners take seriously the Arab extremists' obsession with reclaiming *al Andaluz,* the vast portion of Spain where, from the eighth through the tenth centuries, Islamic civilization reached its pinnacle. The dream of lost Andalusia is an opiate for the disappointed souls of the Middle East—even though Cordoba's rulers would have rejected Osama bin Laden's puritanism as well as his demonic will to destruction.

But the dream has little to do with any reality, past or present. The fanatic's vision ignores the tale of how Moorish Spain was lost. It wasn't Christian knights who wrecked the grandeur of Muslim

Cordoba and Seville. Berber fundamentalists from North Africa shattered the golden age of *al Andaluz*, invaders whose vision of Islam—like that of today's terrorists—did not include Aristotle, astronomy, and tolerance.

The faithful slew the faithful. The Berber invasions enabled still-weak Christian kingdoms to nibble their way southward. For five centuries after the fundamentalist triumph, feudal strife, not strict religious wars, plagued the Iberian peninsula. Moorish and Christian nobles switched sides again and again.

Mercenaries from both faiths fought for gold, not God. The legendary Christian hero El Cid drew his title from an Arabic word for "leader"—after fighting in Moorish employ.

In 1492, Grenada, the last Moorish kingdom, fell. Weakened from within, it needed only one last blow from without.

It's a universal story. Constantinople, bastion of Christianity for a thousand years, fell to Ottoman armies aided by Italian gunners and Christian engineers—after being sacked by Western Crusaders. Following the Mughal invasions of India, Hindu princes danced over to the Muslim side. Within every faith, believers have been ready to slaughter their own kind over the number of imams in a religious succession or the contents of the communion cup.

There is guilt and blood and loss on every side. And the past cannot be changed.

As a student of history alert to ugly surprises, my fear is that Islamic extremists may arouse passions dormant in the West. Muslim terrorists might do well to recall that there are far more Christian holy places in the Arab world than there are Muslim vestiges in Europe.

Suppose the Christians of tomorrow were provoked to demand the return of the apostolic churches of Asia minor? Or the vast lands of Orthodox Byzantium? Of historical Armenia? Or of Alexandria, the city that dominated early Christian thought? Before Mohammed's triumph, even Mecca had a Christian minority—and Jews had a vital presence in Medina.

The game of "this was mine and must be mine again," whether structured along religious lines or in terms of national identity, is as dangerous an enterprise as any in history. One great American strength has been our willingness to leave "the old country" behind, abandoning all claims to repossession.

Wherever opposing factions claim the same land for their gods, conflicts are insoluble without extremes of bloodshed. When we insist on chaining God to any patch of earth, we make Him as small as us.

Islamic terrorists will not reconquer Spain. But they may do colossal damage to their faith.

A few weeks ago in Istanbul, I paid my admission to St. Sophia's again. For perhaps the tenth time, I wandered alone through the vestibules and galleries, with the grand space beneath the dome pierced by the morning light and the luminous shafts of history. After the fall of Constantinople, *Aya* Sophia became a mosque for five hundred years. Enormous shields with Koranic inscriptions hang above the remaining Christian mosaics.

But no congregation of either faith can claim the cathedral nowadays. Seventy years ago, with the wisdom of Solomon, Kemal Ataturk decided that Saint Sophia's would be a mosque no longer, but neither would it revert to Christian use. Despite the anger of Islamic clerics, the building became a museum, open to all.

Ataturk's gesture was as visionary as it was courageous. If I see the ghosts of Christian martyrs inside those massive walls, Muslims see the shimmer of Ottoman glories and the shadows of the empire of faith. The compromise decreed by one great man allows us all to look beyond the masonry to another, better world.

In *this* world, every claim staked to a patch of "holy" earth reduces God to the status of a landlord. For my part, I hope to visit Istanbul's greatest museum in peace for years to come—as Muslims may visit the museum in Spanish Cordoba that once was the greatest mosque upon the earth.

He Who Hesitates

New York Post

April 27, 2004

Our troops in Iraq are fighting a twenty-first-century war. And they're winning on the battlefield. But they're being defeated by diplomats seeking a twenty-century peace.

Paul Bremer, Washington's scoutmaster in Baghdad, is a solid, hardworking twentieth-century bureaucrat. But the future of Iraq—and the entire Middle East—demands a twenty-first-century strategist who can escape the cant of the foreign-policy establishment and the lure of failed models of nation-building.

We created the problem of Fallujah through neglect. Had we had adequate forces on hand a year ago in the immediate aftermath of combat to permeate the Sunni Triangle with troops, and had the administration had the clarity of vision to declare martial law, the current violence would have been averted.

Instead, we handed gold-plated lollipops to killers and worried about hurting the feelings of Saddam's hard-core supporters. We looked away as the terrorists gripped one Iraqi city after another—because we lacked the forces to put a military "cop" on every beat. Our enemies didn't need to hide—we weren't around often enough to see them.

Nonetheless, when the revolt began in Fallujah earlier this month, our Marines, supported by the U.S. Army, hammered the terrorists into the dirt. We took casualties—but the losses were overwhelmingly on the enemy's side, as they always should be.

The Coalition Provisional Authority's response? And the Bush administration's? They made the Marines stop well short of the goal post. Listening to Iraqi leaders who have their own personal power—not Iraq's interests or ours—at heart, our civilian leadership ordered the Marines to break off combat operations before the job was finished. We let the terrorists off the ropes, granting them time to recover for another, inevitable round.

Next, I suppose we'll establish a DMZ.

Since the cease-fire, our troops have had to endure the ludicrous charade of "negotiations" with the Fallujah city fathers—breaking the rule that we never negotiate with terrorists or their surrogates. The resulting "agreement" to turn in heavy weapons led to the mockery of sending the Marines a pickup truck full of junk while the terrorists gained weeks to prepare their defenses, construct ambushes, and organize a far tougher resistance than they could have presented two weeks ago.

Our enemies are laughing at our folly, while creating a myth of heroic resistance in Fallujah—for which we will pay dearly in the months and years ahead.

Make no mistake: There can be no compromise in Fallujah. If we stop one inch short of knocking down the last door in the last house in the city, our enemies will be able to present the Battle of Fallujah to their sympathizers as a great victory: They fought the Americans to a stalemate (with the implication that, next time, the Americans will be defeated and driven from the Middle East).

Of course, we could defeat them. We know that. But in the broken world between the Bosporus and the Indus, seductive lies trump hard facts. Our insipid diplomacy plays into the hands of our enemies: It looks like cowardice. And it is.

We must not only win, we must be *seen* to win, graphically and decisively.

"Experts" warn that we mustn't alienate the hard-core Sunnis or the fundamentalist Shia's. Wake up and smell the cordite: They're already alienated. They'll never love us. So we'd better make damned sure they fear us.

The Battle of Fallujah isn't about one city. It's about the future of the entire Middle East. Despite the low number of casualties in historical terms, this could prove to be one of the decisive battles of history in its long-term effects.

We *must* win. If the enemy fights from mosques, level the mosques. If they fight from hospitals, gut the hospitals. If they open fire from orphanages, turn them into blackened shells. We cannot allow terrorists any sanctuaries. The men we face—and the watching world—interpret our decency as weakness.

The diplomats have had their chance. Now it's time to fight. Unfortunately, our Marines and soldiers are in the position of a man in a fistfight in an alley. The other guy has total freedom of action, while our man's "friends" keep tugging at his arms and trying to restrain him. Guess who gets his teeth knocked out?

The president needs to lead, not equivocate. If there is any emerging resemblance to Vietnam, it isn't on the battlefield, but in the White House, where no one seems to have the will to win.

The terrorists pull the triggers and detonate the bombs. But the Marines and soldiers who come home in flag-draped coffins are Donald Rumsfeld's dead and Paul Bremer's corpses. President Bush is listening to the kind of men who destroyed LBJ's presidency and ravaged a generation of young Americans.

We cannot waste the lives of our troops for yesterday's bankrupt theories of international relations. Stop worrying about making our mortal enemies happy. We must either make up our minds to win or bring our soldiers home.

An American Disaster

New York Post

May 1, 2004

The United States just experienced its first true disaster in Iraq. As news of the disgraceful mistreatment of prisoners by American soldiers sweeps the world, our enemies celebrate a major propaganda gift. Even our friends cannot defend the indefensible.

On the battlefield, we must be fierce. But once an enemy becomes a prisoner of our military, he must be treated justly and humanely. Strictness, yes. Abuse, no.

The rogue American soldiers and renegade contractors involved committed two sets of crimes.

The first—the physical maltreatment and humiliation of prisoners—was against the Uniformed Code of Military Justice and the Geneva convention. If convicted, the accused soldiers need to see the inside of a military prison themselves. As for the contractors involved, our country either must find a way to prosecute them—or stop employing contractors in conflict zones. Evident attempts to sweep this part of the scandal under the rug are intolerable.

The other set of crimes, while harder to prosecute, will have a vastly more powerful effect than the direct abuse of individuals. Our laws and codes haven't begun to catch up to the pace of technology, but those who tormented the Coalition's prisoners have done immeasurable damage to our country and our efforts to advance the cause of freedom—in Iraq and around the world.

A time-tested military saying runs, "One aw-s#8@ cancels a hundred attaboys." This particular debacle canceled thousands of hard-won successes, great and small.

Thanks to the power of the globalized media and the internet, those images of prisoner abuse will be immortalized, their effects inflated far beyond the truth—which was bad enough. Anyone in the Arab world who sought "evidence" that Americans are nothing more than imperialist bullies just got it.

Those Europeans for whom anti-Americanism is a cult, if not an outright religion, are already having a grand time. Quibbling that no prisoners were killed or maimed won't help. For those who wish to believe ill of America, the abuse photographs can be conflated with Europe's own far greater crimes.

No one died in those brutal antics in the Abu Ghraib prison. But the global left will treat these events as if they were the Holocaust and the Gulag combined.

It's just possible that no soldiers in U.S. history have done more damage to our country's cause than the Gang of Six from the 800th Military Police Brigade. But it's not just about the soldiers directly involved. These crimes demonstrate an utter failure of the chain of command. All the way to the top.

Why did it happen?

Yes, there are always bad apples in any organization. But that excuse is unacceptable. The truth is that this was a *systemic* failure—one that could have, and should have, been prevented.

We never had enough troops in Iraq. Nor do we have enough in the Army and Marines overall. When Baghdad didn't turn out to be Orlando, after all, those brilliant civilian thinkers in the Office of the Secretary of Defense continued to try to do things on the cheap militarily.

The reservists guarding those prisoners weren't trained for the job. They were thrust hastily into duties that require specific skills, great personal and unit discipline, and supervised experience. Then contractors—so beloved of OSD in every sphere—were allowed to run wild in the prison, answering to no one.

Had properly trained, active-duty MPs been running that prison, it's unlikely that such events could have taken place.

But we don't have enough active-duty MPs. Or infantrymen. Or even truck drivers in uniform. The mantra from this administration's apparatchiks has been, "Outsource it." Well, they just outsourced America's honor.

There are no words adequate to describe the damage done by these crimes against Iraqi prisoners. Killing all the terrorists we can in combat is one thing—and a good thing, at that—but after the shooting stops, we must always behave humanely. It's not just about laws and conventions, but about the basic decency that makes us Americans.

Overwhelmingly, we get it right. But you can't get it wrong even once. An out-of-control gang in uniform just made a mockery of those Americans who have died to bring a better future to Iraq. They shamed every soldier serving today. And every one of us who served in the past.

If you still need one more example of how irresponsible OSD's approach to the occupation of Iraq has been, consider *where* the prisoner abuses took place: The Abu Ghraib prison was the old regime's most notorious atrocity workshop. We shouldn't even have used it as a latrine. But our general unpreparedness for the occupation—and mindless expedience—had us take it over almost before the blood of Saddam's victims dried on the walls.

Now our enemies can point to American crimes in the same notorious halls. Yes, our deeds were isolated and less than lethal. Frankly, it doesn't matter. In the battle for the soul of the twenty-first century, perception trumps facts.

The thugs of Abu Ghraib—the *American* thugs—just dealt the greatest blow to America's prestige since the fall of Saigon. In the Middle East, this story will morph into myth and outlast our lifetimes. It will haunt our every effort. And yes, it will recruit terrorists.

At least some of the accused enlisted soldiers are likely to spend time behind bars. Their leaders should, too. And not just those in uniform.

Best We've Ever Had

New York Post

May 2, 2004

Our soldiers stood out in downtown Kirkuk. Not only because of their uniforms and weaponry, but because of their discipline and bearing. Anyone seeing our troops at a checkpoint or guarding a public building in Iraq knew instantly that America had sent her best.

The soldiers I saw weren't "elite" in military terms. They were just line doggies—infantrymen doing the tough, routine work of occupation, support troops making the military machinery go, or public-affairs soldiers doing their best to help a ravaged population come to terms with freedom.

I didn't bother them, except to thank them briefly for serving our country. They had better things to do than chat with yet another scribbler. As a former soldier, I could read what I needed to know from their body language—the alertness, rigor, and pride—or from the wary relaxation of the soldier coming off his post in a dangerous world.

I was indescribably proud of them. Anyone reading this paper would have been proud of them, too. Our politics don't matter. Those troops are serving us all. They didn't have a voice in the strategic decisions, wise or not, that sent them to those foreign streets. Young and splendid, they were doing their best not only for their country, but for humankind.

While in Iraq, I heard plenty of complaints about the Coalition Provisional Authority, its willful blindness, vanity, and ineptitude. But I never heard a single word criticizing our soldiers. Our troops were held in respect. And, sometimes, in awe.

Paul Bremer isn't our most important representative in Iraq. GI Joe is. And we couldn't ask for a better one.

In that ravaged sliver of the world, words are almost as cheap as human life. But good examples endure. One old Kurdish warrior simply marveled at the way our troops followed orders. In their long guerrilla struggle against Saddam, Kurdish commanders negotiated orders with one another, partisans in several senses. The promptness and vigor with which an American unit moved out when ordered to go—second-nature to those of us who served in American uniforms—amazed him.

That was the kind of military the old veteran wanted for his country's future.

For all the damage done to America's image by Hollywood trash, one good sergeant can change the fate of a village. And an honorable general can save an entire population from destruction. The world sees far too much of a phony America, all sex, violence, and greed. It needs to see more, not less, of America's soldiers.

Much is made—justifiably so—of the "greatest generation" that fought World War II. Korean War vets belatedly got the recognition they deserved all along, and our nation is finally paying its proper respects to those who gave their best in our Indochina wars. But the truth is that, man for man and woman for woman, the United States has never fielded a finer military than the force we have today.

Every man and woman serving is a volunteer. That makes an enormous difference. In any draftee military, no matter the crisis or the cause, you have a disaffected element, those who don't want to be there. A draft is good for our country in many ways, but it isn't good for military effectiveness.

Despite the sometimes deadly challenges our soldiers face today, and even with repeated and painful separations from their families, today's troops are reenlisting. And more young people are signing up to become soldiers, Marines, sailors, and airmen, or to serve in that most underrated service of all, our Coast Guard.

The drama is in Iraq these days—at least that's what's reported. But journalists are herd animals, elbowing each other for a twist on the same headline. Meanwhile, the vital efforts of our troops in Afghanistan only make the news when a combat fatality turns out to be a patriot who turned his back on a multimillion-dollar sports career.

An Army buddy of mine now serving in Kosovo tells hair-raising tales of greater strife than recent reports indicated. The reporters were all in Baghdad. No one writes about the routine heroism of our troops serving in the Balkans.

Nor will you read much about the quiet but indispensable efforts of our special-operations forces around the globe. Yet these men daily risk their lives pursuing the worst enemies of our country and civilization. Not a few die in secret clashes, their stories forever untold.

For every brave Marine you see laying down a base of fire in Fallujah, other service members around the world are making our military system go. To really get a sense of the breadth and depth of our war against deadly evil, you have to look behind the battlefield and study the troops stationed here in the United States.

They aren't at peace. There are no more Sergeant Bilkos or Beetle Baileys. Those who aren't at war are preparing for war—or, all too briefly, recovering from it.

After returning from Iraq, I visited Fort Huachuca, Arizona, the Army's intelligence schoolhouse, to speak to the officers and enlisted soldiers in training. I was supposed to be teaching them, but the truth is that they taught me.

The lieutenants looked impossibly young; all had joined the Army after 9/11. They knew what they were facing. The junior enlisted soldiers had all joined after Operation Iraqi Freedom. They were under no illusions about the dangers ahead.

But they joined. And they're proud. They were the best-motivated soldiers I can remember. Almost thirty years ago, I was a private myself at "Fort We-gotcha." The truth is, we were sad sacks compared to the soldiers now filling the ranks. Today's troops are fitter, smarter, better educated, better disciplined, and far more motivated than those I served with during my enlisted years.

From the Arizona desert, I was privileged to go to Fort Bragg, North Carolina, the home of Army Airborne, of Special Forces, Delta, and other elite units; now I was talking to Special Ops generals and colonels. They were the finest group of senior officers I can remember—commanding the best of the best but asking themselves how their organizations could become still better. Fighting today, they also bear responsibility for shaping the forces our country will need tomorrow. There was no slack anywhere. And no soldiers ever took their mission more seriously.

From those generals down to the privates, you hardly sensed they were at home—and they certainly were not at peace. Wherever I traveled, it was clear that the Army was at war. Soldiers of every rank were committed to giving the best support they could to their brothers and sisters deployed to combat zones. Leaders struggled to improve training, to refine doctrine, to question organizational structures, to increase effectiveness and efficiency—with increasingly strained resources.

And it isn't just the Army. Behind the security guards at Quantico or any other Marine base, you'll find a force at war. While the rest of us enjoy the pampered lives of twenty-first-century Americans—even our poor are rich compared to so much of the world—our finest fellow citizens guard the gates against the new barbarians.

Some die. Others suffer wounds from which they will never fully recover. And I have not heard one soldier complain. In Iraq, the common response of wounded troops is to ask to return to their units as soon as possible.

But we don't have enough of these soldiers or Marines. We're running these great troops ragged. Morale remains remarkably high, in Iraq and at home, but our men and women in uniform deserve better treatment. And simple fairness.

This promises to be by far the longest of our nation's wars. There are no end-zones in sight, no Berlins or Tokyos. Those who volunteered to serve under our flag have a right—and a need—to see their wives and children now and then, to catch their emotional breath between our nation's battles.

We need more troops. Please don't believe the lies of those for whom outsourcing has become a pagan ideology or whose priority

will always be to pour money into the pockets of the defense industry. We need more troops. Not gold-plated junk. Troops.

Write to your senator or congressman. Write to the president. It
doesn't matter whether you're a Democrat or Republican. The
blood of our soldiers doesn't come in party colors. Don't just say
you support our troops. Do something about it. Tell our nation's
leaders to give our troops what they need.

Our men and women in uniform are dying for us each day. The
least we can do is to make sure there's enough of them.

Look Who's Crying "Abuse!"

New York Post

May 11, 2004

The events in Abu Ghraib prison shamed America and our military. The mistreatment of prisoners is utterly unacceptable. And we *haven't* accepted it.

As a nation, we've taken responsibility for the tragic actions of a few. Our military has been investigating the misdeeds for months. The initial report was brutally frank. There's no hint of a whitewash. The guilty parties will be called to justice.

Even given the strategic damage done by those horrid photos, the fact is that we Americans can be proud our system does *not* tolerate such behavior. It's an exception, far from the rule. We're genuinely shocked that even a few of our soldiers could behave so grotesquely.

Now consider our loudest critics, those governments expressing outrage over the crimes we've been investigating of our own volition.

Start with the Arab world. There is no Arab country—none—in which prisoners aren't treated immeasurably worse than the victims of the sadists in uniform at Abu Ghraib. The torments inflicted on our prisoners came as a shock to us. In the Middle East, torture and even murder remain business as usual behind prison walls.

Can anyone imagine Egypt, or Syria, or Iran, or Saudi Arabia, or even Turkey holding public, televised hearings to grill senior government officials about conditions in their prisons? And prisoners

147

of their militaries are unmentionable. Can any reader name one Middle Eastern state, other than Israel, in which prisoners have any real hope of redress?

Would any of the world's enthusiastic critics of America like to spend time behind bars in any state between Morocco and Pakistan? Without excusing the behavior of those renegade military police in Iraq, isn't there some slight difference between humiliating enemy prisoners and torturing one's fellow citizens to death?

And let's not leave our sanctimonious European friends off the hook. When French intelligence agents blew up a Greenpeace vessel not so long ago, it was treated as little more than a case of littering in the *Bois de Boulogne*. And when, almost fifty years after the events, a retired French general published a book admitting the extent of French torture and extra-judicial murders in Algeria, the French government's first impulse was to prosecute him for telling the truth.

Asia? How many public investigations have there been into the Indian military's extra-judicial killings in Kashmir? What of those Indonesian generals who barely got a tap on the wrist for the atrocities of East Timor? Of course, the Chinese People's Army is a model observer of human rights. . . .

As an American, I *want* my country to be held to higher standards—we can live up to them. Proudly. But we don't need any more hypocritical charges from states with no standards at all.

The international media have been no better. It's certainly fair to criticize America. Our system's robust enough to stand up to even the most bigoted scrutiny. But when stations from al Jazeera to CNN International cover the misbehavior of a few U.S. prison guards with more fervor and airtime than they did Saddam's mass murders (or the ongoing crimes in virtually every other state in the Middle East), then, as an American, all I can do is tune them out.

All those who opposed the removal of Saddam, from the BBC to Egyptian state television to the *New York Times,* act as though the events in Abu Ghraib prove that they were right all along.

No. They weren't right. And no amount of disingenuous "reporting" or feigned shock on the part of newsreaders can change the fact that America behaved nobly and bravely in Iraq—

or that we continue to struggle to do the right thing, if sometimes ineptly.

We've made mistakes. We'll make more. We're human. But it's never a mistake to fight for freedom. If the Iraqis make a mess of their one great chance, it won't be our fault. But it *will* be the fault of those regional governments and the global media who encourage anti-American hatred at every opportunity, pretending that terrorists are freedom fighters.

Although those photos from Abu Ghraib are disgusting, it's far more appalling that so much of the world doesn't want a free Iraq to succeed, that jealousy of the United States is so great that TV commentators, heads of state, and many a common citizen would gladly write off the twenty-five million people of Iraq just to give America a black eye.

But black eyes heal. Much more quickly than the scars left by institutionalized torture and murder, state oppression, decades of censorship, imprisonment without hope of trial, religious bigotry, and ethnic cleansing. That, too, is a lesson of Iraq.

Even human-rights advocates seem vastly more concerned with sticking it to America than with the suffering of millions of prisoners in countries that wouldn't let foreign activists near their prisons. Attacking America makes headlines. Taking on the government of Egypt gets you nowhere. In the quest for renown, justice falls by the wayside.

Human-rights critics were in Iraq because we let them in. Perhaps they should try Saudi Arabia next.

The headlines now wounding us will not soon go away. The media, foreign and domestic, will twist every drop of blood from this story of an American misstep. But no matter how much more there is to come, we Americans will admit our errors and fix them. Then we'll move forward, no less determined to do the right thing.

How many other nations in the world could claim as much?

Throwing Victory Away

New York Post

May 13, 2004

Quiet isn't the same thing as peace. As a column of Marines paraded through Fallujah this week, it was done at the sufferance of our enemies. We lost the battle of Fallujah. By surrendering.

The Coalition Provisional Authority insists that quiet streets are what matter. But the streets were quiet under Saddam, as they may one day be quiet under religious fanatics. Is that our sole remaining goal in Iraq? A phony calm that leaves terrorists in power?

We bragged publicly that we would avenge the mutilation of those four contractors at the hands of Fallujah's thugs. We told the world we would not stop until the city was cleansed of insurgents. And, of course, we swore we would never negotiate with terrorists.

What did we actually do? We negotiated with terrorists, reempowered Saddam's thugs in uniform, and ran away as quickly as we could go. The Marines insist they could have won, had they been allowed to fight. That's unquestionably true, but, as North Vietnam's senior general once pointed out about a different war, it's also irrelevant.

The diplomats claim we backed down to spare the innocent people of Fallujah. But they didn't lift a finger as the city's Arab fanatics drove out Fallujah's Kurdish population. And how does it benefit the average citizen to leave gunmen in control—protected now by Ba'athist thugs who tell us mockingly that there "aren't any foreign fighters in the city?" Right. And there are no politicians in Washington.

Our threats have begun to sound as hollow as those made by Khadafy in his prime. Our power means nothing unless we are willing to use it decisively. The truth is that those heroic young Marines who died in the initial combat encounters in Fallujah lost their lives for nothing. Frightened, politicized leaders squandered the advantages gained by their sacrifice.

And our enemies are telling the Muslim world that they fought the U.S. military to a standstill. For once, they're telling the truth. It doesn't matter that they won politically, not militarily. They *won*.

We'll pay for our failure in Fallujah for years to come. The message our enemies took from their success was that Americans don't have the stomach it takes to win. Far from fostering peace in our time, our cowardice in Fallujah will encourage no end of attacks on Americans.

Oh, yes. Fallujah's quiet this week. But the triumph of the Sunni-Arab thugs reinvigorated the rising by Muqtada al Sadr's Mehdi Army. The Shia's now have to prove that they can defeat the Americans, too.

And just by the way: It's now perfectly acceptable to saw the heads off living American captives. The Americans will squawk and call the perpetrators names (sticks and stones . . .). But if only you murder enough Americans, we'll build you new power plants, sewage systems, factories, hospitals . . . and guarantee you an honored place at the bargaining table.

At present, U.S. Army troops are engaged with the fanatics led by Babyface Sadr, a gangster in religious robes whom even the Iraqis despise. We're winning. But the danger is looming yet again that the failed civilian leadership in Baghdad will step in and call off our troops before the job is finished.

If, having lost Fallujah through timidity, we back down on our promise to bring one murderous renegade cleric to justice, our credibility will collapse entirely.

Cowardice isn't a strategy. Weakness isn't a virtue. Caving in to killers isn't a demonstration of humanity. When fighting monsters who decapitate living prisoners in front of video cameras, you are, literally, in a knife fight to the bone. If we aren't willing to fight such enemies to the death, we might as well stay home and hide in a corner, waiting for them to come after us, which they will.

A fundamental problem is that our military is fighting twenty-first-century conflicts, while our diplomats and bureaucrats are still mired in twentieth-century models of how the world should work (but doesn't and won't). In an age of deadly terror and mass murder, we seek compromise, minimal enemy casualties, and happy faces all around.

For two years after 9/11, President Bush provided us with courageous, decisive, visionary leadership. Then the election approached and he lost his nerve.

Make no mistake: Short-term compromises with murderers to gain a brief stretch of preelection quiet will return to haunt us—soaked with the blood of our soldiers and our citizens.

The president likes to stress that we are in a war, but he's the one who seems to have forgotten it. He needs to take charge of his subordinates, in Washington and Baghdad, and remind them that some things *are* worth fighting for.

Kill Faster!

New York Post

May 20, 2004

In Iraq last month, I learned a great deal about the future of combat. By watching TV.

During the initial fighting in Fallujah, I tuned in al Jazeera and the BBC. At the same time, I was getting insider reports from the battlefield, from a U.S. military source on the scene, and through Kurdish intelligence. I saw two different battles.

The media weren't reporting. They were taking sides. With our enemies. And our enemies won. Because, under media assault, we lost our will to fight on.

During the combat operations, al Jazeera constantly aired trumped-up footage and insisted that U.S. Marines were destroying Fallujah and purposely targeting women and children, causing hundreds of innocent casualties as part of an American crusade against Arabs.

It was entirely untrue. But the truth didn't matter. Al Jazeera told a receptive audience what it wanted to believe. Oh, and the "Arab CNN" immediately followed the Fallujah clips with video of Israeli "atrocities." Connecting the dots was easy for those nurtured on hatred.

The Marines in Fallujah weren't beaten by the terrorists and insurgents, who were being eliminated effectively and accurately. They were beaten by al Jazeera. By lies.

Get used to it. This is the new reality of combat. Not only in Iraq, but in every broken country, plague pit, and terrorist refuge to which our troops will have to go in the future. And we can't change it. So we had better roll up our camouflage sleeves and deal with it.

The media is often referred to offhandedly as a strategic factor. But we still don't fully appreciate its fatal power. Conditioned by the relative objectivity and ultimate respect for facts of the U.S. media, we fail to understand that, even in Europe, the media has become little more than a tool of propaganda.

That propaganda is increasingly, viciously, mindlessly anti-American. When our forces engage in tactical combat, dishonest media reporting immediately creates drag on the chain of command all the way up to the president.

Real atrocities aren't required. Everything American soldiers do is portrayed as an atrocity. World opinion is outraged, no matter how judiciously we fight.

With each passing day—sometimes with each hour—the pressure builds on our government to halt combat operations, to offer the enemy a pause, to negotiate . . . in essence, to give up.

We saw it in Fallujah, where slow-paced tactical success led only to cease-fires that comforted the enemy and gave the global media time to pound us even harder. Those cease-fires were worrisomely reminiscent of the bombing halts during the Vietnam War—except that everything happens faster now.

Even in Operation Desert Storm, the effect of images trumped reality and purpose. The exaggerated carnage of the "highway of death" north from Kuwait City led us to stop the war before we had sufficiently punished the truly guilty—Saddam's Republican Guard and the regime's leadership. We're still paying for that mistake.

In Fallujah, we allowed a bonanza of hundreds of terrorists and insurgents to escape us—despite promising that we would bring them to justice. We stopped because we were worried about what already hostile populations might think of us.

The global media disrupted the U.S. and Coalition chains of command. Foreign media reporting even sparked bureaucratic infighting within our own government.

The result was a disintegraton of our will—first from decisive commitment to worsening hestitation, then to a "compromise" that returned Sunni-Arab Ba'athist officers to power. That deal not only horrified Iraq's Kurds and Shi'a Arabs, it inspired expanded attacks by Muqtada al Sadr's Shi'a thugs hoping to rival the success of the Sunni-Arab murderers in Fallujah.

We could have won militarily. Instead, we surrendered politically and called it a success. Our enemies won the information war. We literally didn't know what hit us.

The implication for tactical combat—war at the bayonet level—is clear: We must direct our doctrine, training, equipment, organization, and plans toward winning low-level fights much faster—before the global media can do what enemy forces cannot do and stop us short. We can still win the big campaigns. But we're apt to lose thereafter, in the dirty end-game fights.

We have to speed the kill.

For two decades, our military has concentrated on deploying forces swiftly around the world, as well as on fighting fast-paced conventional wars—with the positive results we saw during Operation Iraqi Freedom. But at the infantry level, we've lagged behind—despite the unrivaled quality of our troops.

We've concentrated on critical soldier skills but ignored the emerging requirements of battle. We've worked on almost everything except accelerating urban combat—because increasing the pace is dangerous and very hard to do.

Now we have no choice. We must learn to strike much faster at the ground-truth level, to accomplish the tough tactical missions at speeds an order of magnitude faster than in past conflicts. If we can't win the Fallujahs of the future swiftly, we will lose them.

Our military must rise to its responsibility to reduce the pressure on the National Command Authority—in essence, the president—by rapidly and effectively executing orders to root out enemy resistance or nests of terrorists.

To do so, we must develop the capabilities to fight within the "media cycle," before journalists sympathetic to terrorists and murderers can twist the facts and portray us as the villains. Before the combat encounter is politicized globally. Before allied leaders panic. And before such reporting exacerbates bureaucratic rivalries within our own system.

Time is the new enemy.

Fighting faster at the dirty-boots level is going to be tough. As we develop new techniques, we'll initially see higher casualties in the short term, perhaps on both sides.

But as we should have learned long ago, if we are not willing to face up to casualties sooner, the cumulative tally will be much, much higher later. We're bleeding in Iraq now because a year ago we were unwilling even to shed the blood of our enemies.

The Global War on Terror is going to be a decades-long struggle. The military will not always be the appropriate tool to apply. But when a situation demands a military response, our forces must bring to bear such focused, hyperfast power that our enemies are overwhelmed and destroyed before hostile cameras can defeat us.

If we do not learn to kill very, very swiftly, we will continue to lose slowly.

Bravery, Blood, and Lies

New York Post

May 25, 2004

If the recent retreat from Fallujah showed the world how to get counterinsurgency operations exactly wrong, the U.S. Army has been giving lessons on how to do it right in its campaign against Muqtada al Sadr's thugs.

Each confrontation has its own requirements in Iraq. In Fallujah, we had an opportunity to strike swiftly and eliminate several hundred terrorists. Instead, the decision was made to hand the city over to our enemies to achieve a "peaceful solution."

The result? Ambushes and roadside bombs continue to kill Marines in the Fallujah area—Marines who fought bravely and well, only to see victory snatched from their hands by their own superiors.

In the broader insurgency led by the renegade Shi'a cleric Sadr, the military task was more complex. With outbreaks of violence in the holy cities of Najaf and Karbala, as well as in a teeming Baghdad slum, the Army faced the risk of alienating the greater Shi'a population if sacred shrines were violated or civilian casualties soared.

But our commanders on the ground also had advantages, which they seized. Sadr's thugs had no deep support—on the contrary, local people wanted them to leave their neighborhoods and stop misusing sacred sites. No senior cleric supported Sadr, a vainglorious junior mullah. And we had good intelligence—

some of it coming from the population Sadr pretended to represent.

The Army couldn't just blast its way into downtown Najaf or Karbala, given the religious sensitivities involved. Instead, troops from our 1st Armored Division, "Old Ironsides," methodically peeled away one layer of resistance after another. Shrines weren't violated. Civilians were spared. Damage was minimized. Yet, thanks to the skill of our soldiers and their leaders, Sadr's gangsters were slaughtered by the hundreds.

In some Shi'a areas, Sadr's "uprising" proved to be much ado about nothing and swiftly collapsed. Elsewhere, fighting raged. In Sadr City, the Baghdad slum, our soldiers promptly moved to take control—recognizing that Sadr had drawn most of his recruits from its fetid alleys.

Meanwhile, battalion task forces from the 1st AD cordoned the holy cities. With precision and patience, they avoided traps set by the militiamen that would have profaned the sacred tomb complexes. Fighting door-to-door and through a vast cemetery, they staged lightning raids in the hours of darkness, keeping the enemy under pressure.

Whenever Sadr's militiamen made the mistake of coming out to fight, the soldiers from the "First Tank" efficiently helped them achieve martyrdom—with remarkably low friendly or civilian losses.

As weeks of skillful fighting approach a climax, Sadr's thugs have been driven from Karbala, Najaf has quieted, and our forces have punched deep into his stronghold of Kufa. His militia has been broken. His deputies have been arrested or killed. And Sadr himself is cornered, physically and politically.

Now comes the most dangerous phase of the operation. With our troops on the verge of bringing Sadr to justice, the only thing we have to fear is yet another intervention by the guys in ties. If we snatch defeat from the jaws of victory again by letting Sadr off the hook, we will throw away the textbook example of success our Army just delivered.

Sadr needs to come out of his hiding place in handcuffs or in a shroud.

Writing for my fellow soldiers ten years ago, I warned that one of the consistent American weaknesses in the future would be the impulse of our own diplomats to rush to the rescue of our enemies just when our military had them on the ropes. It happened in Fallujah. We can't afford to let it happen again.

Don't worry about making a martyr out of Sadr. Even his fellow Shi'as want him dead. . . . while the media whine.

Americans can be proud of the superb job our troops are doing, not only against Sadr, but throughout Iraq. Yet, revealing their prejudices in an election year, many "leading" media outlets are determined to turn Iraq into a failure.

The endless orgy of coverage of the Abu Ghraib incident, for example, is insufferable. The successes and sacrifices of more than a hundred thousand soldiers go ignored, while a sanctimonious media focuses on the viciousness of a few ill-led criminals in uniform.

The truth is that Abu Ghraib was the story big media longed for, a scandal journalistic vultures could turn into strategic roadkill. Press coverage of our military's many successes has been scant.

Development projects go ignored. If soldiers don't complain, they don't get camera time. When our forces successfully target a terrorist hideout, the evidence doesn't matter. The media leaps to validate enemy lies that a "wedding party" was attacked.

Not one voice in the media raised the possibility that terrorists willing to slaughter three thousand civilians on 9/11 might be perfectly willing to murder a dozen or so Arab women and children to set up a propaganda victory. Increasingly, our enemies make sophisticated use of our own roundheels media—which is always ready to credit evil men with virtue, while assuming that American soldiers are wrong.

Recent press and broadcast stories have focused sympathetically on the plight of military deserters. Ludicrous stories of abuse told by Iraqis looking for a cash handout are presented without the least skepticism. And in the most disgraceful essay of this new century, Susan Sontag, writing in the *New York Times Magazine*, associated the prisoner-abuse affair with the massacres in Rwanda and the Holocaust.

Really? Does Ms. Sontag truly believe that Abu Ghraib equals Auschwitz? Does she *know* a single American soldier? How simple the world must look from behind her desk. . . .

This is not an argument for censorship. America *needs* a free media. But we also need a responsible media. Abu Ghraib was an ugly little story that big media exaggerated into a strategic disaster—with no thought for the consequences for our troops, our country, or the people of Iraq.

For too many journalists, sensation trumps all else. American successes, such as the Army's recent victories, are an annoyance. Doesn't anyone care about the truth?

Killers with Cameras

New York Post

May 21, 2004

Imagine if, on D-Day, the Nazis had been allowed to place camera teams on Omaha Beach—with our suffering soldiers forbidden to interfere. What if, on top of that, the Germans had invented American atrocities against French civilians—and our own officials defended their right to do so in the name of press freedom?

That's the situation with al Jazeera in Iraq.

Staffed by embittered exiles and pan-Arabist ideologues—the last Nasserites—al Jazeera is so consumed by hatred of America and the West that the network would rather see Iraq collapse into a bloodbath than permit the emergence of a democracy sponsored by Washington.

Despite his slaughter of a million-and-a-half Muslims in wars and campaigns of repression, al Jazeera cheered for Saddam during Operation Iraqi Freedom, inventing Iraqi victories. Its staff reacted with horror to the fall of Baghdad—and suppressed film clips of celebrating Arabs.

Since then, al Jazeera has glamorized Islamic terrorists (who, were they ever to come to power, would close al Jazeera and butcher its staff) while portraying the Ba'athist campaign of murder and sabotage as a noble freedom struggle.

Al Jazeera is so bigoted and morally debased that its reporters and producers delight in Coalition casualties, in dead Iraqi doctors and engineers, and (above all) in dead Kurds.

Al Jazeera not only encourages the assassination of American soldiers, but pulls out all the stops to excite anti-U.S. hatred throughout the Arabic-speaking world.

The response of our own officials in Iraq? Al Jazeera is only exercising freedom of the press. Isn't that why we fought to bring down Saddam?

This is idiocy, a perverse political correctness based upon a rejection of common sense.

Press freedom is a treasure of our civilization, but it's also distinctly a product of our civilization—one that doesn't always export well. It works in our society for numerous reasons.

First, despite undeniable excesses, there's a fundamental respect for facts in our media. Second, our press is not rewarded for encouraging mass murder. Third, we have libel and hate-crime laws that work. Fourth, the great majority of journalists take pride in the standards of their profession—despite popular notions to the contrary.

We also have healthy, vigorous, combative competition. In the end, the members of our media keep each other honest. One should never underestimate the jealousy journalists feel toward one another as a factor in exposing fabrications. The glee with which reporters unmask the sins of more successful colleagues is an unappreciated virtue of the profession.

Al Jazeera has no such controls. It's Pravda without the truth—in living color. As long as the network glorifies its host, the Emir of Qatar, and avoids anything beyond the most lightweight criticism of select Arab leaders, it's allowed to incite hatred, assassination, and genocide.

Facts are never allowed to interfere.

When I toured al Jazeera's studios in January, the lack of interest in objective reporting was startling. All the staff cared about was popularity and power. It was *un*reality TV at its worst. They bragged about their technology ("Better than the BBC!") and their influence, but never mentioned integrity, veracity, or responsibility. It was the Nazi propaganda ministry on amphetamines.

Is a media organ that consistently lies, preaches hatred, and encourages political murders entitled to unrestricted access? Iraq's own leaders don't think so. Yet Paul Bremer has protected al Jazeera in the name of some fairyland notion of a free media.

Whether we speak of a free media or a free society, freedom comes with responsibility. Those who decline the responsibility forfeit their claim to freedom. We often forget this elementary contract. Al Jazeera ignores it entirely.

By alarming our closest allies with staged footage and Big Lies, al Jazeera drove the Bush administration to retreat from Fallujah—creating a terrorist city-state, a plague boil on the body of free Iraq. Al Jazeera triumphed by inventing tales of slaughtered infants and rabid attacks on civilians. We let them get away with it unchallenged.

In an age when the global media has become an ever more powerful strategic factor, we need to reexamine assumptions of press freedom so peculiar to English-speaking civilization that they even don't apply fully in continental Europe.

We need not accommodate hate-speech overseas any more than we would tolerate it here at home. And we have every right to demand respect for the truth.

If the rules essential to a free press are ignored by al Jazeera and others, they forfeit any claim to press protections.

Al Jazeera has become the most powerful ally of terror in the world—even more important than Saudi financiers. We're foolish if we do not recognize it as such.

We should not interfere if the new Iraqi government decides to place restrictions on al Jazeera. Soon enough, we ourselves may need to recognize that "journalists" with deadly agendas should be classified as enemy combatants. If the War on Terror really is a war of ideas, we shouldn't let our enemies win with lies.

This is not an argument against freedom of the press, but against murderous propaganda. Despite the quivering alarm such a proposition will excite in the faculty lounge, it really isn't hard to tell the difference between honest attempts to report the news and incitement to genocide.

Apologists for al Jazeera are legion, of course. Even though the network never seriously criticizes Arab terrorists, Arab hate-speech, torture by Arab governments, Arab corruption, or

Arab atrocities. (*Those* are all legitimate forms of cultural expression, you see. . . .)

In the end, the most tragic factor of all is that, while al Jazeera prompts the murder of individual American soldiers, it's simultaneously poisoning the entire Arab world by reinforcing the fatal Arab addiction to blaming others for every home-brewed disaster.

To spite the "Great Satan America," al Jazeera is willing to let the Middle East speed into Hell. We need to apply the brakes.

The Muddle in Iraq

New York Post

September 17, 2004

Fighting terror is like fighting a fire. It's easiest in the early stages, before the flames spread. But if you sit idly by, hoping that the fire will burn itself out, you're likely to find yourself up against an inferno.

Confronted by global terror, the Clinton administration hoped the problem would go away by magic. Faced with incipient terror in Iraq last year, the Bush administration insisted that the magic of freedom would make it disappear.

But policies that rely on magic of any kind beg for disaster.

We don't yet face a disaster in Iraq—thanks to the quality and commitment of our troops. And the Bush administration, despite its errors, has had a great stroke of luck in Prime Minister Ayad Allawi, who has shown not only a solid grasp of the problems Iraq faces, but the will to solve them no matter what it takes.

At the moment, it's almost impossible to find a balanced view of Iraq in America. The partisans of both political parties are out in force, insisting either that Iraq's a magnificent place with a minor litter problem or that it's an inferno where countless legions of terror are being forged.

The reality's in the middle but still more hopeful than not. Despite the lurid media reports, more good things than bad are happening in Iraq. Progress is slow and painful. But it's still progress.

The media report an increase in violence, occasionally noting that the terrorists hope to influence the U.S. election. But there's much more to the carnage than Bush vs. Kerry.

Despite the impression created by intermittent attacks, the terrorists have shifted their priority away from attacking our troops. Every time they go after our soldiers or Marines, our enemies suffer disproportionate casualties. So they're concentrating on killing *Iraqis*—government officials, the police, educators, doctors, and businessmen.

This gains them short-term headlines and creates local chaos, but it's alienating the population. Bombing crowds of young men applying for jobs is not an effective way to win hearts and minds. The Iraqis may not want us to stay forever, but they do *not* want the terrorists in power.

And there's another, more significant reason why the violence has increased: Our troops are on the offensive again, reclaiming towns and cities where terrorists grabbed power after the Bush administration faltered in Fallujah this past spring.

Despite the frantic efforts of the Arab media to stop our destruction of the terrorists and insurgents, Prime Minister Allawi and the key members of his government are hanging tough. They know that Iraq doesn't have a chance unless terror is uprooted. *They* support our troops. In response, the Bush administration has been willing to apply military power again, as long as it doesn't create embarrassing headlines before November.

We're retaking one city after another. But the core problem remains Fallujah, where the administration's surrender—despite the tactical success of our Marines—allowed our enemies to create a terrorist city-state. The violence that seeped across central Iraq over the summer came from terror's safe haven in Fallujah.

Allawi wants Fallujah brought into line. Our military has the muscle. Operations will be harder now than they would have been four months ago, since our enemies have had time to prepare for a siege. But we can do it.

The delay is because the Bush administration wants to avoid serious combat until after our elections. The Bushies are using airstrikes against terrorist safe houses, but that won't retake the city.

The truth is that the terrorists are the lesser problem. The greater impediment to progress has been our presidential elections and the policy distortions they create.

The polarization, dishonesty, and manipulation on both sides aids the terrorists. When John Kerry states categorically that he'll bring our troops home within four years, it promises the terrorists that they only have to hang on. When he declares our efforts a disaster, he encourages our enemies to believe they're winning. And when he promises a "more sensitive" war on terror, it's read as a pending declaration of surrender.

Kerry blathers. Bush delays. Iraq burns.

Meanwhile, our intelligence community has once again shown its weakness by covering its backside, instead of finding terrorists. A National Intelligence Council report revealed this week paints a bleak picture of the future of Iraq. Why? Because the intel bureaucrats don't want to be blamed if things go wrong. There's nothing safer than assuming failure.

I dealt with the NIC during my days as an intelligence officer. I always found it more interested in playing it safe than in serving our country. Clearly, nothing has changed.

October is going to be a bloody month—it may appear to prove the pessimists right. But Iraq's future isn't tied to a 24/7 news cycle. The key event is going to be the election. Not *our* election, but the Iraqi vote scheduled for January.

Nobody else in the Middle East wants that election to take place. The U.N. is warning that security conditions may prevent voting—giving the terrorists hope. But the Iraqi interim government is staying the course.

Fallujah is the military test of our resolve to secure the future of Iraq. But the January election is the strategic test. We must not let ourselves become discouraged. Those ballots are worth fighting for. No matter how bloody and flawed, an Iraqi vote held on schedule would be a tremendous victory for freedom.

Our enemies and fair-weather friends alike will try to disrupt the voting. Our response may decide the future of the entire Middle East.

And Now, Fallujah

New York Post

November 4, 2004

Tuesday's decisive popular vote wasn't just for George W. Bush. It was for our troops, as well. The American people sent a message to the world: *We* know we're at war. And our men and women in uniform are going to win.

We, the people, voted to fight.

The first military mission facing the president is the destruction of the terrorist presence in Fallujah. That city-state of terror has become the unifying symbol for our enemies, more vital to the Middle East's fanatics than the fate of Osama bin Laden.

Last spring, the administration made a fateful mistake, stopping short when our Marines were on the brink of victory. This time, our president—with a mandate from the American people—isn't going to stop until the last assassin lies dead in the last cellar.

But he needs to get on with the job. We should move against Fallujah immediately—with the support of Iraq's interim prime minister. We have an ideal window for action while our enemies, from al Qa'eda and the French to al Jazeera and the BBC, are bewildered by their failure to dictate our election's outcome. Their vicious attempts to change our government failed. Now they're wondering what on earth to do.

While they're scrambling, we should be shooting.

And when the president gives the order to finish the job in Fallujah, the Washington civilians need to get out of the way of our Marines and soldiers. Send the lawyers on a Caribbean cruise. Our troops know how to do this job. We need to trust them.

We must not be afraid to make an example of Fallujah. While we always seek to fight humanely, the most humane thing we can do in that tormented city is just to win, to burn out the plague of fanaticism and prove to Iraq's people that the forces of terror will not be allowed to enslave them.

We need to demonstrate that the United States military cannot be deterred or defeated. If that means widespread destruction, we must accept the price. Most of Fallujah's residents— those who wish to live in peace—have already fled. Those who remain have made their choice. We need to pursue the terrorists remorselessly.

That means killing. While we strive to obey the internationally recognized laws of war (though our enemies do not), our goal should be to target the terrorists and insurgents so forcefully that few survive to raise their hands in surrender. We don't need more complaints about our treatment of prisoners from the global forces of appeasement. We need terrorists dead in the dust. And the world needs to see their corpses.

Let potential terrorist recruits get a good, hard look at their probable fate. And let them see a U.S. Marine standing proudly and fearlessly in the center of Fallujah.

Many other difficult tasks lie ahead, from helping the Iraqis conduct their country's first free national elections, through assisting the Afghans as they consolidate their remarkable progress, to hunting down Islamic terrorists wherever they go to ground.

We can do it. And the American people know it. They just said so.

Even if Fallujah has to go the way of Carthage, reduced to shards, the price will be worth it. We need to demonstrate our strength of will to the world, to show that there is only one possible result when madmen take on America.

Our troops in Iraq have been energized by the election results. They understand that each vote cast for Bush was a vote of confidence in them. They never trusted the phonies who slapped on bumper stickers that read "Support our troops, bring them home."

Those who voted for President Bush are the real supporters of bringing our troops home. *After* their work is done. In Fallujah. And wherever terror threatens the cause of freedom.

Finishing Fallujah

New York Post

November 9, 2004

The most decisive battle since the fall of Baghdad has begun. Thousands of U.S. Marines, Army units, and Iraqi government forces have moved into Fallujah. Now we need to finish the job swiftly, no matter the cost in death and destruction, before the will of our civilian leaders weakens again.

Stopping even one building short of the annihilation of the terrorists and insurgents would be a defeat. Al Jazeera will pull out the propaganda stops, inventing American atrocities. The BBC will pressure Tony Blair to rein in our president. Iraqi faction leaders will press Prime Minister Ayad Allawi to accept a cease-fire for "talks."

The weight of the free world is on the shoulders of our Marines and soldiers—and on the backs of our Iraqi allies. They've got to wrap up major operations in a week.

We can do it. Our troops are the best in the world. The early phases of combat last night showed solid intelligence work and adept planning. The terrorists spent months preparing defensive traps, but our combat engineers—key members of the team—blew right through the roadside bombs and barricades. We're off to an impressive start.

U.S. and Iraqi forces are attacking on multiple axes, keeping the terrorists off balance. Key sites within the city already have been seized—including a hospital that cared more about propaganda than its patients. Iraqi national forces have performed solidly thus far. A win in Fallujah will mark the birth of their new nation—one that never really existed in the past, when Iraq was held together only through oppression.

Significantly, the main assault began after darkness fell. Following months of preparatory airstrikes and unpublicized raids by U.S. special operations forces, the night attack instantly put the terrorists at a disadvantage. Although our enemies may have acquired a few night-vision devices, our troops are superbly equipped and trained as night stalkers.

In the irregular wars of the past, the guerrillas owned the hours of darkness. Not anymore. GI Joe is the Midnight Master.

Expect round-the-clock ground and air operations that give the terrorists no rest and deprive them of the initiative. Our troops *know* how important this battle is. They'll fight ferociously. The Marines, especially, are itching for revenge after being deprived of victory for political reasons last April. They only need to be allowed to do the job right this time.

It's up to President Bush not to let them down. No matter what happens, no matter who complains or balks, no matter the false accusations from Al Jazeera and the BBC, our president needs to stand firm until the job is done. By quitting in April, we created the terrorist city-state of Fallujah. Now we need to shut it down for good.

Meanwhile, be prepared for media monkey business. No matter how well things go, we'll hear self-righteous gasps over the inevitable U.S. casualties. The first time a rifle company consolidates a position long enough to bring up ammunition, we'll hear that the attack has bogged down. If commanders on the ground decide to shift forces from one axis of advance to another, we'll be told that our troops couldn't make progress against "dug-in terrorists."

If four Iraqi units out of five perform well in battle, but one outfit fails or flees, we'll be bombarded with reports insisting that our training program hasn't worked, that the Iraqis aren't really with us, that the interim government has no grassroots support (sort of what the Dems said about George W. Bush).

And if Operation Phantom Fury goes miraculously well, we'll be criticized for waiting too long to go in, for exaggerating the threat, and for knocking over a stop sign with a tank.

The global media lost the U.S. presidential election. They'll do their best to win the Second Battle of Fallujah for the terrorists.

The truth is that war is cruel. And difficult. And complex. It's never as smooth as it is in a film or a video game. In real life, heroes get killed, too—sometimes by friendly fire. Mistakes are made, despite rigorous planning. The enemy shoots back. And sometimes the enemy gets lucky. Tragedy is war's inseparable companion.

We cannot foresee all the details of the combat ahead. The fight for Fallujah may prove easier than we feared, or tougher than we hoped. Time will tell. Meanwhile, don't let your view be swayed by the crisis of the hour. Have faith in our troops and their leaders.

In return, I can promise you one thing: If we don't fail our troops, they won't fail us.

Victory in Fallujah

New York Post

November 11, 2004

In the Second Battle of Fallujah, military operations are ahead of schedule. Our casualties have been blessedly light. The terrorists who haven't fled are being killed by the hundreds. Our troops will soon achieve their goal of eliminating Iraq's key safe haven for terrorists.

Our Marines and soldiers have carried the ball inside the ten-yard line. The media's response? Move the goalposts.

The legions of pundits ("Will talk for food") now suggest that a win in Fallujah will be meaningless because we failed to kill or capture the terrorist leadership, because some of the thugs ran away, and because Fallujah won't resemble Darien, Connecticut, by next Sunday.

On Tuesday, as our troops handily pierced the defenses terrorists had spent months erecting, the *New York Times* carried *two* front-page stories implying that our forces were facing possible defeat. The *Times'* military analysis was incompetent and just plain wrong. And the photo its editors ran above the fold showed a Marine curled in a ditch under enemy fire.

It wasn't reporting. It was a mix of anti-American propaganda and wishful thinking. Al Jazeera couldn't have done it better.

Now that our troops are winning so lopsidedly that it can't be denied, the *Times* likely will tell us that Fallujah didn't matter, anyway, that our efforts were wasted. Then Seymour Hersh, the *New Yorker's* greatest living fiction writer, will follow up with a fairy tale called "Failure In Fallujah."

What's *really* happening?

We're winning a critical victory. Since the political decision to stop short in Fallujah last April, the terrorists had bragged to the world that the city would never fall to the infidel. Abu Musab al Zarqawi and his thugs turned Fallujah into a vast dungeon, complete with torture chambers and execution halls. The terrorists stockpiled weapons and ammunition, welcoming thousands of international "jihadis" and using the city as a base to spread terror across central Iraq.

Fallujah became the new world capital of terror. And Allah's butchers proclaimed that they'd slaughter U.S. troops in the streets, if they tried to enter the city.

Guess who's dying now?

By fleeing without fighting to the death as they promised they would, the terror-masters discredited themselves. After Coalition leaders lost their nerve last April, the terrorists portrayed themselves as having faced down America's military might. This time, they ran away, leaving untrained recruits to take the bullet train to paradise.

The swift fall of Fallujah is not only a practical disaster for the terrorists, but a massive loss of face for them throughout the Muslim world.

Plenty of tough street fighting remains, but three-quarters of the city is under the control of Coalition and Iraqi forces. Contrary to smug media predictions, the Iraqi units didn't run away. They did their part to free the city and save their country.

What have we found in Fallujah? Hostage slaughterhouses— butcher shops for human cattle. Stockpiles of ammunition and explosives in mosques. And a city scarred by all the marks of an Islamic reign of terror.

Talking heads may smirk and say that we'll still have to fight the terrorists elsewhere. True enough. But no one claimed that Fallujah would be the last battle. Of course, the terrorists who ran away will try to refurbish their image with more bombings, assassinations, kidnappings, and beheadings.

But they've lost their greatest stronghold. They've lost their sole tangible symbol of success. And they've lost their image as dauntless warriors able to stand up to the U.S. military.

In this imperfect world, where results are never what amateurs demand, the Second Battle of Fallujah is already a huge win for the good guys—even before the shooting's over.

In the coming weeks, the terrorists will try to reinfiltrate the city. They'll stage photogenic car bombings and assassinations. Then we'll be told that we still don't control Fallujah, that we've failed. But a city where terrorists have to sneak in to plant a bomb is a far better place than one in which they rule.

Meanwhile, our troops and their Iraqi allies remain engaged in brutal street fighting. The remarkably low friendly casualty list is bound to grow. But no one need doubt the outcome. Our troops will complete the mission they were given.

But the media need to stop inventing missions of their own, then blaming our troops for not accomplishing them.

Down and Dirty

New York Post

November 14, 2004

It all comes down to the grunt. Our military assault on Fallujah employed spectacular military technologies and innovative teamwork between services, thorough planning, and overwhelming force. But the Infantry squad still decides who wins or loses.

Setting aside the greater issues of defeating terrorism and promoting a free Iraq, the Second Battle of Fallujah has been remarkable on a purely military level. Beyond the sophistication of our weaponry and even the valor of the American soldier, the fighting affirmed that our armed forces are very good at learning while at war.

The German Field Marshal Erwin Rommel supposedly said of American GIs that he'd never seen troops so green, but had never encountered troops who learned so fast. Well, today's U.S. soldiers and Marines don't go into war half-trained as they had to do in World War II—we now have the best-prepared forces in the world—but they still learn quickly on the battlefield.

Doctrine has rarely been an American strength. We've won our battles and wars through pragmatism, casting aside what didn't work and improving the methods that did. Instead of the inflexibility that outsiders attribute to our military, our armed forces are brilliant improvisers, ingenious at coping with war's surprises.

In Fallujah, cooperation between the services—the Marines, Army, and Air Force—took a major step forward, with Army heavy metal supporting the Marines, while Air Force fighters flew holding patterns overhead, waiting to deliver precision strikes in support of ground operations.

Unmanned aerial vehicles (UAVs) were used to an unprecedented degree, increasing our battlefield surveillance and targeting capability dramatically—some UAVs can even attack the enemy positions they locate. Robotics have begun to play a role in down-and-dirty combat in the streets.

Enhanced communications and battlefield-awareness technologies reduced friendly-fire incidents while allowing commanders a clearer picture of the battle than any leader has had since the days when the warlord stood on a hill and watched the slaughter unfold before his eyes.

But it *still* comes down to the young Americans who signed up for the Infantry.

Urban warfare is formidably difficult and dangerous. The utility of our wonder-technologies plummets when we have to fight inside wrecked industrial plants or in the labyrinths of ancient cities. Past a point, the intelligence systems can no longer see. The troops at the tip of the spear engage enemies at short range in abruptly chaotic circumstances. Who lives or dies is decided with rifles, grenades, and automatic weapons.

Viewed from a distance, our victory in Fallujah was impressive from the opening round. But the sense of ease we get from 24/7 summaries isn't shared by the Infantrymen fighting their way through a booby-trapped city defended by enemies who seek death as a blessing.

In urban combat, the physical difficulties and psychological stresses soar. There are few clear fields of observation and fire. Everything seems a deadly muddle. The enemy might appear from any angle, in front of you, behind you, or on a flank, firing from a window or a rooftop, waiting in a ruin to detonate a booby trap or popping up from a tunnel or a cellar with a rocket-propelled grenade.

For the Infantry squad—sometimes reduced to a half-dozen members—there's no time-out. Even during pauses to bring up ammunition or water, the danger meter always pegs out. The adrenalin rush of combat alternates with weariness of body and soul. Nerves move outside the skin. All senses intensify.

There are two tactical challenges for the Infantryman fighting in a city: crossing open spaces and clearing buildings.

The enemy will always try to control the best fields of fire, but American soldiers have a long history of cracking the code on how to continue the advance. In the battle for Monterrey, during the Mexican-American War, the enemy positioned cannon to sweep the streets down which we had to pass. In response, our soldiers dug and blasted their way through the walls of the city's densely built houses until they emerged behind the Mexican gunners.

In Fallujah, our tools are far more advanced, but the key remains the creativity our troops bring to the battlefield. Left to his own devices, the American soldier will figure out a way to get the job done that the generals never considered.

The other challenge is clearing buildings. We're good at it. But death still lurks behind the walls and doors. And the soldier must guess right. Even though most of Fallujah's civilians have fled, our soldiers and Marines still have to wonder whether the noises in the next room come from an enemy strapped with explosives or from a terrified mother and child.

That's when training and discipline really tell. The unprecedented low numbers of friendly and civilian casualties thus far writes a new page in the long and savage history of urban warfare.

And if the soldier makes the right decision in that hallway— tossing in a grenade to kill a suicidal opponent, or risking his own life to spare the innocent—there's a next time just minutes away. There's another building to be cleared down the block. Then another.

Once the industrial areas have been left behind and the houses begin to crowd together, as the avenues fade into alleys snaking between multiple-story houses whose roofs nearly touch overhead, technology dead-ends.

Air controllers can't call in precision weapons. The gunships can't pick out the targets. Helicopters can't get in close enough. Artillery barrages would have to be fired "danger close" and would slaughter civilians. The recon drones can't weave through the passageways and courtyards. Tanks can't enter the narrow passageways. The dense construction interferes with communications.

And the Infantry squad shoulders all the weight of war. Combat comes down to shouts and hand signals, dashes between doorways, and covering fire directed toward invisible opponents. With all the noise and echo, it's hard to pinpoint a sniper or get a fix on enemy fighters shifting between buildings.

That's when all the rhetoric about "bands of brothers" gets real. Each soldier must trust his life to the handful of young men with whom he's trained, lived, argued, shared, and suffered. Junior NCOs barely older than those they lead must command the confidence of their subordinates. Battle drills have to work, the soldiers have to function as a team and follow procedures instinctively. And if one goes down, bleeding in a gutter, the assault can't stop.

More shouting. Orders can barely be heard. But the squad seems to share a common intelligence. Weapons bark over the clink of empty shell casings. Fresh magazines snap into rifles. Fire teams work their way forward, a machine gun is rushed to a rooftop. The rifleman in the best position to take out the target is out of grenades. Another soldier thinks he hears firing behind him. Someone yells that friendlies are in the field of fire. . . .

The sniper's killed. Or he fades away. The squad leader calls in a status report, if the buildings don't block his transmission. The soldiers take up firing positions on a rooftop. Ammunition is shared—"cross-leveled." The Marines or soldiers are hungry, but too wired to realize it. They're thirsty, and they *do* know that much.

Second squad needs support. Move out. A burst of fire tears into the wall ahead of the soldier on point. And it all begins again. . . .

This isn't even a hint of the war the infantryman must fight. No words written in the comfort and safety of America could do justice to the young men who faced the streets of Fallujah.

This is war's guts, where all of the wonder weapons give way to flesh and blood. This is warfare as it was in Jericho and Jerusalem, in Aachen and Manila, in Hue and Mogadishu.

And it will always require an infantryman.

Nothing Islamic About Human Sacrifice

USA Today

November 17, 2004

Suicide bombings. Assassinations. The wholesale murder of prisoners. The mass slaughter of 9/11. Videotaped beheadings and the execution studios recently discovered in Fallujah. We describe it as "Islamic terrorism."

And we're wrong.

The hard-core terrorists spawned by the breakdown of the Middle East quote the Koran. They wear Muslim garments. They perform the daily rituals prescribed by the faith into which they were born. But all of us, in the West and the Middle East, have mistaken the identity of these butchers.

For all of their Muslim trappings, the terrorists of al Qa'eda and its affiliates have returned to preIslamic practices, to behaviors that Moses, Christ, and Mohammed uniformly rejected: They practice human sacrifice.

The grisly decapitations caught on film and the explosives-laden cars driven into crowds, the bombings of schools and the execution of kidnapped women are not sanctioned by a single passage in the Koran. Nor are they political acts committed by freedom fighters. These are the actions of a resurrected blood cult that has nothing to do with the message of the Prophet Mohammed and everything to do with the bloodthirsty winged devils and gory altars that haunted the ancient Middle East.

The terrorists may believe that they're good Muslims—self-awareness is not a widespread human trait—but their deeds are those of the pagans Mohammed condemned.

We live in an age of change so profound that entire cultures cannot cope with the stress. In the Middle East, we see more than the routine "clash of civilizations." Instead, we are eyewitnesses to an event without precedent: the crash of the once-great, still-proud civilization of Middle Eastern Islam.

IMPULSES FROM THE PAST

In the Middle East, the heavens are falling, and the Earth is wracked by failure. The result was predictable, had we been willing to open our eyes. From the confusion of Reformation-era Europe to China suffering the advent of Western gunboats, history saw human beings react to cultural crises by fleeing into cults that sought revenge.

Instead of returning to a "pure" Islam, the terrorists are building a blood cult, a deformed offshoot of their faith that revives the most primitive and grotesque of religious practices. Human sacrifice pervaded early societies, from preColumbian America through Europe and across Asia. Yet we have grown so accustomed to gentler forms of religion that the discovery of a ritually murdered corpse in alpine ice shocks us. When bones unearthed in the American Southwest bear the markings of ceremonial murder and cannibalism, the politically correct shout their denials. But the truth is that our ancestors bribed their gods with blood.

A paradox of this era of technological wonders is that its dislocations have conjured primitive impulses from the past. This is the great age of both satellites and revived superstition, of all-seeing sensors and blind faith.

Every one of the great religions is under siege. But the crisis is nowhere as intense as in the Middle East, where treasured values and inherited behaviors simply do not work in the twenty-first century.

Nor is the cult of human sacrifice unique to "Islamic" terrorists even now. What was Jonestown but the murder of hundreds of humans in service to a warped religious vision? From spaceship cults in California to the killing of "witches" in the developing world, the impulse to please one god or another by spilling blood remains more deeply ingrained than we like to admit.

"Experts" schooled in the failed dogmas of the past century say Osama bin Laden and his ilk are political actors driven to violence, that the religious trappings of terror are only superficial. They're utterly wrong. The terrorists' relationship to their god is fundamental.

It's time to put aside the international-relations texts that have failed the world so miserably. We must confront the elementary problem of our times: Frightened human beings and the longing for easy answers that lead to the most repugnant forms of faith.

The Aztecs are back.

ISLAM'S WORST ENEMIES

You don't need to understand Arabic to get the message of those videotaped beheadings, with their rituals and liturgy. The sermon precedes the sacrifice. Then the human calf, shivering with terror, has his throat slit by the "priest." We might be watching a ceremony from four thousand years ago.

The attack on 9/11 was not a political act. It was a religious act. But it wasn't Islamic. The Koran forbids the murder of innocents (as well as the taking of hostages and the abuse of prisoners). The 9/11 attacks were cult behavior from the dawn of civilization, employing modern tools.

We must cut through the layers of intellectual nonsense piled up by academics and pundits to get at the essence of this new—and very old—reality. When the terrorists we face invoke the names of "Allah" or "Mohammed," they are blaspheming and corrupting a great faith. The prophet was appalled by the religious practices of the early desert peoples. Those who murder in his name today have rejected his message even as they claim to revere it.

The terrorists we face aren't super-Muslims. They're Islam's worst enemies. They don't seek to turn back the calendar to the tenth century. They're reaching back to the sordid epochs when gods drank human blood.

Finding True Islam

New York Post

November 22, 2004

Last week, I had an inspiring conversation with a Muslim-American. An immigrant from Pakistan, he hadn't yet been granted citizenship, but he had more faith in America than our native-born elite does.

"I write to my brothers and sisters," he said, "And I tell them that they do not know true Islam. If you want to see true Islam, you must come to America."

He meant the social justice and the respect for the individual, rich or poor, prescribed by the Koran. He had not found those qualities in the land of his birth. Nor do they prevail in any Muslim state between Casablanca and Karachi.

Islam sets high standards for the daily behavior of its adherents—but all too often the Koran's calls for fairness, charity, and common decency are rejected in favor of social strictures misinterpreted by bitter old men and fanatics. The oppression of women, terrorism, and the police states of the Middle East were not part of the Prophet Mohammed's vision.

My Muslim friend had recently found yet another reason to believe in America—in a place the rest of us would overlook. Coming from a land where the rich can even murder with impunity, he was thrilled that Olympic swimmer Michael Phelps had to face drunken-driving charges.

"Seven gold medals!" my friend said. "He is a hero, sir! And still he must face the court!

"It is not hidden away because he is powerful. This is very good, this is Islam."

The crime and possible punishment of young Mr. Phelps looks very different to a man born where the poor are eternal victims.

Nor is this soon-to-be citizen an exception among our immigrants. In his personal life, he follows the trail that so many newcomers of various faiths walked before him. He works two jobs. Family finances are tight, but he discourages his sons and daughters from working part-time jobs, insisting that they concentrate on their studies.

The result? His eldest son is studying business and accounting in a good university. The younger kids are determined to emulate their big brother and make the honor roll at school. One boy is a gifted athlete.

In this country less than five years, they're as American as overpriced coffee.

Not all of our fellow Americans who happen to be Muslims are as vocal as my pal, but I believe that they overwhelmingly share his affection for their new home. The headlines will always go to the bad apples, but the very few American Muslims who've engaged in extremist behavior are often converts to the faith, jailbirds, or troubled young people of the sort drawn to the worst elements in any belief system, from white supremacists to Islamic extremists.

No matter their backgrounds, new immigrants have to work through a period of disorientation. Emotional ties to their native cultures tug hard in difficult times—and no one likes to be vilified over an accident of birth.

Personally, I wish more American Muslims would speak out publicly against extremism, against the punitive visions that disfigure Islam, and against the oppression they felt compelled to flee. But I also recognize that these new Americans have been badly shaken by the events of recent years. They're not sure where they stand, or if they'll ever be truly welcome. They're wary of criticizing their own kind, partly from shame and partly because their community is their only safety net.

We need not gloss over the failings of our newest immigrants, whether Muslim, Catholic, Hindu, or any other religion. But we *do* need to have faith in the transformative power of America.

Whenever I hear a "native born" American complaining that our country is "being taken over" by the latest arrivals, I know that the speaker is blind to our country's strengths.

America makes Americans. And it makes *good* Americans. This country is magic, and the magic is growing stronger, not weaker.

Mexican-Americans don't want to take back our Southwest for Mexico. They want Mexico to become more like our Southwest, where a man or woman can build a decent life, where he or she doesn't have to pay bribes at every turn, and where even the poor man's home is his castle. Irish-Americans may have great affection for the land of their ancestors, but they're not moving back there in droves. I don't know any French-Americans who feel a deep allegiance to Jacques Chirac.

Trust America. And believe in our fellow Americans. A tiny minority of Muslim immigrants may preach hatred (thanks not least to Saudi funding) or dream madly of "reestablishing the caliphate." With the indestructible idiocy of youth, some Muslim-American kids may get off on fundamentalist rap music (yep, it really exists) or feel compelled to horrify their parents by growing beards. But most of the Muslims who live among us just want to live better lives than they could have built in the lands of their birth, to see their families thrive and their children prosper.

The American dream doesn't change, only the complexions and accents of the dreamers. Contrary to an old saw from the left, bigotry isn't as American as apple pie. Bigotry is a universal human disease. Being a good American is the most effective cure.

So the next time you hear some bag of wind condemning every Muslim-American because of the misbehavior of a very, very few, do something truly American: Tell him he's a jerk.

Osama's Nightmare

New York Post

December 29, 2004

Monday's message from Osama bin Laden told us what he fears: a vote.

Condemning any Iraqi who goes to the polls as an infidel, the terror master hopes to derail the elections. He knows that every ballot cast is a defeat.

Anyone who dismisses the importance of the upcoming Iraqi elections need only listen to Monsieur bin Laden's urgent plea for a boycott. Osama praised the atrocities of Abu Musab al Zarqawi, a hands-on executioner, and welcomed his collaboration in efforts to block the balloting.

Islamic terrorists distrust the common people. They dread the strength of those who might think for themselves. Convinced that men and women must be governed fiercely from above, the terrorists are the gory religious incarnation of thousands of years of tyranny. Their god is a savage dictator in the clouds.

Osama and Zarqawi share an understanding of their weakness. Given a choice, few men and women prefer to be oppressed. Elections are the best weapon humanity has developed against the age-old hierarchies that concentrate power and wealth in the hands of a few, letting grim old men exterminate simple joys.

The Islamic-extremist vision of a world governed by the harshest interpretation of their faith could not survive where people pick their own leaders. The terrorists know it. And they fear it. Like

187

other self-appointed elites, they pretend to speak for the average man while despising him as unworthy of having a voice in his own affairs. (A reality-TV show about Islamic terrorism might be called "Intellectuals Gone Wild.")

Osama possesses no religious authority to condemn Iraqis for voting. Pretending to revere Islamic tradition, he and his fellow terrorists make up the rules as they go. The slaughter of the innocents, videotaped executions, kidnappings, and the assassinations of political candidates have no basis in the Koran. Terrorist Islam is a primitive blood cult.

That cult could not survive in a Middle East where elections became the norm.

The upcoming vote in Iraq will be messy, at best. Sunni Arabs may stay home, intimidated by terror and poisoned by demagoguery. But that would no more invalidate the election results than a boycott by college professors would negate the legitimacy of a U.S. election. In a democracy, those who lack the courage or will to vote must bow to the ballots of those who take a stand.

The choices Iraqis will make next month may appear as much a rebuke to America as to the terrorists. That, too, is democracy. Instead of worrying about the short term, we should focus on the long term: Democracy is addictive. As we just saw in Ukraine, democracy allows voters to learn from past mistakes. *Any* vote is an ultimate win for America.

Despite the cries of the experts-for-rent for whom imperfect results always mean failure, we should take heart from Osama's latest message: If any confirmation were needed of the importance of holding elections in Iraq, we just got it. If the terrorists thought they had a chance at the polls, they'd be campaigning instead of killing.

Washington simply needs to stay on course. Last-minute jitters must not persuade us to seek an election delay. We should encourage the government of Prime Minister Ayad Allawi to keep the vote on schedule. The only valid reason for a postponement would be if the Iraqis themselves determined a delay was crucial.

The terrorists would see even a brief postponement of the voting as a victory for their desperate campaign of assassinations and bombings. Delayed elections would strengthen the terrorists and insurgents, not weaken them, while even voting that seemed a bloody mess to outsiders would be a milestone for the entire Middle East.

The elections will be the most important test yet for the people of Iraq—Arabs, Kurds, Turcomans, and others. We can't predict the outcome of the elections because the Iraqis themselves don't know what's going to happen.

Will they turn out in masses, defying the prophets of doom as the Afghans did? Will they choose religious leaders over secular technocrats? Will elections be used to settle old scores or to make a new start?

How many Sunni Arabs will defy the terrorists and vote? How many Iraqis will die as they stand in line at the polling stations? Will other Arab governments—terrified of democracy themselves—condemn the results no matter how much courage Iraqis demonstrate? Will a successful election intensify the cruelty of the terrorists?

The only thing of which we may be certain is that our deadliest enemies are doing all they can to stop Iraq's elections. It's the one goal on which the various terrorist factions and insurgent groups agree. If we needed any further proof that our struggle against terror is about human freedom and the dignity of the common man and woman, our enemies are laying it in front of us.

Let Iraqis Vote

New York Post

January 14, 2005

Is Iraq ready to hold perfect, orderly, all-inclusive elections? Of course not. But by the unfair standards critics are raising, the United States might not qualify for nationwide balloting, either.

Iraq's elections are going to be deadly, disorderly, and deeply flawed. And they will still be the most open and authentic elections ever held in the Arab world. Anyone who needs proof of the importance of these polls need only look at the ferocity and duplicity of those intent on delaying or preventing them.

From Islamic terrorists to the *New York Times,* the enemies of free elections in Iraq have a common goal: They desperately want the American experiment in bringing democracy to the Middle East to fail—the first for reasons of power, the latter to regain its lost prestige.

The terrorists' alarm is understandable. Ditto for the Sunni-Arab insurgents. They could never win an election in Iraq, and they know it. The terrorists believe in religious tyranny, while the insurgents believe in secular tyranny. Neither care in the least about the aspirations of the common people.

For its part, the *Times* believes in the tyranny of the intelligentsia. Blinded by its hatred for the Bush administration, it attempts to portray every development in Iraq as a disaster. Even marginally successful Iraqi elections would prove it wrong yet again.

Shouldn't we raise an eyebrow when we find America's self-proclaimed "newspaper of record" shoulder-to-shoulder with Abu Musab al Zarqawi and the leftovers of Saddam Hussein's regime? Does the *NYT* really want the terrorists to win? Is their editorial vanity so great?

American critics of the elections lately have shifted to complaints that the Sunni Arabs may not be adequately represented in the voting. In other words, if less than 20 percent of potential voters choose not to participate, it negates the election's validity. By that measure, the United States hasn't held a valid election in living memory.

The critics whine that the poor Sunni Arabs aren't ready. The truth is that the Sunni Arabs, who benefited under Saddam at the expense of the majority Shi'a and the Kurds, will never admit that they're ready for elections. Elections mean they lose.

If the elections were postponed for a decade, the Sunni Arabs would still argue that they needed more time. Well, if they refuse to vote, it's a lick on 'em. And if they're too cowardly to vote, they don't deserve the benefits of democracy.

Let those who brave the bullets and bombs shape Iraq's future.

The truth is that some Sunni Arabs *will* show up to vote, at great risk. But even if not one participated, it would still leave us with over 80 percent of Iraqis anxious to go to the polls.

The days of the dictatorship of the Sunni-Arab minority are over in Iraq. They don't like it. And that's just tough. The Sunni Arabs need a dose of reality, not coddling. The U.S. occupation was far too indulgent toward them from the beginning. They need tough love, not crocodile tears.

The issue the critics avoid like a leper's kiss is that any delay would hand the terrorists a victory. Wringing their hands about the level of violence in Iraq, democracy's opponents on the Upper West Side insist that voting requires higher levels of security.

Do they imagine that an election delay would make the violence subside? On the contrary, the terrorists and insurgents would believe—rightly—that they had triumphed. Attacks would increase, more recruits would flock to terror's cause (everybody loves a winner), and democracy would recede beyond the far horizon.

Less than a year ago, the same critics wailed that democracy couldn't work in Afghanistan, that Afghans would be too afraid to vote or would vote for bigots and warlords. Instead, millions turned out to elect a moderate technocrat backed by the West.

Iraq is more complex than Afghanistan. The election may disappoint us, in its conduct, its results, or both. But you have to start somewhere. You can't play the intellectual's game of endless procrastination, sunk in dreams of impossible perfection. There is no substitute for the courage to act.

We may find ourselves facing a postelection government less receptive to our ideas, more fractious, or even hostile to our presence. That's democracy. Let the people speak.

But don't listen to the terrorists, the insurgents or the *New York Times,* all of whom are committed to denying a voice to the majority of Iraqis.

Thirty-one Fewer Good Men

New York Post

January 27, 2005

Yesterday, our country lost thirty-one patriots at one blow. A Marine Corps transport helicopter went down in the dark in western Iraq. There were no survivors.

Although the crash is still under investigation, the initial information suggests an accident, not hostile fire. The tough Iraqi environment, perhaps even a sandstorm, may have contributed to the loss, but such tragedies don't occur only in war zones.

The defense of freedom is dangerous work even in the absence of an enemy. Our aging military helicopters have crashed on training missions in Texas and North Carolina, in Germany and elsewhere. The Marines we lost yesterday were aboard a CH-53 Sea Stallion, an aircraft that first flew in 1964 and entered the operational force in 1966.

The Sea Stallion's been upgraded over the years, but it's a safe bet that the airframe that went down was older than most of the Marines aboard.

It's not only combat that puts our troops in danger—training with aging equipment takes lives as well. Marines and soldiers die during administrative lifts from a base to an exercise site.

No matter how good the maintenance, the crew's training, or the safety procedures, old aircraft go down. And those in uniform die unheralded.

There's something else at play, as well, when we lose yet another bird in Iraq or Kentucky: Our aging fleet of transport helicopters is a symptom of the neglect of practical military needs in favor of glamorous fighter aircraft and submarines of no real use.

Our land forces have been treated as stepchildren far too long. We see the price daily in Iraq, where too few soldiers and Marines, not always adequately equipped, are in battle on freedom's frontiers.

The Marines have been good stewards of our tax dollars. As a former Army officer, I've long been impressed by the Corps' determination to get every last ounce of value out of the materiel entrusted to them. The Army is also underfunded, but the Corps is virtually monastic in its poverty. They suck it up and do their best.

Still, there's a point at which aging combat systems must be retired, no matter how devoted their care has been.

We owe those who serve in uniform our gratitude. But we also owe our warriors more than applause: We owe them the tools they need to do their jobs, and those tools should be reasonably up-to-date and dependable.

Our Marines and soldiers never let us down in war. But we routinely let them down in peace. Few voices demand that our troops be provided with that which is essential, rather than with the frivolous junk craven defense contractors foist on them—with Congressional help.

Our troops risk all they have to keep us safe. And we send them to war in aircraft models that entered the force when LBJ was president.

The Marines who went down in western Iraq deserved better. Even if we ultimately learn that the helicopter was hit by a missile smuggled over the Syrian border, the fact remains that we sent those Marines to war in an aircraft designed before shoulder-fired missiles became a threat.

For all the money wasted in Defense budgets, we didn't provide our troops with the essentials: body armor, vehicle armor—or transport aircraft fit for the twenty-first century.

Nor were those thirty Marines and the sailor aboard that helicopter the only casualties yesterday. Four other Marines were killed in Iraq, and the Army lost two soldiers. We can't prevent all combat losses. But we should be ashamed if we can't keep our troops alive when the guns aren't blazing.

The Truth About War

New York Post

February 6, 2005

In San Diego on Tuesday, I had the privilege of sitting beside Lieutenant General Jim Mattis, a Marine who knows how to fight. We were on a panel discussing future war. And Gen. Mattis, a Marine to the marrow of his bones, spoke honestly about the thrill of combat.

Mattis has commanded at every level. In Desert Storm, he led a battalion. In Afghanistan and then in Iraq, he led with inspiration and courage. Everyone on our panel had opinions about war, but that no-nonsense Marine knew more about it than the rest of us combined.

In the course of a blunt discussion of how our military has to prepare for future fights, the general spoke with a frankness that won the hearts of the uniformed members of the audience. Instead of trotting out politically correct clichés, Mattis told the truth:

"You go into Afghanistan, you got guys who slap women around for five years because they didn't wear a veil . . . it's a hell of a lot of fun to shoot them."

The language wasn't elegant. But we don't need prissy military leaders. We need generals who talk straight and shoot straight, men who inspire. And I guarantee you that any real Marine or soldier would follow Gen. Mattis.

What was the media's reaction? A B-team news crew saw a chance to grab a headline at the military's expense (surprise, surprise). Lifting the general's remarks out of context, the media hyenas played it as if they were shocked to learn that people die in war.

Combat veterans are supposed to be tormented souls, you understand. Those who fight our wars are supposed to return home irreparably damaged.

Hollywood's ideal of a Marine is the retired colonel in the film *American Beauty*, who turns out to be a repressed homosexual and a murderer. Veterans are supposed to writhe on their beds all night, covered in sweat, unable to escape their nightmares.

War does scar some men. Most vets, though, just get on with their lives—scratch a veteran looking for pity and more often than not you'll find a supply clerk who never got near a battlefield. And some who serve—the soldiers and Marines who win our wars—run to the sound of the guns, anxious to close with the enemy and kill him. They may not love war itself, but they find combat magnetic and exhilarating. They like to fight.

That's fine in movies featuring Brad Pitt as a mythical Greek hero. But God forbid that a modern-day Marine should admit that he loves his work.

Well, Marines and soldiers don't serve full careers because they *hate* their jobs. In peace or war, the military experience is incredibly rich and rewarding. And sometimes dangerous. Goes with the territory. But for most of the young infantrymen in Iraq, their combat experience will remain the highpoint of their lives. Nothing afterward will be as intense or exciting. And they will never make closer friends than they did in their rifle squad.

Gen. Mattis may have been unusual in his honesty, but he certainly isn't unusual in our history. We picture Robert E. Lee as a saintly father figure, but Lee remarked that it's good that war is so terrible, since otherwise men would grow to love it too much. He was speaking of himself. Andy Jackson certainly loved a fight, and Stonewall Jackson never shied from one. Sherman and Grant only found themselves in war.

We lionize those who embraced war in the past, but condemn those who defend us in the present. George S. Patton was far blunter than Jim Mattis—but Patton lived in the days before the media was omnipresent and biased against our military.

The hypocrisy is stunning. Gen. Mattis told the truth about a fundamental human activity—war—and was treated as though he had dropped a nuclear weapon on an orphanage. Yet when some bozo on a talk show confesses to an addiction or a perversion in front of millions of viewers, he's lionized as "courageous" for speaking out.

Sorry. It's men like Jim Mattis who are courageous. The rest of us barely glimpse the meaning of the word.

We've come to a sad state when a Marine who has risked his life repeatedly to keep our country safe can't speak his mind, while any professor who wants to blame America for 9/11 is defended by legions of free-speech advocates. If a man like Mattis hasn't earned the right to say what he really believes, who has?

Had Gen. Mattis collapsed in tears and begged for pity for the torments war inflicted on him, the media would have adored him. Instead, he spoke as Marines and soldiers do in the headquarters tent or the barracks, on the battlefield or among comrades. And young journalists who never faced anything more dangerous than a drunken night in Tijuana tried to create a scandal.

Fortunately, Lt. Gen. Mattis has three big things going for him: the respect of those who serve; the Marine Corps, which won't abandon a valiant fighter to please self-righteous pundits whose only battle is with their waistlines; and the fact that we're at war. We need more men like Mattis, not fewer. The public needs to hear the truth about war, not just the crybaby nonsense of those who never deigned to serve our country.

In my own far humbler career, the leaders I admired were those who had the killer instinct. The soldiers knew who they were. We would have followed them anywhere. They weren't slick Pentagon staffers anxious to go to work for defense contractors. They were the men who lived and breathed the warrior's life.

Table manners don't win wars. Winning our nation's battles demands disciplined ferocity, raw physical courage—and integrity. Jim Mattis has those qualities in spades.

Semper fi, General.

Terror's New Frontier

New York Post

February 9, 2004

Mosul is the good girl who went bad. Quiet in the early days of the occupation, the violence-ravaged Iraqi city has become a must-win battlefield for our enemies. The terrorists and insurgents will throw all they have left into the fight.

There's no mystery involved: Mosul's the decisive point in northern Iraq. Over the long term, the city's vastly more valuable than Fallujah.

Insurgent attacks, terrorist bombings, and assassinations erupted last autumn and continue on a regular basis. They're not going to stop soon. After Baghdad, Mosul will remain the most bitterly contested Iraqi city in the months ahead.

Every blast and tactical ambush has a strategic purpose. The Sunni-Arab insurgents *need* control of Mosul to remain viable. And the international terrorists want to deny it to all but Sunni Arabs.

We failed to see how much we changed Iraq. Mosul is now a frontier town, at the northern edge of the Sunni-Arab world.

With a strong Kurdish tradition, a location astride the Tigris River, and control of the key route from Turkey, the city's strategic importance was obvious from the eighth-century caliphate of Harun al Raschid to the era of Saddam Hussein. Saddam gave his military officers homes in Mosul and encouraged other regime supporters to homestead. He was determined to conquer the city demographically, to make it incontestably Arab, instead of the poly-glot mix it long had been.

It was an old trick. The Romans, Byzantines, Arabs, Crusaders, and even the nineteenth-century Russians used military colonies to augment or substitute for expensive frontier garrisons: Get the sol-diers to put down stakes and the land becomes your own.

Mosul became so heavily populated with military and secu-rity officials that Saddam's sons, Uday and Qusay, chose it as their hideout—and died there. The city remained calm in the early months of the occupation because Saddam's loyalists felt confident that the struggle could be won elsewhere—they preferred to ravage the cities of others, rather than risk their own retirement homes.

The Ba'athists assumed that Mosul would be theirs again after the Americans fled Iraq. But they got an unpleasant surprise: The Americans showed no sign of leaving. Meanwhile, the Kurds grew in strength and confidence.

With elections looming, it was obvious that the country's Shi'a majority would dominate the polls, while the Kurds would vote a united ticket and place second. Our enemies saw what the media could not: They were losing. So they began to execute Plan B.

The insurgents and terrorists alike recognize Mosul as the vital outpost of their blood and faith. If Iraq remains whole, the Sunni Arabs need to dominate Mosul for political leverage. Should Iraq break into three pieces, Mosul would be strategically and economi-cally essential to a Sunni-Arab state.

We see Mosul as a set of tactical problems. Our enemies view it as an indispensable fortress-city on the edge of the Sunni-Arab world.

Mosul dominates northern Iraq. It threatens the primary bor-der crossing with Turkey at Zakho, which provides the Kurds with an economic lifeline. It was Saddam's military base for repeated attacks on Dohuk and Irbil, two of the three Kurdish provincial cap-itals, and it dominates the most direct route from Turkey to Suleimaniye, the third. The Sunni Arabs know they've lost the oil-rich Kurdish city of Kirkuk, at least for now, but possession of Mosul would guarantee them effective control of the pipelines that carry Kirkuk's oil.

The insurgents and terrorists had to make their move. And they can't quit, despite heavy losses. Our enemies will stop at nothing to prevent Iraqi security forces from gaining traction. They have to sustain the myth of a malevolent occupation. They like to kill us, but they *need* to kill and discourage the Iraqis who stand against them.

Mosul is the single city our enemies can't afford to lose, the key to all of northern Iraq. Without Mosul, the Sunni Triangle is a shrunken, economically impotent territory, dependent on the mercies of the central government.

The Sunni Arabs retain demographic control of cities such as Ramadi, Baquba, Tikrit, and Fallujah, and they've given up the Shi'a south for now. But Mosul contains a combustible ethnic mix. The insurgents are determined to keep the matches coming.

For their part, the international terrorists see Mosul as the border fortress of true Islam. Although the Kurds are overwhelmingly Sunni Muslims, they're far too secular and tolerant for the extremists—and, at its heart, the terror campaign spearheaded by Abu Musab al Zarqawi in Iraq is a racist, Arab movement. The terrorists are as hostile to the independent-spirited Kurds as Saddam ever was.

Watch Mosul. From the raids on police stations to suicide bombings and mortar attacks on our bases, preventing the pacification of Mosul has become the primary operational goal of both the insurgents and the terrorists.

What will our enemies do now, after the election? Everything they can to create casualties, stir unrest, and prevent the normalization of Mosul's economy. The Sunni-Arab insurgents will attempt to exacerbate Turkey's fears about Kurdish power and independence, while the terrorists will continue to send in suicide bombers.

In the wake of the widespread displays of courage in Iraq's first free elections, the insurgents and terrorists feel themselves pressed against the wall. In response, they'll lash out madly—to include attacks against moderate Sunni Arabs.

Our enemies fantasize about turning Mosul into another Mogadishu or Beirut. We need to prevent it from turning into another Fallujah. The odds are on our side, not theirs.

But be prepared for more bloodshed in Mosul. If our enemies lose the city, they've lost Iraq.

Now, the Horse-Trading

New York Post

February 15, 2005

The results of Iraq's first free elections are in. They're better than any realist could have expected. And, predictably, the media are grasping at every possible negative.

Let's look at things honestly.

The United Iraqi Alliance, endorsed by the Grand Ayatollah Ali Sistani, got 48.2 percent of the vote. That's enough to please the party's wide array of Shi'a backers, but it's not enough to govern without a coalition.

Interim Prime Minister Ayad Allawi's Iraqi List came in third, with 13.8 percent. This largely Shi'a party also includes Sunni Arabs and will act as a secular counterforce to the UIA's religion-tinted coalition.

Vitally, the Kurdistan Alliance took second place with a startling 25.7 percent. This not only demonstrates the power of Iraq's most pro-American element, but grants the Kurds the role of political kingmakers. Both of the major Shi'a parties will court them.

Muqtada al Sadr, the bigoted thug who cast himself as the voice of Iraq's Shi'as? His party gets three seats out of 275. So much for Shi'a extremism.

Democracy works.

When all of the horse trading for ministerial positions is over, we'll be miffed at some of the appointments. But it's critical for Iraq's democracy to be as inclusive as possible. Given the new government's mission of drafting a constitution, a big-tent approach, encompassing everyone from theocrats to ardent secularists, offers the best hope of a peaceful future.

Dismiss the media nonsense about the Sunni-Arab failure to participate invalidating the elections. The Sunni Arabs know they blew it. Their most promising politicians are maneuvering for a role in writing the new constitution. And the Shi'as and Kurds will bring key Sunni Arabs into the process. They know their society better than the pundits do.

You can also disregard the warnings that Iraq will turn into another Iran. Ain't going to happen. The Grand Ayatollah Sistani, Iraq's most revered figure, is well aware that Iran's theocracy has failed miserably—tarnishing the faith he loves. As a result, Sistani has set a rational course that will endure beyond his death.

The constitution may end up with more strictures than we like. But the odds are that the document will be a sensible compromise—with every party grumpy but content. Clerics will have influence but won't rule.

Much can still go wrong, of course. But the prophets of doom were mistaken about the war, about the insurgency's appeal, and about the enthusiasm of the Iraqis for elections. There's no reason to believe that their critiques of the election results are any wiser.

And the critics seem determined to ignore the most encouraging outcome of all: No Iraqi voting bloc handed power to fanatics or demagogues.

Arabs and Kurds alike chose coalitions, not rigid parties. Kurds put longstanding rivalries aside, while Shi'as voted for a range of interests under two umbrella organizations. And although the United Iraqi Alliance drew almost half of the votes, it may not even survive to the next election.

In short, the wheeling and dealing won't only be between parties, but within them. That means compromise, then more compromise. And once all the romance and rhetoric fades, it's compromise that lets democracy work.

Who will govern? Who will draft the new constitution? Shi'as and Kurds, of course. But both groups realize the importance of including Sunni Arabs in the process. And they will. Other minorities, such as Turkmen and Arab Christians, will also have a voice.

The Kurds will probably gain the presidency. This would be not only an act of justice and redress, but a tremendous step forward for the Middle East. At present, the region's thirty million Kurds are excluded from executive power. An Iraqi president selected from the country's six million Kurds would be an inspiring new beginning.

A Shi'a will become prime minister, the government's key position. Several candidates are in the running, with views ranging from the pious through the moderate and secular. (Even that hustler extraordinaire Ahmed Chalabi is angling for the job.) The likeliest result? A new prime minister acceptable to the clerics, but not a cleric himself—one whose loyalty is to Iraq, not to Iran.

We'll hear no end of protests and complaints (although they won't be as nasty as those directed at President Bush after our own elections). The Turks will pick endlessly at the scab of their fears of Kurdish freedom. And the insurgents, backed by Syria, won't give up—although more and more Sunni Arabs will turn away from them. Dreading democracy, the terrorists will keep sending disturbed young people to their deaths as suicide bombers.

And the Iraqis will build a democratic government.

This is only the start, of course. Much could go wrong. All of the courage and sacrifice might yet end in another classic Middle-Eastern disappointment. But there's more reason to be hopeful about Iraq today than there ever has been before.

And it isn't just Iraq: A new spirit has appeared in the heart of the Middle East, a sense that, just maybe, freedom is a possibility for hundreds of millions of Muslims.

As for all those disingenuous demands for an American "exit strategy"? We have one. It's called "Democracy."

Terrorist vs. Terrorist

New York Post

March 2, 2005

Osama bin Laden gets it. The terror-master understands that the campaign of bombings and assassinations has backfired in Iraq, erasing popular support for Islamist fanatics and unleashing the forces of freedom.

So World Terrorist No. 1 sent a message to Regional Terrorist No. 1: *We're losing. We need a different strategy.*

Osama wants Abu Musab al Zarqawi to shift his sights from Iraq's population, to help carry the struggle back to American soil. With the old order beginning to crack in the wake of Iraq's elections, bin Laden sees that his last, desperate hope is to hurt America so badly that we quit the fight.

Osama is a strategist. He may not be a very *good* strategist—he called the aftereffects of 9/11 utterly wrong. But he thinks in global terms, in timeframes that look decades into the future and centuries into the past. He's a big-picture guy.

Zarqawi is a hit man. He thinks tactically. Faced with the humiliation of eight million Iraqis defying his threats and lining up to vote, his instinctive response is to lash out, to punish, to kill without stopping. Monday's bombing in Hilla took 115 Iraqi lives. It was a classic Zarqawi operation.

Osama and Zarqawi are both frustrated by the series of reverses they've suffered. But their perspectives on the Islamist war against modern civilization differ profoundly.

Even in hiding, Osama has managed to build an accurate picture of events in the greater Middle East, where his cause is on the ropes. He's realized that Zarqawi's program of videotaped beheadings, suicide bombings against civilian targets, and the assassination of teachers, doctors, and local officials hasn't won hearts and minds.

Zarqawi has become a menace to Osama's vision. The new guy on the block is out of control. He's hitting the wrong targets.

Osama is a long way from disavowing Zarqawi—he'd rather use him. But an eventual split could come, if the Jordanian doesn't read between the lines of the big guy's message. Osama wants a change in tactics. *Now.* Three years ago, people in the Middle East were cheering and naming their babies after him. Now he's losing his star quality.

The people of the Middle East are voting in Iraq and the Palestinian territories, toppling a puppet government in Lebanon, agitating for elections in Egypt—and even casting ballots for municipal representatives in Saudi Arabia. Syria looks shaky, and Iran's youthful population wants the mullahs gone. Sunni and Shi'a Muslims may even learn to cooperate.

Whether Osama's sitting in Karachi, in the mountains bordering Afghanistan, or even in Iran, he sees that the West is winning. The infidels are turning the heads of the faithful.

It must eat at him like cancer.

Bin Laden knows that his movement can't afford a further hemorrhage of popular support. In his gory way, Zarqawi is becoming a more immediate threat to al Qa'eda than America. By killing so many Muslims, Zarqawi has destroyed the folk-hero image of Islamist terrorists, reducing them to nothing but renegade murderers.

Zarqawi may blow Osama off. His resources and interests are regional, not global. He doesn't have the temperament to call off his private war and try again elsewhere. Zarqawi's a gritty, furious field officer who wants to get at the enemy right now. Osama's the general with the broader grasp of events.

Osama's real message to Zarqawi isn't *Hit America instead.* It's *Stop what you're doing, brother.*

Our homeland will be hit again. By someone. Sooner or later, the bad guy lands a punch. Meanwhile, we should take heart from the latest evidence—delivered by Osama himself—that the cause of freedom is even more powerful than we thought, that democracy *is* contagious.

Osama's message to Zarqawi was one of despair—and a tribute to the millions of Arabs who are turning against his kind.

It Was Worth a War:
Iraq, Two Years Later

npr.org

March 20, 2005

The Bush administration got many of the details painfully wrong in its design to change the Middle East, but it got the big issues right: Saddam Hussein was an intolerable tyrant; the oppressed do yearn for freedom; and the roots of Islamist terrorism lie in the region's comprehensive stagnation.

Change was essential. But change on a grand scale doesn't come without costs. A lurid 24/7 news cycle made the price we paid in the wake of Operation Iraqi Freedom seem exorbitant, yet given the magnitude of the endeavor, we've gotten off lightly by any historical standard. The potential return on our strategic investment has begun to look enormous.

Contrary to the views of its supporters and detractors, the Bush administration is neither saintly nor evil.

Inept decisions on the part of Secretary of Defense Rumsfeld and his acolytes exacerbated the occupation's difficulties. In the wake of a spectacular battlefield victory, our soldiers often died needlessly and Iraqis suffered more severely at the hands of terrorists and insurgents than would have been the case had our government heeded expert advice instead of closing its eyes and touching wood.

Nonetheless, the administration's overarching vision, the dedication of our troops, and the determination of the Iraqi people produced free elections that set a new standard for the Arab world—providing a catalyst for the reforms that have lately begun to spread across the region. Future historians won't complain of the twenty-two months between the fall of Baghdad and those inspiring, defiant elections. The interval will seem brief when viewed dispassionately.

What President Bush undertook was more difficult than he imagined—but the world can be grateful that he rejected traditional diplomacy and acted. Those critics who insisted that "war doesn't solve anything," or that Arabs don't want democracy (a despicable, racist argument), or that dictators are entitled to the protections of sovereignty will be judged far more harshly by history than those who supported regime change in Iraq.

At their worst, the administration's opponents seemed to long for the Iraqi experiment to fail—just to spite the Bush administration. We need to put such hypocrisy behind us. We must have the individual and collective integrity to recognize that great, positive changes appear to be under way in the Middle East—triggered by America's engagement in Iraq.

Those who remain incapable of granting the current administration any credit should at least honor the eight million Iraqis who defied terrorist death threats to vote in their first free elections. Surely, we can praise the hundreds of thousands of Lebanese who put their own ferocious past behind them to topple a puppet government in Beirut. The region's valiant reformers no longer appear to be anomalies, but prophets.

There is genuine, if tenuous, hope for peace between Israelis and Palestinians. Young Iranians want to be rid of their dictatorship of mullahs. Egypt's President Mubarak promises steps toward democracy. And even Saudi Arabia's ruling family—a grotesque mafia—has begun to experiment with low-level elections.

All of this is only a beginning, of course. The Middle East remains socially decayed, economically incompetent, and politically brutalized. But what we have seen in the past two months is more than the most optimistic among us thought possible in so short a time.

Much could still go wrong. Ethnic and religious rivalries may yet poison Iraq's future. Autocrats will maneuver to retain power. Terrorism will linger. And if any single factor can impede progress across the entire Middle East, it's the endemic culture of corruption—a cancer that goes far deeper than the topical symptom of terrorism.

Nothing can be taken for granted. If the pessimists were wrong thus far, the optimists had best remain sober. Every breaking indicator suggests that the people of the Middle East are willing to sacrifice for change, but great dreams have been frustrated before and not all of the changes we'll see will be pretty ones. Religious fanaticism still haunts Muslim civilization. We may hope that the region has begun to shake off its deadly malaise, but there will be plentiful disappointments along the way. Euphoria remains as ill-advised as unyielding pessimism.

Yet hope now exists in a region long deemed hopeless. That much is undeniable. For the first time in history, the common people of the Middle East have an outside chance to build a humane future. Tyrants are falling, terror has failed, and democracy just might work where it long was scorned.

It was worth a war.

Gitmo Cocktail

New York Post

June 16, 2005

The demands to shut down our Guantanamo lockup for terrorists have nothing to do with human rights. They're about punishing America for our power and success.

From our ailing domestic left to overseas America haters, no one really cares about the fate of Mustapha the Murderer or Ahmed the Assassin. The lies told about Gitmo are meant to undercut U.S. foreign policy and embarrass America.

The Gitmo controversy is about many things, from jealousy of the United States and outrage that we refuse to fail, to residual anger that we won the Cold War and exploded the left's great fantasy of a dictatorship of the intellectuals. But the one thing the protests aren't about is human rights.

Except, of course, as a means to slam the United States.

Torture? Who and when? Koran abuse? I'd rather be a Koran in Gitmo than a Bible in Saudi Arabia. Illegal detentions? Suggest a better way to handle hardcore terrorists. Maltreatment? Spare me. The food the prisoners receive is better than what I had to eat in the Army.

Another thing: Would it be more humane to incarcerate the declared enemies of civilization in northern Alaska, rather than on a Caribbean beach?

Has the Bush administration made mistakes regarding Guantanamo? You bet. The biggest one was attempting to placate the critics. By launching a new investigation every time a terrorist had a toothache, our government played into the hands of its enemies.

The truth is that the terrorists and their defenders have something in common. It's not courage, which is one quality violent fanatics don't lack. It's that neither can be appeased.

Any concession only increases their appetites. The Clinton administration's reluctance to respond to terrorist strikes encouraged al Qa'eda. If the Bush administration closed the Guantanamo facility, any alternative holding center would be attacked just as rabidly and dishonestly. If we put our captives up at the Four Seasons, we'd be condemned because somebody smelled bacon at breakfast.

You can't negotiate with terrorists. And you cannot reason with ideologues—whether they're Islamist fanatics or pathetic old lefties fishing for a cause to give meaning to squandered lives. Terrorists, French and German neo-Stalinists, and our own democracy-hating intelligentsia aren't interested in facts. It's all about the comfort of *belief.*

Let's get this straight: Nothing we could do would appease those who feel a need for our country to fail. We must stop trying to satisfy them.

There's a military maxim that applies to all the nonsense about Gitmo: Don't let the entire battalion get bogged down by a sniper. By attempting to respond to the wild charges leveled by those who offer no solutions themselves—who have no interest in solutions—we've allowed anti-American basket cases from Harvard Yard to the German parliament to create an issue from nothing.

Oh, and thanks to the "mainstream" media for assuming that our country's always wrong.

There *is* a culture of torture in the world. Blessedly, America isn't part of it. When a few of our troops make mistakes, they're punished. Given the magnitude of our task and the unprecedented conditions we face, it's remarkable our errors have been so few.

What should enrage every decent citizen is that the real torturers—from Zimbabwe to China, from Syria to North Korea—get a pass from the political left. If terrorists behead defenseless captives on videotape, it's simply an expression of their culture. But if a handful of U.S. troops play an ugly round of Candid Camera, that's a new gulag.

As someone who takes human rights seriously, I'm appalled by the lack of sympathy the left feels toward the victims of any regime other than the Bush administration. Let's shout it to prisoners everywhere: If you're not harmed by an American, your suffering doesn't count.

The left's hypocrisy is immeasurable. The grandchildren of those who defended Stalin are mortified that Saddam Hussein will stand trial. By taking such irresponsible voices seriously, we grant our critics a strength they otherwise lack and simply help them keep their lies alive.

No matter what our country does, we will never please a global intelligentsia outraged that all their theories came to nothing. We can't satisfy al Qa'eda, and we can't please those discontented souls who need to blame the United States for their personal inadequacies. It's time we stopped trying.

What should our nation's leaders say about Guantanamo and our treatment of captured terrorists? A lot less.

When comments are unavoidable, try this: "We're human. We make mistakes. We fix those mistakes. And we move on. Nothing will divert us from our mission of defeating terror and keeping our country safe."

Misreporting War

New York Post

July 1, 2005

Pop quiz: Which issue matters more to America's future: the remarkable progress made in Afghanistan or the disappearance of a teenager in Aruba?

Obviously, the latter. Over the past month, TV news has devoted more airtime to a missing girl than to Afghanistan and Iraq combined. It took the loss of a special operations helicopter and the sixteen personnel aboard to get our Afghan success story back in the headlines—as bad news.

The relentless quest for sensation (and ratings) hurts us badly in Iraq, where a torrent of negative reporting creates an alternate reality in which terrorists dominate the country. The coverage of Afghanistan is even more lopsided.

Yes, Afghanistan has problems. It will have problems beyond our lifetimes. But the country is vastly more peaceful, humane, and hopeful than *ever* before in its history.

The disparate regions composing Afghanistan have always been lawless beyond the city limits. Tribes, not governments, ruled. The current blips of back-country violence are nothing compared to the country's gruesome past. This is a horribly wounded society that's healing faster than we had any right to expect.

Sit back and press the memory button. Remember how, in the wake of 9/11, the experts warned that we'd suffer devastating casualties when our "soft" troops came up against the "battle-hardened"

Taliban? We were assured our efforts would fail, that we'd wind up as badly burned as the Soviets and Brits before us; the entire country would take up arms against any foreign invaders.

Didn't happen. Our military and the CIA delivered a swift, stunning triumph. And our troops are actually welcome.

No one held those errant experts accountable. Now they're back, pouncing on every scrap of bad news in the hope they'll be able to say, "We told you so."

And here's how our media deal with the undeniable progress made in Afghanistan:

Tens of thousands of girls enrolled in schools? *Who cares.* Peace in most of the country? *Boring.*

Democratic elections? *Nonstory.* Economic progress? *Less than a nonstory.*

A construction boom in Kabul? *About time journalists had a nice hotel.* Afghan troops defending their elected government? *Zero interest, dude.*

Sixteen GIs lost in a helicopter shot down by terrorists? *Now THAT'S news.*

It *is* news, of course. We mourn the loss of every one of our servicemembers. And although every American casualty, colonel or corporal, counts equally, the loss of a team of Navy SEALs is an operational blow. We want to know what happened.

The problem is the imbalance in the reporting. My friends who serve or served in Afghanistan are bewildered by the only-bad-news-counts coverage. By any objective measure, Afghanistan's an incredible, they-said-it-couldn't-be-done success story. But we only hear that the Taliban is back.

Well, the Taliban never went away entirely. The movement may never fully disappear—no more than nutty white-supremacy groups will vanish completely from the U.S. scene. But we're better off now than in the heyday of the Ku Klux Klan, and the Taliban's been reduced to a local nuisance.

The Taliban's supporters are drawn to disciplinary religion and social repression. Low education levels and ethnic fissures help them survive. International terrorists provide support. But compare today's beggarly Taliban with the power that ruled the country less than four years ago.

We can't expect perfect solutions to the world's problems. The current skirmishing in Afghanistan involves classic frontier-bandido clashes, reminiscent of our own past. Apache raiders would strike in our southwest, then flee across the border to Mexico—just as the Taliban flees into Pakistan.

The Apaches remained a local problem for decades, but they never threatened our government's survival. And the Taliban won't return to rule in Kabul.

But the Taliban have an ally the Apaches never dreamed of— the media. Make no mistake: Our Islamist enemies are as media-savvy as the top Hollywood agents. They know they can't defeat us militarily, so attacks aim to influence opinion polls and decision-makers in the United States. Calls for withdrawal timetables and partisan declarations that we're failing only encourage our enemies to kill more of our troops.

This week, we lost sixteen fine Americans in the Afghan mountains. They deserve to be mourned, and their sacrifice merits respect. But the failure to provide balanced reporting from Afghanistan—and Iraq—is nothing less than spitting on their graves.

What's the Value of Victory?

USA Today

July 13, 2005

In classical economics, an item's value is determined by the price someone will pay for it. By that measure, Iraq is the world's most valuable real estate to Islamist terrorists.

Critics claimed that Iraq was a diversion from the war on terror. Yet the terrorists are committing all the lives they can muster and every resource they command to prevent the emergence of a rule-of-law democracy in Baghdad. Even the recent bombings in London seemed to be intended to drive British forces out of Iraq.

If Iraq doesn't matter, why are Islamist terrorists so desperate to dislodge us?

When defeatists insist that Iraq has cost us too dearly and we need to set a timetable for withdrawal, consider the price our foes have been willing to pay: Tens of thousands of terrorists and their allies have died or been captured. The situation looks far bleaker from our enemy's vantage point.

If Iraq's various ethnic and religious communities build a reasonably equitable democracy that broadly respects human rights, it will be the greatest success Arabs (and Kurds) have seen in seven hundred years. And Arabs need a win. Behind all their protests and posturing, they're afraid that they can't build a decent, modern state where elections count and a constitution prevails. Even an imperfect result in Baghdad would give the Arab world a level of moral refreshment that no authoritarian regime could ever deliver.

The terrorists understand that. The fanatics who believe in a bloodthirsty, disciplinarian God realize that a popular, tolerant state in the Middle East would kill their dream of winning over the masses. Corrupt, oppressive governments plowed the soil for the extremists. Saudi and Gulf-Arab funding provided the fertilizer. The seeds of hatred grew wildly as we looked away. Now, the terrorists want to harvest the crop.

FAILURES OF THE RIGHT, LEFT

Terrorists know how much is at stake and they're united behind their cause. Meanwhile, we've become a house divided, allowing the debate over Iraq to be hijacked by ideologues on both the right and left.

First, consider the sins of the right. Although the Bush administration did a great thing in deposing Saddam Hussein, the Rumsfeld Pentagon did it with astonishing ineptitude. From the refusal to deploy enough troops to the willful neglect of occupation planning, ideologues set us up for a protracted struggle and unnecessary casualties.

The administration got the big picture right but ignored the troublesome details. The president and his deputies further harmed their cause by refusing to admit that mistakes were made. From the floundering early days of don't-call-it-an-occupation through the incompetence of the young political activists sent to staff the Coalition Provisional Authority, willful errors have been redeemed only by the valor—and blood—of our troops.

For their part, demagogues on the left mirrored the sin of the neocons in the Pentagon: They insisted that the world is as they wish it to be, rather than as it is.

Saddam was a Hitler clone. Iraq was a massive death camp. Had President Clinton invaded Iraq, the American left would have declared him the greatest liberator since Lincoln. Liberals allowed their distaste for a president to confound them into a mindless defense of evil.

Today, some left-wing opinion-makers appear to be rooting for Iraq to fail. Every call for a timetable for the withdrawal of our troops is a gift to the terrorists. Speeches on Capitol Hill insisting that Americans are tired of the war, that our casualties are too high, and that we need an "exit strategy" provide aid and comfort to media-savvy enemies. Scoring political points in wartime kills American soldiers.

The let's-embarrass-Bush voices must consider the consequences of partisanship. If we promise that our troops will leave by a given date, we have effectively surrendered. The fanatics have only to wait until we leave. The subsequent bloodbath would be stunning—and could lead to a regional war.

As for disingenuous calls to "support our troops, bring them home," they always seem to come from those who never served in uniform themselves. I spend a great deal of time with our soldiers. They believe in their cause. Recruiting may be tougher in wartime, but our combat troops are reenlisting at higher rates than in peacetime.

THE PRICE TO QUIT IRAQ
Yes, this war damaged our military. That's what war does. But far from "breaking" our armed forces, our commitments have given us the world's most experienced military.

If those on the right have lied about the administration's frequent incompetence, those on the left need to weigh the price we would pay for quitting Iraq. The terrorists would have won the strategic Super Bowl. Progress in the Middle East would collapse. Fanaticism would spread as never before. And newly confident terrorists would strike our homeland again.

The situation in Iraq is far from ideal. But it isn't remotely as bad as the relentlessly negative media reports imply. Good news isn't news. So we're bombarded with breathless reporting about casualties and car bombings or the murder of the Egyptian ambassador, but we get no sense of the far more complex reality. This struggle is so difficult because our enemies view it as decisive. They'll pay any price to win.

We need to get beyond our partisan quarrels. The terrorists lack the power to defeat us. But we certainly have the power to defeat ourselves. The greatest danger is talking ourselves into failure.

The Real Target

New York Post

August 4, 2005

In Iraq yesterday a roadside bomb killed fourteen Marines. Two days earlier, six Marines from the same outfit were ambushed and killed. Yet those Marines were not the terrorists' primary target.

You were.

Our enemies know the Marines won't quit. But they hope you will.

The terrorists realize now that they can't defeat our military. Instead, they hope to achieve what the North Vietnamese did: To blur the reality on the ground and convince the American public that we're losing.

Those Marines were tactical targets of opportunity. You're the strategic target. The terrorists hope that our media will create an atmosphere of failure—and that you'll give in to a sense of defeat.

The Marines are looking for a few good men (and women). The terrorists are looking for headlines.

The Marines who died on the Euphrates River battleground were closing down crucial smuggling routes from Syria. Recent operations have made life ever more difficult for the terrorists. Our enemies are fighting fiercely because they're cornered.

They certainly want to kill Marines. But that doesn't require video cameras. The rush to document and publicize their occasional successes makes it clear that the terrorists are fighting, above all, a media campaign. It's their only hope.

That's no comfort to the families of the Marines we lost, of course. And the fact that twenty fatalities within three days came from the same Ohio-based reserve unit, the 3rd Battalion of the 25th Marines, magnifies the pain.

But the unit's losses reflect the importance of its mission.

The terrorists want to hit that battalion as hard as they can, to break the unit's morale and gain some breathing space. They've been doing what any thinking enemy would do—concentrating their resources on a decisive point. They probably studied the forces tightening the noose around them and decided that hitting a reserve unit offered the best chance of success.

They don't know the Marines.

Our troops will keep the pressure on even as they mourn. The Marines have faced far tougher enemies—not least the suicidal Japanese, another enemy who showed no mercy (and beheaded prisoners, as well).

The difference is that the extremists in Iraq don't expect a battlefield victory. They're fighting for time. They hope to wear us down, to maintain a level of photogenic chaos in just enough of Iraq to keep the media hot. They'll keep chipping away at our forces, praying that our will will prove far weaker than our weapons.

They don't expect to force out our military through violence. They hope our political leaders will withdraw our troops. The terrorists have done their homework. They know that a disheartening number of our politicians share one of their beliefs: a low opinion of the American people, a notion that we're weak, that we're quitters.

The terrorists know that our Marines aren't afraid of them. But they believe that our politicians are terrified. Of you.

So you're the target of every bomb, bullet, and blade our enemies wield. Those Marines were killed to discourage *you*. They were targeted to ignite political discord in the United States. They died to give ammunition to those in Washington who view our dead only as political liabilities.

There are many practical military issues the administration hasn't addressed. Our forces in Iraq always have been too few. Much of the equipment with which our Marines and soldiers are equipped is old, inappropriate, and inadequate. We went to war with a military designed by defense contractors, not by warriors.

But while those issues are real, we can't afford to play politics with the vital global struggle of our times, the battle with the psychotic strain of Islam that generates terror. Ultimately, the fate of Iraq won't be decided by our enemies. And it won't be decided by our troops. It's going to be decided by you. By your voice and your vote.

The terrorists mean to help you make your decision.

Count on the Cavalry

New York Post

September 13, 2005

Perhaps the only blessing of Hurricane Katrina was that the media, smelling blood at home, reduced their attacks on our efforts in Iraq. Meanwhile, over the past few weeks, our troops conducted one of the finest operations since the fall of Baghdad.

The city of Tal Afar near the Syrian border had become a terrorist refuge. Foreign fanatics wanted to turn it into a new Fallujah. But they repeated a mistake they've increasingly made: They alienated the local population.

Tal Afar needed a cleanup. But it had to be done cleverly. Fallujah was a fortress. Tal Afar was a city held hostage. Firepower had to be used wisely. Leveling Tal Afar wasn't the answer.

Enter our 3rd Armored Cavalry Regiment. Teaming up with the 3rd Iraqi Division, the 3rd ACR faced the mission of defeating the terrorists without destroying the city.

In addition to the finest soldiers in the world—our own—and Iraqis willing to fight for their country, we had another ace in our tactical pocket: a brilliant regimental commander of a distinctly American breed.

Colonel H. R. McMaster planned to take the city in stages. A tough fighter when he has to be, McMaster is also the sort of leader who never wastes a life. With Iraqi troops leading many of the tactical actions, the 3rd ACR bit chunks out of the city until all that was left was a sprawling neighborhood stronghold of international terrorists.

Even then, McMaster and his team didn't want to win the battle but lose the population's future support. In a fight like Fallujah, you have to do it fast and hard, but in Tal Afar there was time to draw the civilians away from the pockets of resistance.

When the operation climaxed last weekend, the combined U.S.-Iraqi forces had captured hundreds of terrorists, killing more than 150. Half a dozen terror chiefs lay dead. One American soldier fell in combat. The nationalist Iraqis lost a few men, too. There are fights when casualties can't be avoided. But a good commander knows the difference.

Col. McMaster understood his enemy, his own forces, and the civilians caught in between. He was playing chess, not checkers. The end result: Our forces entered the last quarter of the city virtually unopposed. The terrorists not yet captured or killed had fled. And Tal Afar is free.

Inevitably, we'll hear complaints about terrorists getting away. But the few who did escape were a small cost to pay for preserving most of the city. Every battle has its own terms. You've got to know when to hold your fire and when to kill everything that moves. Restraint is the hard part.

For all his abilities on the battlefield, McMaster has another side that may surprise civilians: Far from the swaggering, blustering commander Hollywood loves to mock, he's a soldier-scholar with a doctorate in history. He's also the author of the most respected book written by any military officer of his generation—*Dereliction of Duty: Lyndon Johnson, Robert McNamara, the Joint Chiefs of Staff and the Lies That Led to the Vietnam War.* It's a courageous book. Soldiers read it. But McMaster rarely mentions it.

During his months in Iraq, he surely felt a sense of déjà vu, given the tragic similarities between the McNamara and Rumsfeld Pentagons. But Iraq isn't Vietnam. The stakes are higher, for one thing. For another, we're winning. Thanks to leaders like H. R. McMaster and American soldiers like the troopers of the 3rd ACR.

Nor was Tal Afar another operation in which our troops did all the heavy lifting: The Iraqis fighting beside us performed professionally, standing up in the line of fire for their new government.

And the Western media continues to insist that Iraq will fail. Although the noise level dropped in Katrina's wake, we're being warned that Iraq's Sunni Arabs, registering in large numbers, are going to vote against the draft constitution.

Wait a minute—isn't that what democracy's about? A few months ago, the media's complaint was that the Sunni Arabs wouldn't participate in elections. Well, they intend to participate this time. And if they vote down the draft constitution, maybe Iraq will disintegrate. But there's also a good chance that the Sunni Arabs will see that democracy works and join the political battle, instead of battling with bombs.

We *must* stop being impatient with the Iraqis and insisting that their every effort is doomed. Despite great difficulties, the Iraqis continue to move their country forward. Not one of the "expert" claims that Iraq would fail has yet come true.

So what's happening in Iraq while recovery efforts from Katrina also defy the doomsayers? A combined U.S.-Iraqi force cleaned out the terrorist base at Tal Afar with remarkably low losses. Sunni-Arab "rejectionists" are preparing to join other Iraqis at the polls. International terrorists have become hated in Iraq. The number of tipoffs we receive has soared. And the country just plain refuses to fall apart.

At this rate, the media may have to send the mayor of New Orleans to Iraq. Just to foul things up and make some headlines.

Snubbing Democracy

New York Post

September 21, 2005

For fifty years, the American left complained that we supported dictators instead of backing human rights and democracy. On Sunday, the lefties got yet another dose of what they used to demand: Free elections in Afghanistan, long the victim of tyranny.

The left's reaction? Ignore the success of the balloting and explain away its importance by bending the truth until it's as twisted as an arrow designed by a liberal-arts faculty.

Why? Because Afghan democracy was enabled by the U.S. military—and by that devil incarnate, George W. Bush.

Leftists care nothing for real human beings. They only care about causes in the abstract—and *who* does a thing is far more important than what actually gets done.

It's disheartening to see our lefties reject every worthy value they once professed, switching their support to psychotic terrorists and dictators (well, they always *did* like Stalin and Mao . . .). But the rest of us can take heart from the Afghans' courage, from their determination to assert their political liberty.

Even major U.S. news outlets, disappointed by the lack of Election Day bloodshed, relegated the voting to the inner pages or to a brief mention well along in the broadcast. Heroism in the cause of democracy doesn't merit headlines.

Instead, we heard whining that just over 50 percent of eligible Afghans voted, that there were too many candidates, that warlords were allowed to run, that the Taliban's back in business, and generally, that Afghanistan still isn't a replica of Vermont four years after its liberation.

OK. Let's consider the complaints.

• If "only" 50 to 60 percent of the potential voters cast a ballot, that's better than a political environment in which nobody gets to vote. Turnout is a *lot* lower in most U.S. congressional and local elections—and we don't have to brave threats of death and trudge over some of the world's harshest mountains to cast a ballot. (Mostly, we won't even drive to the polling place down the street.)

• Too many candidates? During our last presidential election, I, for one, would have liked more choices than our two party monopolies offered. Afghans are learning as they go. At this stage in the country's development, inclusive elections are better than exclusive ones.

• Warlords running for office? Is it better just to have them running guns? Let's see who won after the votes are tallied. Let the people choose.

• Taliban back in business? They never went away completely—and they won't. You can no more eradicate all bigotry and hatred than you can wipe out crime.

Americans reduced the once-powerful Ku Klux Klan to a laughingstock, but a few grown men still parade around in sheets. The Taliban will lurk on the fringes of Afghan society for years, representing a small, virulent constituency. But they'll never come back from the fringes.

And just by the way: In the southern provinces where the Taliban once was strongest, higher-than-average numbers of women registered to vote. Think they want Mullah Omar & Co. back?

• Is Afghanistan imperfect? You bet. But its government doesn't look bad compared to Louisiana's. Afghanistan will *never* be Vermont. The issue is whether or not it will be a better Afghanistan. It already is.

Afghanistan never had real democracy before the election that chose President Hamid Karzai. This is a largely illiterate country where only 6 percent of the people have electricity. Far from being cause for discouragement, the fact that so many Afghans turned out to vote should make us cheer the magnetism of democracy, the human longing for self-determination.

Despite all the Taliban threats of Election Day violence that tantalized the media, the polling hours passed without a single major attack. Nationwide, nine people died in isolated incidents of violence.

The "resurgent" Taliban couldn't even muster one good suicide bomber. Wasn't *that* worth a headline?

As a young soldier on a weekend pass a quarter-century back, I woke after an interesting night in Paris to read that the Soviets had invaded Afghanistan. Later, as an intelligence officer, I monitored the Kremlin's occupation. After the Soviets fled, I watched the Taliban. I read Afghan history and visited the region. I never dreamed that so broken a country could make such rapid progress toward democracy.

Sunday's elections were a testament to sheer human resilience.

We *all* should be exhilarated by the valor and spunk displayed by Afghan voters. Left or right, we should be heartened by the yearning of human beings to control their own destiny, to cast off ancient traditions of oppressive governance. And we should be boundlessly proud of our troops, who gave the Afghan population this opportunity.

Instead, we get shrugged shoulders and cheap criticism. The noncoverage of Sunday's elections said far more about us than it did about Afghans.

Protest Therapy

New York Post

September 27, 2005

Last weekend, a hundred thousand Americans protested in Washington, demanding that we bring our troops home now. It was a fascinating installment in our nation's self-therapy craze.

Set aside the get-Bush-at-any-cost political hustlers, the earnest college students not yet seasoned by reality, the Jew-baiting free-Palestine detachments, and the very few who have thought seriously about the war and found it lacking.

You're left with the legions of Cindy Sheehan wannabes—meandering souls who, were they only capable of honesty, would be wearing T-shirts that read, "It's not about the war, it's about me!"

Were we able to psychologically profile the demonstrators, we'd find that most of them have a great deal in common: Disappointing lives, failed relationships, and the desperate need for a cause of any kind. If we weren't at war, they'd be marching to save pinworms from drug-company aggression.

Of course, opposing a war involving American troops is the best cause of all. Our country has disappointed the protesters intimately—failing to hand them, free and clear, the lives to which they feel themselves entitled. So forget that our troops are reenlisting at record rates and willingly risking their lives in a war they believe in. The self-satisfying cry of the demonstrators is "Bring Our Troops Home Now!"

It would be far easier to be sympathetic if a single spokesperson for the media-amplified antiwar movement laid out a convincing model of what would *happen* in Iraq or Afghanistan if our troops just came home.

Please, tell me: What becomes of Iraq if we just pull out? Does Atlantis rise from the Tigris to inaugurate the Age of Aquarius in the Middle East? Would grateful terrorists teach us folk dances? Or might the terrorists and insurgents be emboldened, resulting in a bloody civil war, acts of genocide, and far worse abuses of human rights than the shabby nonsense at Abu Ghraib?

I'm ready to listen. Convince me. Was Saddam's rule better? Where were you when he was gassing the Kurds and butchering the Shi'a? Are the fates of foreign peoples only important when our troops can be blamed?

And how about Afghanistan? Where was dreary old Joan Baez when the Taliban banned Afghan folk music, jailing and torturing musicians? Where were the advocates who believe that every fourth-grade reading list should begin with *Frodo Has Thirteen Mommies* when girls were forbidden education of any kind? Were Afghans better off under the Taliban?

Answer me, please.

The reason no protester has described what would follow a withdrawal of our troops is that no one on the left can face the answers.

Who needs responsibility, anyway? The protesters are cocooned in a society that minimizes consequences. If anything goes wrong, it isn't their fault. The answer is never personal responsibility, but joining a support group.

The protesters get their wish, our troops leave, and a bloodbath erupts, drawing in Turkey, Syria, and Iran? Just reach for a glass of sauvignon blanc and speed-dial a like-minded pal for reassurance. Genocide isn't your *fault,* girlfriend. You did what you felt was right, don't be so hard on yourself.

No consequences. At least not for us.

If the demonstrators believe so firmly that our government and military are wrong, shouldn't they follow the example of the earlier leftists who formed the Lincoln Brigade and *fought* against fascism? Couldn't they at least muster a Jane Fonda battalion of artists, actors, and professors to deploy to Iraq and bore our troops into surrendering?

The truth about those who would abandon the people of Iraq and Afghanistan to terrorists and thugs is that their spiritual ancestors aren't the men of the Lincoln Brigade, but the thousands of Americans who joined the German-American Bund in the 1930s, arguing that American interests lay in peace with *Reichskanzler* Hitler, one swell guy.

A popular theme last weekend was "War, what is it good for?" Well, the answer is that war's good for plenty of things. It freed and forged our nation. War liberated millions of black Americans from bondage. War stopped Hitler, if too late for many millions of his victims (peace at any price tends to have a very high price, indeed).

And our troops liberated fifty million human beings in Afghanistan and Iraq—who are far more grateful than the protesters or our media will accept.

In this infernally troubled world, war is sometimes the only effective response to greater evils. And there *is* evil on this earth. It would also be easier to sympathize with the antiwar protesters if they occasionally criticized the terrorists who bomb the innocent.

But the protesters don't really care about Iraqi suffering, or terror, or the Taliban's legacy. They're a forlorn mix of Bush-haters who reject election results that they don't like and drifting souls yearning for a cause to lend their failed lives meaning.

As for the pathetic Ms. Sheehan, since she insists on speaking in the name of our troops, let me suggest that she does not even speak for her own son, a man who joined our military of his own volition and who died for a cause far greater than any represented on the National Mall last weekend.

Iraqi Vote Victory

New York Post

October 18, 2005

Risking death, Iraqis of every background came out to vote on Saturday. Terrorists proved powerless to halt the country's progress. The final count isn't in, but the people appear to have approved a new constitution.

Never before in the Arab world have a country's citizens been permitted to vote on the laws that would govern them. Even had the draft constitution been rejected, this would have been a historic moment in the Middle East and beyond.

Our media's response? The vote doesn't matter. The constitution's flawed. Iraq's Sunni Arabs will resort to civil war. Enormous problems remain.

Well, big problems *do* remain in Iraq. There's certainly a potential for more internal strife. The constitution *isn't* perfect.

But to suggest that at least nine million Iraqis casting peaceful ballots don't matter is just sour grapes on the part of those journalists and editors who have been relentless in predicting failure in Iraq—and who've been wrong every single time.

If the day comes when the last U.S. troops leave a peaceful, democratic, prosperous Iraq, the headlines will read: "Failure in Iraq: Three Sunnis Still Unhappy."

Iraq may yet fail as a unified state. Violence will continue. But what's frustrating is the determination of so many in our media to convince the American people that Iraq's a hopeless mess. It's an example of vanity, selfishness, and spite virtually without precedent in the history of journalism.

The greatest tragedy imaginable for our "mainstream media" would be to have to admit that President Bush was right about Iraq.

A startling number of editors and opinion columnists have been wrong about every development in Iraq (and Afghanistan). First, they predicted a bloody, protracted war against Saddam's military. Then they predicted civil war. They insisted that Iraq's first elections would fail amid a bloodbath. Then they declared that Iraq's elected delegates would not be able to agree on a draft constitution. Next, they thundered that Iraq's Sunni Arabs wouldn't vote.

Most recently, the sages of the opinion pages declared that the proposed constitution would be defeated at the polls by the Sunni Arabs. All along they've displayed a breathtaking empathy with the Islamist terrorists who slaughter the innocent, giving Abu Musab al Zarqawi a pass while attacking our president and mocking the achievements of our troops.

A herd mentality has taken over the editorial boards. Ignoring all evidence to the contrary, columnists write about our inevitable "retreat" from Iraq, declaring that "everyone knows" our policies have no chance of success.

That isn't journalism. It's wishful thinking on the part of those who need Iraq to fail to preserve their credibility.

We are dealing with parasitical creatures who, never having done anything practical themselves, insist that the bravery and sacrifice of others has no meaning. Their egos have grown so enormous that they would sacrifice the future of Iraq's twenty-six million human beings just so they could write "I told you so." And, of course, the greatest military experts are those who never served a day in uniform.

The mission we've set for ourselves in Iraq is a tough one. Mistakes made it even harder. But any man or woman of integrity would have to admit that our troops have performed with remarkable skill and tenacity—and that the Iraqi people have displayed confounding courage in their efforts to build a just government for themselves.

There are two things the "mainstream media" are simply unwilling to face regarding Iraq. First, the stakes are immensely high and the premature withdrawal demanded by the pundits would fatally increase the power and allure of Islamist terrorists. Second, we're not only asking a major state to change its form of government—we're asking people to fundamentally alter a failed civilization.

Such a goal cannot be accomplished overnight. Or even in the course of a single administration. Iraq is about the greater fate of the realm of lethal failure stretching from Gibraltar to the Indus.

But we won't see a rational discussion of the roots of the Middle East's cultural collapse—such honesty is taboo. Instead, we'll just hear more about our own "failure" in Iraq, no matter how many successes there are on the ground. Our columnists and editors resemble those diehard communists who kept on praising Stalin right through the purges, the Molotov-Ribbentrop Pact, and the revelations about the Gulag.

We'll hear that Iraq's new constitution is flawed (so is ours—that's why we have amendments). We'll be told that the Sunni Arabs are dissatisfied (so are many American Democrats). Allegations of electoral fraud will never go away (sound familiar?). And political partisans will continue to claim that our military efforts are useless (as demagogues have claimed since the Civil War).

Despite the attacks by international terrorists and the media, Iraq continues to move forward. The process is imperfect, as are all things on this earth. But the bravery and determination that Iraqis displayed at the polls again last weekend deserve better analysis than smug pundits' party-line declarations of failure.

Exploiting the Dead

New York Post

October 20, 2005

We'll soon reach a total of two thousand dead American troops in Iraq. You won't miss the day it happens. The media will pound it into you.

But no one will tell you what that number *really* means—and what it doesn't.

Unable to convince the Bush administration or our troops to cut and run, the American left is waging its campaign of support for Islamist terror through our all-too-cooperative media. And you're the duck in the antiwar movement's shooting gallery.

Breathless anchors and voice-of-God columnists will suggest that two thousand dead is an exorbitant price to pay in wartime, that reaching such a threshold means we've failed and that it's time to "support our troops and bring them home."

All lies. Certainly, the life of every American servicemember matters to us. But the left's attempt to exploit dead soldiers and Marines for partisan purposes is worse than grave-robbing: Ghouls only take gold rings and decaying flesh; the left wants to rob our war dead of their sacrifices and their achievements, their honor and their pride.

Those who died in Iraq have *not* died in vain. Even should Iraq fail itself in the end, our courageous effort to give one Middle-Eastern Muslim population a chance to create a rule-of-law democracy has been worth the cost—for their sake, but also for ours. Without a transformation of the Middle East, we shall see no end of terror.

As a former soldier whose friends still serve under our flag, I'm especially disgusted by the pretense on the part of those who never served and who wouldn't dream of letting their own children serve that *they* speak for the men and women in uniform.

Our troops speak for themselves. By reenlisting. And returning to Iraq to complete the mission for which their comrades gave their lives or suffered life-altering wounds.

Two generations of politicians and pundits suffer from their avoidance of military service. They speak of war in ignorance and view our troops—whom they quietly despise—as nothing more than tools of their own ambitions. After deploring body counts during their Vietnam-era protest years, today our leftists revel in the American body count in Iraq.

The left has been infuriated by its inability to incite an antiwar movement in our military—forgetting that this is an all-volunteer force whose members believe in service to our country. The best the Democrats can do is to trot out poor Wes Clark, an ethically challenged retired general who will say anything, anywhere, anytime in return for five more seconds in the spotlight.

As for that "unacceptable" number of casualties, let's put it in perspective: Our current loss rate in Iraq from combat and noncombat deaths is 765 per year. That's painful for individual families, but we would have to remain in Iraq, taking casualties at the same rate, for *seventy-six years* to rival our loss of more than 58,000 Americans in Indochina.

And Vietnam wasn't remotely as important to our national security. The terrorists we face today are more implacable than any of the enemies from our past. Even the Germans didn't dream of eradicating our entire population. The Japanese hoped to master Asia, not to massacre every man, woman, and child in America.

We would need to continue our efforts in Iraq and the greater War on Terror for 532 years to suffer the 407,000 dead we lost in less than four years in World War II.

And what about our greatest struggle, the American Civil War? We would have to maintain the status quo in Iraq for 470 years just to rival the number of Union dead and for 729 years to equal our total losses, North and South.

Even our Revolutionary War, in which fewer than five thousand Americans died in combat (many more, unrecorded, fell to disease) has to be judged in terms of the population at the time—just over two million. Equivalent losses today would be over a half-million dead Americans.

The point isn't to play hocus-pocus with statistics. That's what the proterrorist left is trying to do—betting that you know nothing of military history. Two thousand dead isn't a magic number. Our first loss was as important as the last. We must not make a mockery of our fallen by treating them as political rag dolls to be tossed around the media playroom. Great causes incur great costs.

In historical terms, our losses in Iraq have been remarkably light, given the magnitude of what we seek to achieve. The low casualty rate is a tribute to the skill and professionalism of our troops and their battlefield leaders. None of us should breathe a word that undercuts them while they're fighting our war.

If the American left and its media sympathizers want someone to blame for our combat losses, they should begin with themselves. Their irresponsible demands for troop withdrawals provide powerful encouragement to Muslim fanatics to keep on killing as many American servicemembers as possible. On the worst days the terrorists suffer in Iraq, our "antiwar" fellow citizens keep the cause of Islamist fascism alive. Their support is worth far more to Abu Musab al Zarqawi than any amount of Saudi money.

It would be wonderful to live in a world in which war was never necessary. But we don't live in such a world. And there are no bloodless wars. We should honor every fallen American. But we also must recognize that, on this maddened earth, only the blood of patriots shed abroad allows us to live in safety here at home.

PART III

Eyes Open

Information Is Not Intelligence

Army Magazine

January 1986

Written over twenty years ago, this article is included to demonstrate that a number of us were well aware of the intelligence system's deficiencies but could not budge the mammoth bureaucracy. It's heartbreaking how little has changed in two decades.

If, on the eve of World War II, a French intelligence officer had evaluated the *Wehrmacht* using our preferred methods of quantitative analysis, he would have found no cause for alarm. The Germans were outnumbered and outgunned. French tanks were technologically superior. France could rest easily behind the Maginot Line and a reassuring web of alliances.

Mere numbers, however, revealed little of consequence. It was not the quantity or quality of German material that conquered, but the relatively brilliant, daring manner in which those austere assets were employed.

Consider a few of our own mere desperate hours. Would Kasserine Pass or Pearl Harbor have been predictable if quantitative methodology had been used? Did the diet-of-facts whiz kids do very well on the outcome of our Vietnam experience? Would lowest-common-denominator techniques, such as those prescribed by intelligence preparation of the battlefield, have put us on the scent of the German Ardennes counteroffensive?

The answer, in every case, is no. Furthermore, the roster of supporting examples is by no means exhausted.

Approach the problem from the positive side. How many of our most remarkable military feats, such as the American Revolution, meet quantitative criteria? The Normandy invasion and the landing at Inchon were quantitatively doomed to disaster. Try running Major General Thomas J. (Stonewall) Jackson through a computer to see if he had any chance of success in his Valley campaign. Major General Ulysses S. Grant's maneuvers of genius in the closing phases of the Vicksburg campaign were as unsupportable quantitatively as they were logistically.

Yet the direction in which our military intelligence effort is headed is increasingly signposted with force ratios and gadgets, while our strategic analysts too often seem to equate analysis solely with mathematics. We cower behind unreliable computers running faulty programs, disguising our inability or unwillingness to think incisively behind an intimidating mastery of detail.

Our excellent signals intelligence effort is increasingly clouded because we expect it to supply miraculous answers instead of the simple data of which it is capable. Machines supply raw information—men must supply the answers.

We continually insist on blurring the distinction between information and intelligence in practice, even though our often inept intelligence doctrine explains this distinction clearly on the printed page. At our worst, we seem determined to take hard thought and the well-developed human mind out of the analytical process entirely

Certainly, there are some partially understandable reasons behind this ominous trend. First and foremost, timely, incisive analysis is just plain tough to do, and it always will be. Even with the most highly skilled and talented analyst, it remains an imperfect art. Our best answers will always be flawed.

We have so often allowed third-rate minds to do our analysis for us that conceptual projections of enemy intent and capabilities have gotten a bad name When the combat commander demands hard, cold facts—numbers and nothing else—it certainly is not because he has no interest in the way the enemy thinks or approaches the tactical or operational situation. Rather, it is because ill-trained intelligence officers have so often given him pathetically bad answers.

Secondly, we will always have a greater need for intelligence officers than we will have a supply of especially talented men and women to fill the critical positions. Our society offers too many richer enticements to good minds. In this respect. our entire military system is somewhat the victim of the glorification of other walks of life.

You can teach the average educated person to template—to match information against standard profiles—and read tables, but you cannot teach talent to someone who does not have it. Talent can be developed, but the dormant quality must exist in the individual. It cannot be injected, not even in the best of causes.

To compound the problem, the unusual talents that make a good intelligence analyst are maddeningly hard to identify by normative testing, so we choose to pretend our way around our difficulties. The notion that some of us are inherently more capable than others does not sit well with our democratic outlook—especially if we are not those graced with the particular talent in question.

This is especially difficult to get past because it is possible to be extremely intelligent, sensitive, and well educated without possessing any real imaginative ability. Mediocrity often bears impressive credentials.

Our approach, then, is to write off the rare analyst who might foresee the daring, illogical counterattack, or who might intuit where the baffling operational piece fits into the strategic puzzle, in favor of bringing the average officer up to a bare minimum of peacetime competence. Men of vision make us nervous anyway. A polished imagination—so vital to analysis—is the natural enemy of the bureaucratic status quo.

Finally, quantitative methodology does have many meaningful applications, and these tend to mask its deficiencies, especially in peacetime. Ideas about the enemy's ideas will never squeeze dollars out of Congress the way clear-cut (and occasionally tailored) force ratios will.

You cannot convince the layman that the key issue is some untested new way of *understanding* the battlefield. But he can grasp the argument that "his tanks have bigger guns and he's got more of them."

Even the way we train our combat staffs for war places a disproportionate value on quantitative analysts. Our most frequently played war games are mathematics driven. Furthermore, the "Red commanders" across the game board are normally under so many restrictions and are so militarily inept that they are unlikely to employ their assets in a manner that is operationally coherent, let alone in one which reflects the likely actions of a talented enemy commander.

We Americans are downright allergic to nuance and ambiguity. Quantitative methods of conducting intelligence analysis, lethally deficient though they may be, give us something into which we believe we can get our teeth. It is all testable, sort of. Numbers are still there, more or less, in the morning.

Concepts and ideas, however, have an elusive quality that makes them hateful to us. Struggling to think clearly through complex problems is as appealing as going to the dentist. Even our promising Airland Battle doctrine has a "how-to" quality that ignores the infinite variables of the battlefield. We are further seduced by mumbo jumbo about a "computer age."

There is no computer age. This age still belongs to mankind, for better or worse. Computers are just here to help us. Wonderful tools in the right hands, they remain no more ready to fully replace the requirement for rigorous thought in military operations than they are ready to take over full responsibility for the arts.

Beware of the analyst who expects the computer to do more than save him time and help him remember. His mental sloth and lack of moral discipline may cost more lives in wartime than he can input through his keyboard.

At the heart of the problem lie misunderstandings as fundamental as they are unnecessary. As mentioned above, we too often do not adequately differentiate between information that is of intelligence value—what we call combat information at the tactical level—and actual intelligence, which is the result of data fermented, however briefly, in a good mind (or minds). It is the difference between grape juice and wine.

Consider another analogy: In our insatiable appetite for data useful for briefings, we often resemble an architect who spends so much time inventorying the available building materials that he never gets around to designing the building.

It is instructive to read our keystone manual on military intelligence, *Field Manual (FM) 34-1,* while on the lookout for certain key words. "Think," "understand," "comprehend," and "imagine" occur rarely or not at all. The manual exists in a perfectly quantifiable universe. In this respect, as well as in others, it is worrisomely inferior to the 1973 manual on combat intelligence it sought to replace, *FM 30-5.*

It is absolutely wrongheaded to approach intelligence as a just-plain-facts business. Intelligence work inevitably involves intellectual (and sometimes physical) risk taking. It is devilishly tempting in a peacetime military system to play it safe, briefing the commander only on what is positively known, verified, and cross-referenced.

The commander, however, does not need an intelligence specialist to read printouts, inventory tanks, and parrot reports to him. It is the intelligence professional's duty, first of all, to acquire by every possible means the most thorough understanding of his work he can; then, secondly, to be willing to stand in the fire and tell the commander and planner what he, the analyst, *thinks.*

Certainly, the analyst must clearly define for the commander that which seems known and verifiable, those scraps of data on which his analytical construct is based, but he also owes an answer as to what it all means. This may seem obvious, but we are in fact wasting a lot of paychecks on intelligence specialists who have been conditioned to play it safe and creep up the rank structure.

A classic example involves a recent, much-heralded, multivolume study of Soviet military capabilities and trends projected through the next few decades. Years in the preparation and published with handsome glossy covers, the books said virtually nothing that had not been said more articulately by others (and often at a lower classification or even at the unclassified level). The series restated that which was "definitely" known, projected a few "safe" figures on hardware, and avoided any meaningful or stimulating attempts to identify shifting Soviet priorities or perspectives.

Above all, insight was lacking. Told to describe how a man lives, analysts of this school would content themselves with measuring the outside of his house. We spent a good bit of the taxpayers' money to run up pocket calculator figures on hardware, without troubling our brains to consider how the flesh-and-blood enemy behind the new weapon system might attempt to revolutionize its employment. We have grown gun shy when it comes to the critical analysis of enemy doctrine, pure or applied. We prefer that which is countable, on our fingers.

Another symptom of this malaise is especially evident in the intelligence estimates of units subordinated to U.S. Army, Europe (USAREUR). There is a quixotic quest for the "perfect" intelligence estimate, resulting in estimates that are updated too infrequently, that are published late and are often outdated by the time they reach the user, and that are routinely generalized to the point of worthlessness. Even given the severe political constraints within USAREUR, we are capable of turning out far better products. Currently, the best estimates rarely go beyond the cataloging of enemy capabilities to seriously consider operational and tactical scenarios that make sense within an overall concept of the battlefield. The alacrity with which units toe the "party lines" of higher headquarters prevents the healthy dialogue that should result from the articulation of divergent views within the intelligence community.

The pretense that there can be one definitive intelligence estimate—and that all others must agree even as to local particulars—guarantees stasis and brings us dangerously close to the "emperor's new clothes" syndrome. Part of the problem, once again, is that bureaucrats fear disagreement from below, *especially since the subordinate may prove to be right.*

Our classic doctrine tells us that an intelligence estimate is a living document. Consider how foolish it is to imagine that there must be one and only one perfectly definitive intelligence estimate at any level.

If the Soviets have made a joke of centralized planning, we are growing vulnerable in the area of overcentralized operational intelligence. Regurgitating the estimate from higher, without any meaningful critical input, is a criminal abdication of the local intelligence officer's primary responsibility. When that anonymous author of our earlier doctrine wrote that the intelligence estimate was a living document, he displayed an astonishing amount of common sense. We seem determined to ignore it.

As a necessary aside, there are some units within USAREUR—those privileged to have intelligence-oriented commanders—who are more concerned with having an intelligence estimate that makes military sense and shows a spark of life than with chasing perfectionist mirages.

In the best, most self-confident organizations, there is always room for dialogue, and the goal is to continue to evolve rather than to achieve some inspection-ready stasis. It is a wonderful thing to serve a commander who expects his intelligence officers to think.

Are we so infected with bureaucracy that we are damned beyond hope? Is the intelligence community as terminally ill as so many civilian "experts" would have it? (Indeed, those civilian "defense analysts" often behave as though they were relatives impatiently awaiting an inheritance.)

Of course there is hope. But there is no prospect of a pleasant-tasting overnight cure. We may hope that a healthy change in direction will come from above. In the meantime, however, the junior and midlevel intelligence analysts must aim for their own small victories. Awareness is a start. Honesty always helps.

In our American love of good-guy/bad-guy divisions of the world and all things in it, however, we must be careful not to carry intelligence efforts to an equally dangerous extreme, where the genuinely useful aspects of computers and quantitative methodology are rejected out of hand by military romantics whose imaginations are characterized by occult disorder. Plumed hats and more swagger will not help.

Gathering and sorting data are lower-rung functions in which electronics are already a marvelous help to us, and we have only begun to explore the computer's military possibilities. As we train our intelligence personnel, however, we must be careful to make them understand that techniques such as templating and graphic-terrain highlighting are only useful as training tools or initial steps toward mature analysis.

Instead of becoming enslaved by gee-whiz programs and elegant, useless overlays, we should use them to give wings to the critical mind, a mind developed by rigorous training, study, and experience.

Finally, the analyst must consider everything he does in a relentlessly critical light. He must never allow himself to grow content, to cease searching for a better way, for deeper knowledge and understanding. Just as he must attempt to thoroughly understand all aspects of his mission, he must struggle to know himself, his own quirks, deficiencies, and predispositions. There is a fine old military maxim that he who does not know himself will never understand his enemy.

This is a plea for balance, good sense, and recognition of our failings and limitations. We need to consider once again what we really mean by intelligence and what we expect it to do for us in peace and war. Many of our limitations are self-imposed.

Somewhere, between the electronic grand *vizier* who is going to solve all of our problems if we just fund one more hopelessly complex system and the military Luddite who expects to destroy the enemy through the use of a little mental Kentucky windage, there must be room for intelligence personnel who can draw on the wonderful capabilities of our modern reconnaissance and automatic data processing systems, but who will not be so in awe of the whistles and bells that they fail to take the critical step beyond merely compiling data to deciding what these data mean.

Electronics, computers, and quantitative methodology may ultimately tell us where our enemy is, what his present strength is, and even what he theoretically can do. They will never, however, account for an enemy's genius.

The Case for
Human Intelligence

Armed Forces Journal

July 2005

Stalinist collectivization programs hoped to make human beings as interchangeable as machine parts. People would become uniform, reliable, and predictable. Rational principles would rule and technology would overcome human inadequacies. Norms would be fulfilled, with the individual's importance minimized. Political reliability trumped genius—a suspect trait. Divergent thought equaled deviant thought. Anyone who resisted the judgment of the collective would be eliminated.

That is a nearly perfect description of our government's approach to intelligence.

Soviet collectivization failed, at a terrible cost. Although charges of "intelligence failure" are often overstated, our intelligence system remains disappointing. Even its successes are a dubious bargain at more than forty billion dollars per year. For a tenth of that, we could buy off most of the enemies our satellites can't find.

Our intelligence agencies share other similarities to high-Stalinist institutions. Against all evidence, they insist that human beings are rational—or can be forced to become so. They are crushingly bureaucratic. Their faith in science and technology divorces them from the reality of sweat and blood. Originality alarms them.

This industrial-age mentality leaves us with an intelligence community that is far less than the sum of its exorbitant parts. We have carried to a new level of perversity the Stalin-era conviction that humans can be turned into machines, accepting as an article of faith that technology is superior to humanity. It is a belief as hopelessly mired in the last century as the collectivization of agriculture.

The machines *lost*. Humanity is back, from the alleys of Baghdad to Darfur, from hate-fueled madrassahs to mass graves. No machine can comprehend the ineffable complexity of the human spirit and the inexhaustible human capacity for mischief. For all its technological adornment, the postmodern age is a new age of muscle and blood. Yet the way we recruit, train, utilize, and promote intelligence personnel is based on industrial-age models. In the twenty-first century, America's intelligence bureaucracy embraces quantitative measurements, uniformity of credentials, and conformity of thought, rejecting notions of unique talent, instinctive understanding, or innate ability.

At a time when the grimmest threats we face arise from souls ablaze, we respond with arithmetic.

BASIC PRINCIPLES

Our extravagant intelligence architecture rests on a flawed foundation: The indefensible conviction that human beings are rational actors. Humans aren't even rational when they buy automobiles, choose mates, or just pull out a credit card. Stir in fear, jealousy, religion, ethnicity, propaganda, information-overload, and violence, and you had better not expect logical responses to crises 100 percent of the time.

Individuals and entire civilizations are often profoundly—murderously—irrational (or subject to a greater rationality that eludes our primitive behavioral sciences). No student of history can make a case that objective calculations of self-interest shaped humanity's past. Indeed, the last century, that great age of "rational" theories of social organization, proved to be the most lethal and maddest of all.

Why do we succumb to the myth that humanity is rational and that all threats can be explained logically, if only we find the right calculus? Because it's comfortable, intellectually easy, and politically correct (no matter that it fails when the chips are down). Not least, a formulaic view of humanity suggests that we can reduce our reliance on the pesky human factor in intelligence work and turn instead to technology, that seductive American cult.

Intelligence bureaucrats place an almost religious trust in machines, but they're wary of flesh and blood. In the intel canon, machines are angels, while people are dangerous sinners. We never question the machine's commandments as harshly as we do the analyst's beliefs. So we bomb decoys, misread weapons programs, and fail to understand the enemy's nature.

Decisionmakers can be impressed by intercepts of intimate conversations and dazzling images harvested from space. Naturally, the defense industry argues for the preeminence of technology, since it makes enormous profits from black programs. Personnel are regarded as a nuisance. Members of Congress may publicly deplore our lack of human intelligence, but they vote to fund satellites, not competitive salaries.

The Cold War excited the American taste for technical solutions to intelligence challenges, since the threat lent itself peculiarly well to abstract measurement. How many missile silos? How many submarines? How many tanks in a tank regiment? Codes could be broken and installations imaged. Telemetry provided useful data.

Of course, we *never* knew what went on inside the Kremlin. We missed the speed of the Soviet collapse. The eruptions of the post-Soviet world caught our intelligence system by surprise (analysts who forecast the coming violence were ignored). Twisting a line from Dylan Thomas, we knew everything about the Soviets but *why*.

We didn't just neglect the human factor. We actively tried to eliminate it. From the rampage of the Carter years, when our clandestine services were gutted, to the ludicrous U.S. Army proposal to commission only lieutenants with science degrees into military intelligence, every problem was supposed to have a technological solution. People were messy, technology was clean, and the pork was delicious.

Then the world changed. Instead of facing another superpower, we found ourselves up against atavistic hatreds and passions academics had declared vanquished: religious fanaticism, ethnic prejudice, nationalism, genocide. All the satellites could do was to image the burning villages.

When you speak to intelligence bureaucrats, they insist that our agencies and staffs have "gotten religion" since September 11, 2001. But all they do is sing different hymns in public. Their faith in technology and disdain for the human factor still dominate their beliefs.

Just follow the collection plate.

PEOPLE AGAINST PEOPLE

The recent move to increase the number of personnel within the CIA is a step in the right direction, but an inadequate one. Once again, the system assumed that quantitative measurements are decisive. While we do need more bodies, the appropriate talents matter far more than raw numbers—but we don't even know how to identify potential top performers in the intelligence sphere. Our testing system is virtually useless and our recruiting criteria are as likely to hinder our search for the best hires as to help. The default position is to hire unblemished children to take on terrorists, fanatics, and mass murderers.

Our preference for recruiting graduates of "top" universities simply means that we get trainees more conversant with theories than with reality. It's grimly amusing to watch Ivy League kids confronted with the world's complexity—their response is to cram the vastness of humankind into the narrow theories professors inflicted on them. Faced with threats from globo-criminals, religious extremists, and ethnic hate merchants, I would bet on a rough-and-tumble graduate of a blue-collar college over a pampered kid who's never been in a fistfight.

Consider the essence of intelligence work: At the top of the game, it requires knowing what your enemy will do before he has reached a decision himself. It means developing a visceral understanding—a knowledge beyond reason—of your opponents. It demands the ability to suspend your own character and beliefs in order to inhabit the personas of human monsters.

Whether speaking of agents, analysts, or interrogators, intel work demands a level of empathy and a suite of instincts that no academic background can guarantee. A great intel hand can inhabit the enemy's soul. Instead, we have intellectual plagiarists who recycle each other's reports.

The core vocabulary of intelligence should be "talent, instinct, empathy, imagination, experience, and courage." But we'll settle for a squeaky-clean past and a solid grade-point average.

If there is a single crippling failure within our intelligence system, it's the unwillingness to accept that intelligence professionals *must* possess special talents—"gifts," to use an unfashionable word. We accept that even the best-trained professional athletes were born with inherent skills, that concert musicians require unique talents, and that military leaders must possess instincts that rise above the common run. Yet the intelligence system pretends that anyone with a degree in international relations can probe the bloody gutters of the soul.

If only we could return to the wonderful days of the Cold War, when a satellite image seemed worth a thousand words, our resistance to change might appear marginally defensible. But we no longer live in the age of tracking fleets and counting divisions. Our security problems have to do with the devils that crouch in men. We still haven't got a satellite that can spot them.

TALENT AND EXPERIENCE

Even were we to develop a test for the unusual qualities of mind essential to a top intelligence professional, innate ability still isn't enough. Talent must be developed through exposure to the world beyond our shores. But our system offers few serious programs to plunge intelligence personnel into the realms we expect them to understand.

There is no substitute for time spent outside of our own civilization. Intelligence professionals—and not just agents—*must* immerse themselves in foreign cultures for extended periods. A week at the embassy isn't enough. The system needs sufficient redundancy to send career personnel back to their target region time and again for extended stays. (If they don't want to go, they're in the wrong business.)

At present, only the U.S. Army has a first-rate program to develop regional experts, but the Foreign Area Officer specialty is so small it barely merits a file cabinet of its own. The CIA has specialized training capabilities for field personnel, but no commensurate commitment to analysts.

Such training costs money, as bureaucrats will hurry to point out. Fine. Skip the next generation of satellites. Put the money into people. I guarantee you that our nation, if not the defense industry, will be better off for it. And we'd have billions left over for a party.

Technical data are meaningless unless a human being grasps their import. We are all too ready to accept that data equal intelligence. They don't. We need to send intelligence personnel overseas by the thousands so they can develop the tactile sense and intuitive insight that allow top performers to decipher the behavioral DNA of our enemies.

How can we forecast the decisions of profoundly foreign actors when our sphere of experience is limited to Northern Virginia, with occasional forays into Washington, D.C.?

Another problem—perhaps intractable—is that the system has been so self-satisfied and technologically oriented for so long that senior intelligence officials have no idea what intelligence work really means, or how much can be achieved by top performers allowed some leash. On the Army staff in the Pentagon, I served a series of military intelligence generals who understood perfectly how our own administrative system functioned and how to win budget battles, but not one of whom had more than a rudimentary grasp of intelligence work. They knew so little that they couldn't begin to grasp how little they knew.

Or consider the case of an influential government analyst. Patriotic, conscientious, smart, and a master of data, he got the nature of religious extremism completely wrong. Imposing a rational template on men who operate from primal impulses, he concluded that Islamist terrorism can be explained entirely by external factors. Instead of inhabiting the enemy's being, he forced the enemy to conform to his own psychology. It was exactly the wrong way to do intelligence.

On what was his analysis based? On intelligence reports read at his desk. His direct experience with the cultures about which he wrote with such confidence was almost nonexistent. And even that analyst was too creative a thinker for our intelligence agencies.

Contact with the sweat, dust, and hubbub of Arab, Turkic, or Persian societies, or of Pakistan or Afghanistan, might have shocked him into understanding that the rest of the world is not inhabited by Americans in funny costumes. Instead, he read voluminously and failed miserably.

If only we lived in a rational world, analysis would be easy. Those fantastically expensive systems might serve our intelligence community well after all. But the fundamental paradox of the high-tech twenty-first century is that it's also the new age of superstition, of men possessed by devils, of demons at midnight.

And our response is another series of PowerPoint slides.

FINDING THE BALANCE

Technology can be a marvelous aid to intelligence work. Instead, we subordinate intelligence work to technology. We need to return to a more balanced approach, one that accepts that we cannot do without those undependable, erratic, annoying, magnificent human beings who can leap beyond the calculations of the most expensive computer on Fort Meade and look where the most sophisticated imaging satellite cannot begin to see—inside the human soul.

In the 1980s—that great age of intelligence bean counting—senior officers dismissed "predictive intelligence." Their notion of intelligence work was to explain after the fact why something had happened. They weren't doing intelligence work. They were giving history lessons, conducting useless postmortems. They had lost sight of the fundamental reason their organizations existed—to beat the enemy to the punch.

The one lesson we *should* take from history is that attempts to apply scientific principles to humankind always fail, whether we speak of collective farms in the USSR or the collective mediocrity of our intelligence system. In this age of grimly human enemies, we need to respond with flesh and blood of our own—and with extraordinary minds. We need to have the courage to decipher the future our deadliest enemies are already planning.

Hateful as their deeds have been, our enemies have reveled in human genius, from the invention of the suicide bomber—the greatest precision weapon of our time and a dirt-cheap way to have a strategic impact—to the elaborate choreography of September 11. Victims of our own wealth, we assume we can buy a technological solution to any problem. Our enemies have the advantage of poverty—they have to rely on the power of the human mind.

Who gets better value?

Europe: Worlds Apart

New York Post

August 14, 2003

Life may not be predictable, but Europeans are. If we criticize them publicly, they splutter, outraged that we don't recognize their perfection. They can dish it out abundantly, but continental Europeans can no more take criticism than their welfare armies could have taken Baghdad.

The only thing you can get for free from Europeans is advice. And they're always ready to give us plenty of it, as they've been doing for more than two centuries.

Still, behind the easy pleasure of poking fun at European pretensions, there are serious—and hardening—differences between Americans, who embrace the future, and the French or Germans or Belgians who cling to the past.

None of those differences go so deep as our opposing concepts of freedom.

For Europeans—excluding the Brits, who are more like us than they sometimes find comfortable—"freedom" means freedom *from* things: from social and economic risk, from workplace insecurity and personal responsibility, from too much competition in the marketplace or too much scrutiny of governing elites.

Socialism, a doctrine born in Europe, struck very deep roots. The collective takes priority over the individual. The European social contract amounts to this: We will not let the talented rise too high, and we will not let the lazy fall too low. "Equality" doesn't mean equal opportunities, but equal limitations.

For Americans, freedom means the freedom *to do:* To make our own way, to struggle, to achieve, to rise (to climb social, educational, or economic ladders), to move beyond our parents' lot in life and give our children better chances still.

We are products of the immigrant spirit and the pioneer mentality. Our ancestors (as well as today's new immigrants) dared to take a chance, instead of remaining in the "old country," with its degrading social and economic systems.

The Europeans with whom we must deal today are those whose ancestors lacked the courage to pack their bags and board the ships in Hamburg or Antwerp or Danzig. They chose a miserable security over hope that carried risks.

The American Revolution was entrepreneurial and constructive. The French Revolution was vengeful and destructive. Even during the Great Depression, when extremist ideologies achieved their greatest popularity in the United States, nothing approaching a majority of Americans signed up for any totalitarian creed of either the right or left. In the words of Huey Long, who for all his faults spoke for the average Joe, we never stopped believing in the possibility of "every man a king."

Europeans are content with "every man a servant," as long as the terms of service are not too severe and the position comes with job security. Hitler did not cement his hold on power with anti-Semitism—that was an add-on—but with works projects, with jobs for Germans, with a promise of economic security, however low the level.

The Bolsheviks never preached liberty. Their credo was the nanny state, a "fair share" for the workers and the promise that decisions would be made "for the good of all."

We elevate the individual; Europeans worship the group. We dream; Europeans fear. Indeed, the only belief that has been pronounced dead more often than religion is the American dream. Professors write its obituary almost daily. The rest of us live it.

Life isn't fair, of course. But too much enforced "fairness" robs life of its vitality. We Americans live in the one country where each of us, regardless of race or religion, has the chance to realize our potential. Reaching that potential is up to us. But our laws and our culture don't stand in our way.

There are, of course, many further differences between us and the Europeans, but the greatest other distinction relates to the first: American is the land of second chances. And of third, fourth, and fifth chances, if only we have the gumption to seize them.

In Europe, there's little provision for late bloomers. The placement tests the student takes as a teenager determine his or her academic, economic, and social fate to an extent that would spark another revolution in America.

Here, attending Harvard is no guarantee that you'll succeed in life—it just gives you a head start out of the gate. On the other hand, beginning your academic career at a community college doesn't mean you can't climb to the highest income levels.

Europeans accept their fates. Americans make their own.

Most Americans would be astonished if they understood how few opportunities there are for Europeans to pursue adult education, to change careers, to learn new skills—or to recreate their lives. It's an adult version of being forced to retain your identity in junior high school forever.

Europeans demand security, no matter the price. Americans want a shot at the title.

And so it comes to pass that, as America seeks to change the world for the better, Europeans are content to let dictators thrive and populations suffer—as long as Europe's slumber is not disturbed.

Strategically, Europe is in danger of becoming the greatest impediment to positive change in the world. Europe clings to the international status quo, no matter how dreadful, simply because risk has been bred out of its culture. This leaves the United States (and Britain) with the choice of doing that which is necessary and just without Europe's support, or accepting the rules that made the twentieth-century history's bloodiest.

Europeans are correct when they insist that America has become a danger. We are, indeed, a tremendous threat to their self-satisfaction, to their dread of change, to their moral irresponsibility, and to their dreary, state-supported cultures.

Our ancestors chose a new kind of human freedom. Europeans have resisted it ever since.

The Loser's Rant

New York Post

October 17, 2003

Yesterday, Prime Minister Mahathir Mohamad of Malaysia explained the world's problems to the Organization of the Islamic Conference (aka, the "Global Losers' Club").

According to Mahathir, Jews "invented socialism, communism, human rights and democracy. . . . The Europeans killed six million Jews out of twelve million, but today Jews rule the world by proxy. . . . They get others to fight and die for them. . . . "

Never one to back down from a fight when there's no one present to hit back, the prime minister added bravely, "1.3 billion Muslims cannot be defeated by a few million Jews!"

Wrong on all counts, of course. Not least, the last one.

Anti-Semitism Mahathir-style grows more bizarre each time he opens his mouth. It's piggish enough to accuse Jews of designing socialism and communism to further the secret aims of the Elders of Zion, but why should it be an insult to charge Jews—or anyone else—with inventing human rights and democracy?

One suspects that Mahathir isn't wild about either concept.

Except for a convention of European intellectuals, the only place on earth where you could draw applause by damning Jews for their alleged "invention" of human rights and democracy is the Organization of the Islamic Conference, a collection of miserably failed states represented largely by aging dictators.

They're hardly in a position to condemn human rights and democracy, since they've never tried either one.

Nor are these vicious, cowardly men in any position to criticize Jews. Or the AARP, the Rosicrucians, or emperor penguins. Muslim leaders have stolen the oil wealth and squandered the human capital of their people. They couldn't talk straight if they rubbed their tongues with Viagra. No matter what goes wrong at home, they blame Israel and the United States.

And *they*, not the Jews, "get others to fight and die for them." You won't see Mahathir, Bashar Assad, Mo' Khadafy, or any of the potbellied perverts of Saudi Arabia leading bayonet charges against the Israeli army.

The truth is that a few million Jews *can* defeat 1.3 billion Muslims. They've done it repeatedly. And they'll keep on doing it, if necessary.

It doesn't take courage to shoot off your mouth in the presence of like-minded bigots. Rhetoric is the opium of the Islamic elite. They speak madly, then wallow in failure. Their entire civilization has a "born to lose" tattoo.

The saddest part of all this is that Mahathir could've been a contender. Even in his latest Jew-baiting speech—which might have been drafted by the czarist *Okhrana*—he criticized his fellow Muslims, too, for embracing dogma instead of science and progress. In the past, he's accused his fellow Malays of laziness compared to their Chinese neighbors. And he led his country to an impressive, if faltering level of economic success by doing real business, not just by living off petrodollars.

Mahathir understands that education, hard work, sound laws, and real opportunity for all citizens are the keys to success in the twenty-first century. On a good day, he might even admit to the importance of democracy and human rights, as long he gets to call time-out when election results or dissidents make him unhappy.

But he's old and frustrated with setbacks at home—caused not least by Islamic social distortions. He's bitter about the insuperable weakness of the Muslim world. He knows where the problems really lie. But he still can't stop himself from blaming Jews.

All right. Let's frame Mahathir's climactic charge a bit differently: How can a few million Jews so dramatically outperform 1.3 billion Muslims?

Maybe the Muslim world just needs a few more of those notorious Jewish inventions. Like human rights and democracy.

Sound kosher to you?

Why They Hate W

New York Post

November 18, 2003

This week, TV screens will fill with protests against American policy. As President Bush visits Britain, European leftists will gather to denounce him as a threat to world peace. Mock courts will judge our president and find him guilty on every wild charge. But the most instructive demonstrations will be those that *won't* happen.

We won't hear a word about Saddam's tyranny, about his wars or the mass graves still being unearthed. No demonstrator will celebrate the liberation of twenty-five million people.

All we'll hear from the streets is that Bush is bad.

No protesters will chant about the Iraqi families sundered, the fathers tortured and shot, the daughters and wives raped, the use of poison gas against the Kurds, or the million-and-a-half Iraqis, Iranians, and Kuwaitis who died in Saddam's wars.

Bush is worse than Saddam, you see, because he refused to look the other way. His resolve is an embarrassment.

American wars of liberation humiliate the complainers on the left. We've seized their professed ideals and made them a reality. We fought for freedom, while they only chattered. Their protests are the result of wounded egos.

During the Cold War, America was mocked for its ill-judged support of dictators because they were "our dictators." Now our government has left the distortions of the past behind and returned to

America's traditional role of championing freedom. And look how the tables have turned.

Europe's left so hates America and all it stands for that the dictators have become "their dictators." Of course, European intellectuals supported Stalin, too. But it can only amaze anyone who believes in elementary human rights that America is pilloried for putting an end to a murderous regime.

On one level, the European left's protests against all things American are understandable. We won, they lost. All their cherished rhetoric led only to the Gulag in the East and to bankrupt welfare states in the West. Now, the East, where terror reigned, aligns with America, further angering the West Europeans who lived on credit for the past fifty years, loafing in the shade of America's might.

President Bush is an especially appealing target for their scorn, since he's the least European U.S. president since Andrew Jackson. Bush speaks awkwardly but acts powerfully. The European ideal is a politician who speaks beautifully and does nothing.

As the protesters parade in front of the cameras, Americans should be *proud* of the great thing we've done in Iraq. We haven't done it perfectly, but perfection isn't a common human trait. We've served the cause of freedom, even as "Old Europe" accused us of fabricated sins.

What have we *really* done?

• We faced up to our historical and moral responsibilities by removing Saddam from power. Although our past role has been exaggerated, we foolishly supported him in the 1980s. Thus, we had a special responsibility to liberate Iraq (the Europeans bear as much guilt or more but preferred to keep doing business with Saddam).

• We're giving long-oppressed Arabs and Kurds a chance to build a rule-of-law democracy. There are no guarantees that they'll succeed in the end. But simply giving them a *chance* is more than anyone else has ever done for them.

• We've created the possibility of a Middle Eastern success story, of an Arab-majority state that respects its citizens and honors basic freedoms. This is vital. Behind all their feverish accusations against us, Arabs fear they may be incompetent to build a modern, democratic state. We've made a noble effort to plant a garden of freedom amid the briars of oppression. No soldier's life has been lost in vain. Our cause is worthy of comparison with America's finest hours.

Of course, we face no end of criticism, beginning with the complaint that no weapons of mass destruction have *been* found (would it have better pleased the protesters had WMD been found?). Ultimately, this is a minor matter, amplified by the administration's tactical error of using the WMD issue as its public rationale for war.

Had we stressed the need to remove Saddam in the cause of human rights, it would have been much harder for cynical European governments to oppose us. They would have opposed us, anyway. But at least we would have embarrassed them.

Leftists love to retreat into false comparisons, asking, with a smirk, why we chose to depose Saddam when there are plenty of other dictators in the world. It was only because of oil, they insist, ignoring the fact that we'll never recoup our financial investment in Iraq's future.

Why Iraq? Because it was doable, while North Korea isn't. Because we bore a special responsibility, due to our bygone support for the Baghdad regime. Because Saddam had launched wars of aggression unmatched by other contemporary dictators. Because he *did* seek weapons of mass destruction. Because the situation in Iraq continued to worsen. And because you have to start somewhere.

No coward has ever been short of good reasons for doing nothing.

As with Islamic terrorism, European protests against our actions in Iraq are not so much about us as about the protesters' own demons. The current French and German gloating over their belief that we're trapped in a quagmire against which they oh-so-wisely warned us is as shabby as it's fundamentally wrong.

We aren't trapped in a quagmire in Iraq. But the European left *is* trapped in a quagmire of failure, mendacity, and guilt.

How could they not hate the land of the free? Whether we speak of America or Iraq.

India: Democracy Wins

New York Post

May 18, 2004

In last week's elections, the world's largest democracy—India—booted an economically progressive, peace-seeking government that had supported the United States to a degree unprecedented for New Delhi and returned a notoriously corrupt party of obsolete demagogues to power.

It was a triumph for democracy and good news for America.

With Iraq demanding the media's attention, the slight commentaries on India's elections thus far have described a strategic setback for America, given the victorious Congress Party's role in forming the anti-American "Nonaligned Movement" half a century ago.

But the Nonaligned Movement is long dead—and it was never more than half alive. Yes, we'll hear some silly anti-American rhetoric from Congress Party demagogues. But pay attention to what the new government does, not to what it says. Despite the inevitable turbulence attending a change of governments, there is likely to be more continuity in New Delhi than disruption in dealing with the United States.

The current relationship between India and the United States is mutually beneficial, with virtually no downside. The likely new prime minister, Italian-born Sonia Gandhi, is unlikely to kill the goose that keeps laying golden eggs. Expect some feather-plucking in public and some goose-baiting at the United Nations. But don't expect General Electric to be sent packing from Bangalore.

Analysts have also read the election returns as the vote of an underdeveloped countryside against the techno-privileged boom cities, with their prosperous, envy-inducing mix of saris, jeans, and singles' bars. Such jealousy no doubt shaped part of the vote—even though the poverty level in the countryside has been steadily declining. Trickle-down economics work, but in a country as vast, populous, and poor as India, it takes longer than it does on Long Island.

In a sense, the outgoing government was a victim of its success. The techno-boom in cities such as Hyderabad, New Delhi, Chennai/Madras, and even vibrant, appalling Mumbai/Bombay has raised expectations and job envy throughout the country. But no political party could deliver progress at a pace sufficient to fully satisfy the country's pressing needs.

We will likely see continued changes of government as dramatic economic progress nonetheless continues to exclude hundreds of millions of Indians.

Yet, having spent a few months wandering throughout that fascinating country a few years ago, I like to think there was another, crucial factor at work at the polls. The surprise upset of the outgoing government—formed by the Hindu-nationalist Bharatiya Janata Party (BJP)—likely also had to do with the disenchantment of India's burgeoning middle class—the techno-yuppies and entrepreneurs—who were mortified by the anti-Muslim pogroms in the state of Gujarat a few years ago.

Young, educated Indians, especially, felt shamed in the eyes of the world. But the BJP government did virtually nothing to investigate the mass murders or to prosecute those responsible. Instead, the government blamed the victims.

It was a reminder that, for all its liberal economic policies and diplomatic openings, the BJP was grotesquely reactionary on the home front, reigniting not only interfaith but also caste hatreds. The hard-right "Hindutva" or "Hinduness" wing of the BJP is bigoted, ugly, and antimodern, led by ideologues whose extremism is far more dangerous to India and the region than the effete, decayed socialism of the Congress Party.

Yes, the old government opened new doors to cooperation with the United States. Yes, they sought a meaningful peace with Pakistan. Without question, their programs of fostering techno-trade and privatizing moribund state industries were essential. But the hatred they preached in city and village threatened to become a domestic cancer that might have canceled all else.

I believe that some Indians, at least, voted for simple decency. And freedom. And a national unity that includes India's 150 million Muslims.

The BJP government satisfied our immediate interests. But, for all its other failings, the Congress Party shares far more American values: religious freedom, social equality, and big-tent democracy.

India is a remarkable, frustrating, inspiring, infuriating country of almost unlimited human potential. No matter which party takes office in New Delhi, our human ties will continue to expand—to the benefit of all. Indeed, today's Indian-American community is among the most productive immigrant groups in U.S. history—and the values and possibilities they learn in America are having a positive influence back in India.

Expect occasionally nasty rhetoric from the new government in New Delhi as it reaccustoms itself to holding power in a much-changed world. Like many developing countries, India remains in a political transition phase. The old-guard pols, with their left-wing slogans and grasping paws, need to die off and make room for a new generation of educated technocrats. And they will.

Don't worry about the return of the Gandhi dynasty. And don't worry about outdated anti-American rhetoric that may boom from New Delhi. America and India are bound to cooperate. Our futures are intertwined—as the world's two most populous democracies.

Meanwhile, we Americans should applaud *any* country with such a long and continuing tradition of open elections. In the end, democracy abroad always benefits the United States—even if the results disappoint us in the short term (as they may do in Iraq).

Against great odds, India has come so far that no government, right or left, will be able to stop its progress. If they try and the Indian economy slows, well, just wait for the next election.

Reagan to the Rescue

New York Post

June 9, 2004

In 1976, I joined the U.S. Army as a private. Our military was broken. My first unit, in Germany, had trucks built in the 1940s, inadequate winter clothing, inept medical care, and an atmosphere of pessimism. We were not "combat ready."

Crippled by Vietnam, the noncommissioned officer corps had hit bottom—despite a cadre of stalwarts who would not give up. Officers ranged from the shoulder-shruggers to the grimly determined. The barracks were pits. Soldiers made their own survival rules—for example, hashish was OK, but no junkies were allowed on our barracks floor.

Then there were the drunks. Of all ranks. And the overweight and out of shape. As well as good men simply worn out by a long, bitter war.

Had "the balloon gone up," our Infantry would have entered battle in death-trap M113s that were no match for Soviet infantry combat vehicles. Our tanks couldn't rival the firepower of the new Russian models. Our radios were unreliable, and the antique encryption devices rarely worked.

Our war games weren't about winning but about losing as slowly as possible. We always had to resort to nukes in the end.

Our nation had ended the draft and transitioned to an all-volunteer military. But the pay remained at draftee levels. As a sergeant living in an unheated attic apartment, I had no phone and no car.

Once, while we were out on maneuvers, President Carter's secretary of the Army came to visit. He flew in by helicopter, pretended to eat our field rations, spoke to no enlisted troops or junior officers, and left. We didn't exactly feel valued.

Then came Ronald Reagan.

Yes, he raised Defense budgets dramatically. And the money mattered. But the increased funding and higher pay wouldn't have made a decisive difference without the sense that we had a real leader in the White House again. The man in the Oval Office genuinely *admired* the men and women who served. When he saluted his Marine guards, he meant it. The troops could tell.

I attended Officer Candidate School in Georgia during the 1980 presidential election. When I returned to Germany in late 1981, the change in the quality and morale of the "dirty boots" Army was already unmistakable. Even before the new equipment began arriving, the Army was regaining its fighting spirit.

We still had some bad apples—but fewer with every infusion of new, better-educated recruits. Officers were held to ever higher standards. The young sergeants coming up had an energy and optimism that had been missing for years, while the senior NCOs who lasted were the toughest and best of them all. And our new generals, men who had commanded battalions and brigades in Vietnam, had learned the right lessons.

New gear began to arrive. Training budgets increased. We even replaced our janitor-style uniforms with camouflage fatigues. We *looked* like soldiers again.

We had a president who *cared* about us, a man who was proud of us and proud of the country we were pledged to defend. He even understood the power of uniforms and would not enter the Oval Office himself unless wearing a tie.

President Reagan made mistakes. He was human. The intervention in Lebanon ended badly with our precipitous withdrawal after the Marine-barracks bombing. That decision sent a message to the nascent forces of terror that we had no stomach left for a serious fight. The Iran-Contra scandal, although not the debacle the president's detractors tried to make it, was an example of thinking tactically, not strategically. Too much money went into gold-plated weapons systems that never earned their keep.

Yet these were minor matters compared to the fact that this man—this single, remarkable visionary—brought us two world-changing insights: America's greatness remained undiminished, and the Cold War wasn't eternal.

Ronald Reagan brought down the Soviet Union. After all the academic arguments about the USSR's internal weakness and the inevitability of its ultimate failure, the truth is that none of those who speak so knowingly now had the strategic insight of an aging former actor when it mattered.

Which brings me to my confession. Having grown up in the late '60s and early '70s, I carried some of my generation's prejudices along with me into the Army. While I realized that Jimmy Carter had been an inept president (if a good man), I didn't support Ronald Reagan in 1980. I believed that Carter remained the safer of two mediocrities. I bought into the bigotry of those who mocked Reagan as lacking the intelligence to be president.

And it's doubtless true that he didn't possess the highest IQ ever to enter the White House. That goes directly to what Reagan taught me: As we recently saw with another president, the greatest intelligence isn't a substitute for vision, courage, and leadership. Above all, a president needs good instincts, guts, and sound values. The world's overstocked with brilliant people who never get anything done.

Reagan got things done. He gave us the military that serves the cause of freedom so well today. He gave us back our pride. And he gave us back our country.

Like Abraham Lincoln, another self-made Midwesterner mocked by the elites at home and abroad, Reagan's greatness transcended conventional measure. Despite the current outpouring of love and admiration, we have not yet lived long enough to comprehend his full achievement. He was the first among Americans of our time.

If that wasn't clear from the campus, it was obvious to those of us in the mud on the frontiers of freedom.

Mozambique Beats All

New York Post

July 19, 2004

What do you call an African country that suffered under one of the most vicious colonial regimes, was attacked by a powerful neighbor at independence, fought a brutal civil war for more than a decade, and was classified as the poorest land on earth?

If the country is Mozambique, you call it a success story.

I just returned from a stroll through Mozambique with my faith in the human spirit reinforced. Forever starved for tales of woe, our media only tell us of Africa's crises—the last time Mozambique made headlines was during the disastrous flooding in 2000. Yet along with the continent's undeniable problems, there's more than one success story.

After a long civil war—fomented by the old South African apartheid regime—Mozambique almost miraculously converted its warring factions into political parties and held elections. With help from the international community, a model demobilization program turned tens of thousands of unruly soldiers into law-abiding citizens. Even the United Nations came through, removing countless landmines from the countryside.

When the Portuguese revolution of 1974 opened the door to independence, Mozambique was appallingly undeveloped and overwhelmingly illiterate. Then-fashionable socialist theories of regime organization and economics didn't help the new state.

But the country did have one advantage that Western observers misread: The leader of the liberation movement, Samora Machel, was more than a doctrinaire leftist. He honestly believed in racial equality. And in social justice. He wanted to build a country, not a string of palaces.

At a time when African nationalists, from Idi Amin to Joseph Mobutu, were driving out the many hues of talent their countries desperately needed, Machel envisioned a multiracial society that prefigured the achievement of Nelson Mandela.

Machel didn't want to see his country recolonized by the East bloc or the West. He built his own path. The result? The whites-only South African government assassinated him, luring his aircraft into a hillside with a false navigational beacon.

But the seeds he planted took root. When socialist policies failed, Machel's successors switched to a market economy. As in all poor countries, corruption threatened to complete the country's ruin, but enough good men and women fought for the rule of law to move the society forward—including a courageous journalist, Carlos Cardoso, who paid with his life for taking on a Pakistani criminal family whose tentacles had penetrated the government.

Instead of blaming anyone else for their problems, the people of Africa's poorest country rolled up their sleeves and went to work. By the end of the century, Mozambique was posting the continent's highest economic growth rates.

Then the great floods struck, inundating more than five percent of the country, destroying vital roads and rail beds while displacing entire populations.

With international help—including support from the U.S. Air Force—the people of Mozambique struggled through the calamity. When the mud dried, they went back to work.

In the course of my travels, I encountered levels of optimism that seemed almost surreal compared to the boundless whining elsewhere in the developing world. Asked if things were getting better, one young man's response was typical. He thought for a bit, taking the question seriously, and then said, "Sixty-five percent better, I tell you. There is much more to do. We must learn from others, from everyone. But there is peace, no one wants to fight. We will work hard."

By our standards, the schools are impoverished. But they're full. There's a hunger for learning rivaled only by that I encountered in India. With AIDS rampant, health care is abysmal. But it gets a bit better each day. Development programs actually work, with most international assistance reaching the people who need it.

Although the country divides into a heavily Muslim north and majority-Christian south, with native beliefs tenacious throughout the country, the absence of religious strife is noteworthy. Machel set the tone for that, too—his "socialist" vision included religious freedom.

Investment is coming in steadily, especially from South Africa's booming business sector. With twenty-five hundred kilometers of coastline, Mozambique provides the most direct access to global markets for the landlocked countries of southern Africa—with transit and port fees an important source of income. The rail lines may be in need of refurbishment and the roads still bear the scars of war and long neglect, but there's great potential beyond the ruts and potholes.

Natural-gas fields are under development. There may be oil deposits, too. Crime remains low by regional standards. The country has a lively, combative press.

In December, there'll be another presidential election. The incumbent, Joaquim Chissano, is stepping down voluntarily—another remarkable event by African standards. Whether the current ruling party, Frelimo, wins again or the opposition manages a surprise upset, a transition that isn't marred by sour-grapes violence may mark a turning point for the southern half of the continent—sending a message to the neighborhood's oppressive regimes that the people, not aging dictators, are destined to rule.

Things are far from perfect in Mozambique. Life remains hard and poor. Corruption is snapping at the economy's tail. Temptation will be magnified as gas and oil revenues arrive. International criminals exploit the state's lack of resources, using the country as a conduit for heroin and other drugs. The country's remote wilderness could easily hide terrorists.

Still, I'm rooting for Mozambique to prove that failure isn't the region's destiny. From the streets of Maputo, Africa doesn't look like a "dark continent" at all. On the contrary—it's bathed in sunlight. And hope.

Terrorizing Schools

New York Post

September 8, 2004

The horror of the terror attack on a Russian primary school still resounds. From security officers to soccer moms, the sudden question is, "How can we protect our children from terror?"

In the short term, the only conceivable answer is to renew our offensive efforts against these butchers who claim to act in the name of their god. But a crucial part of the long-term answer is perfectly clear to the terrorists, even if we ignore it.

The terrorist assault on civilization and modernity has many aspects, from barbarism toward women to bombings and massacres. But no dimension of the struggle is more important than the Islamist war against secular education. All other progress flows from knowledge. And the terrorists know it.

Last week's school seizure in Beslan, in the rolling fields that rise toward the Caucasus, had layers of intent. First, the Chechen killers and their Arab allies intended to punish Russia as brutally as they could for Moscow's refusal to allow Chechnya to become an independent terrorist state.

As a Russia-hand pal reminded me over the weekend, the Chechens know their enemies: In Russia, the cult of the child is far more pronounced than it is in the most competitive American suburb.

For generations, Russian adults have coped with their dreary lot by placing all of their hopes and dreams in their children. The

Chechens attacked every Russian family's cherished fantasy, responding to their aspirations for better lives for their children by killing the children outright.

But another aspect of the massacre binds it to the terrorist strategy for the Muslim world and neighboring lands where Islam once prevailed: the fundamentalist assault on education.

While the world watched the Beslan tragedy, other terrorist barbarities went virtually ignored. We've become so tolerant of Islamist atrocities that it takes hundreds of dead children to get our attention.

In Afghanistan, Taliban remnants bombed a rural schoolhouse. The handful of dead could not compete with the carnage in Russia, but the purpose of the attack was equally grim. The terrorists killed their fellow Afghans—for the horrendous crime of studying math and science.

That village school had *not* removed Koranic studies from its humble curriculum. Its sin lay in trying to impart useful knowledge *in addition* to the medieval mumbo-jumbo that our Saudi enemies support with global funding.

Children died because they hoped to learn.

That attack was far from the first assault on education by the satanic marauders who pervert their faith. Islamist hardliners would rather see millions live in squalor than have a child learn enough math to survey the site for a sewer line.

In Iraq, the situation is crueler still—and the attacks have been more frequent. The international terrorists our indecisiveness welcomed to Iraq have been targeting Iraqi teachers, university professors, and education ministry officials for the past year.

The Islamists truly believe that ignorance is bliss—that any "education" beyond memorizing the Koran and studying the countless volumes of commentaries upon it is not only unnecessary, but evil.

All cultures have seen assaults on learning, from the persecution of scholars during Europe's Counter-Reformation, through the Nazi bonfires of books, to China's grotesque Cultural Revolution. But the comprehensive Islamist attack on secular education is a first—never before has the "vanguard" of a once-great civilization and one of the world's leading religions tried to eliminate *all* knowledge that isn't shrouded in faith (and girls, of course, don't even get to go to religious schools).

The Islamists are willing to plunge a billion people into darkness in their perverted quest for the light of their god. In doing so, these blasphemers have made an idol of ignorance. This is so deep a tragedy that it can barely be described. If anything could eventually triumph over the passionate ignorance crippling the Middle East, it's education—real education, not religious studies that focus pathologically on the beyond while ignoring the miseries of this earth.

It didn't have to be this way. The Islamic world once was the center of learning its defenders claim. Muslim scholars preserved the classic texts of Mediterranean civilization during Europe's Dark Ages. But the Islamic world made centuries of bad decisions, closing its intellectual gates against the social and intellectual progress that fostered the West's ascent to power and wealth.

Islam once boasted splendid universities, the envy of the world. Today, even the few Middle Eastern universities that offer some hope hardly rise to the level of a third-rate U.S. community college.

A millennium ago, Islam ruled much of this earth—not just with arms, but with knowledge and culture—while the West lay mired in ignorance. Now the situation is reversed. And, instead of laboring to become competitive again, the most dynamic forces in the Muslim world have declared knowledge their enemy. Laying our wishful thinking aside, the truth is that the Middle East may never recover.

Naturally, we focus on the Islamist attacks against our own civilization. But the terrorists are doing far more harm to the Muslim world than they ever have done to us.

The human beasts in that school in Russia—or wherever Islamists seek to stifle learning—weren't just the West's enemies. They're the cruelest enemies Islam has ever faced, worse than the Mongols.

Meanwhile, Islam's most powerful clerics look away. The world is still waiting for Islamic leaders and scholars to condemn the terrorist attack in Russia. Their silence has been heartbreaking.

And silence in the face of atrocity is complicity.

Democracy's Boom

New York Post

December 26, 2004

Challenging growing seasons can produce magnificent wines. Tumult in Iraq, acts of brute terror, and prophecies of doom tormented 2004. Yet it turned out to be a vintage year for democracy.

The "experts" assured us that elections couldn't, wouldn't, and shouldn't work in Afghanistan. Afghans had no tradition of democracy. They were illiterate, tribal fundamentalists resistant to foreign ideas. Grassroots support for the Taliban, widespread violence, and fear were going to frustrate the American folly of believing that Afghans cared about elections.

What happened? In cities and remote villages, the people of Afghanistan ignored grave dangers and turned out to vote by the millions. Desperate to find fault, international critics could cite only minor flaws. And the Afghans elected a rule-of-law president, not a tribal warlord.

Afghanistan still faces daunting problems, but little more than three years ago, it suffered under one of the world's most oppressive regimes, harbored thousands of terrorists, and according to the same experts, could never be subdued by American troops. Now it has a freely elected government—and hope.

Democracy is about the little guy having a voice. Afghanistan's little guys—and gals—took a stand to have their voices heard.

Today, the people of Ukraine are turning out to vote in massive numbers. After a dozen years of post-Soviet corruption and stasis, average citizens decided they'd had enough. They took to the streets in masses last month, protesting a stolen election. Defying homegrown thugs and Russia's president, they demanded freedom and real democracy.

Romania's reform-minded voters got little attention from a press that craves bad news, while Australia's commonsense support for Prime Minister John Howard repulsed the international literati. Spaniards didn't vote the way we would have liked, but they voted fervently as they continued to master the power of representative government after a single generation of democracy.

Half a world away, the people of bitterly poor Mozambique flocked to the polls in December. The results favored sweat-of-the-brow progress over demagoguery. One of the world's poorest nations, Mozambique stood up proudly to prove that democracy isn't only for the Upper West Side. The media ignored this triumph of the human spirit.

In Venezuela, a referendum supported President Hugo Chavez, a man viewed by Washington as Castro-lite (with oil). Despite balloting mischief, the people spoke. We must respect their choice. Building global democracy isn't about short-term gratification for American presidential administrations, Republican or Democrat. It's about *freedom*, with all of its risks, errors, and ultimate glory.

Even when we believe a foreign population has made the wrong choice, we should be grateful that they were able to make a choice at all. In the long run, democracy always benefits the United States of America. Patience is the one strategic virtue we need to cultivate.

Around the world, electoral trends over the past few years upset the doomster predictions of the pundits. Despite solemn warnings that Indonesia or even Malaysia might "go fundamentalist" at the polls, elections in both of these crucial Muslim states resulted in resounding defeats for parties seeking to wield Islam as a weapon.

Again and again, "uneducated" and "unsophisticated" voters chose decency, progress, and opportunity over the pleasures of hatred and blame.

In the end, the greatest electoral triumph wasn't in Afghanistan, but here at home. Our "opinion leaders" backed yesterday's man, a candidate who catered to the prejudices of overeducated baby boomers. John Kerry's supporters believed that America is always wrong. They took no interest in Saddam's mass graves, only in a fair trial for Saddam. They cared nothing for democracy in Afghanistan, but agonized over the treatment of Taliban prisoners at Guantanamo. And they mocked believing Christians as hopeless dunces.

The Democratic Party's message in 2004 was that average Americans need to obey the electoral dictates of blue-state aristocracies.

Online commissars, network anchors, faculty-lounge commandos, and the infernally self-righteous George Soros rallied behind Michael Moore to denounce George W. Bush for liberating tens of millions of human beings, for taking the War on Terror to the terrorists, and for speaking like an average guy, not in the smarmy tones of Harvard Yard.

The result? The American people turned out in record numbers to reelect a man who respects their labor and faith, who believes that freedom is worth fighting for, and who knows that our country is a force for good.

No wonder campus lefties hate democracy. It gives the high-school graduate the same power as the guy with the Ph.D. It offers an identical vote to those who work with their hands and those who never broke a sweat in their trust-funded lives. And it grants the same Election Day authority to the clerk behind the counter as it does to the customer waving the platinum credit card.

Democracy is the ultimate weapon of social justice.

Next year begins with elections in Iraq. Terrorists will do all they can to disrupt the balloting. Iraqis will die for the crime of casting a vote. There'll be local corruption, religious influence, ethnic division, tribal bullying, and polling boycotts. After all of our sacrifices, those Iraqis who manage to vote may favor parties whose agendas frustrate us.

But the Iraqis will *vote*. Not all of them. But millions. Despite the ferocious efforts of the terrorists and insurgents, the Arab world is about to see the first truly free election between the Nile and the Euphrates.

Global pundits will find endless flaws, and many a Washington apparatchik may be troubled by the election's outcome. But the Iraqi elections will be a milestone that no demagogues, America-haters, or instant revisionists will be able to wish away.

Democracy works. It doesn't work all of the time, and it doesn't work everywhere instantly. Sometimes the largest tribe wins and believes it has a mandate to oppress minorities. Sometimes the people choose the hater, not the man of hope. Sometimes the thugs get away with stealing the election.

But consider where this world of ours stood fifty years ago. Or fifteen years ago. Or even in 2003. Democracy's march is long, hard, and painful. But humankind stepped forward in 2004.

A New Strategic Map

New York Post

January 6, 2005

The tsunami's devastation on the Indian Ocean's shores offers a strategic lesson of incomparable importance. Whether or not the Pentagon's current leadership is capable of grasping that lesson is another matter.

The Indian Ocean and its adjoining seas and gulfs form one crucial, integrated strategic theater. The region has been critical to Western dominance for five centuries. Yet when our intelligence services or military planners consider this vast, densely populated region at all, they poke at the different parts and miss the whole.

The Indian Ocean theater contains the world's largest democracy (India), the world's most populous Muslim state (Indonesia), the greatest concentration of oil (on the Arabian Peninsula and in the Persian Gulf), the first Muslim nuclear power (Pakistan), the most progressive economies in Southeast Asia (Singapore, Malaysia, and Thailand), and the greatest concentration of terrorists in the world.

On its eastern extreme, this vast region is bounded by Australia, a sturdy Western outpost. To the west, the Indian Ocean laps the old Swahili Coast and the Republic of South Africa, a state on its way to becoming the continent's first indigenous great power.

No region of the world is so complex, or so thick with both threats and opportunities. The Indian Ocean region is not only critical in detail, but has an overall importance even greater than its parts. From the vital sea lanes that once carried spices and now carry oil, to the competing civilizations on its littorals, the Indian Ocean binds together the world's great passions, needs, and dangers.

This is where Islam must—and can—change, where nuclear weapons are likeliest to be used, where the future economic potential is vast, where the bulk of the world's heroin is produced, and where the heroin of the world economy—oil—could be cut off with a handful of nuclear weapons (think Iran, the Suez Canal, and a few Arab ports).

We have failed to see the forest for the palm trees. Nature recognized what our government consistently fails to understand. The earthquake centered off the coast of Sumatra triggered deadly waves that struck Thailand and Somalia, India and Indonesia, Burma and the Maldives, Sri Lanka and Africa's Swahili coast.

The tsunami drew a strategic map of the twenty-first century. It took a tragedy to inspire serious American involvement in the region (apart from the Middle East, with which we remain rabidly obsessed). While cognizant of the horrors that brought them to Indonesia, U.S. Navy officers are relieved to have a mission at last. Largely excluded from participation in Iraq and Afghanistan because of the reactionary choices the service made, our Navy has suffered from a perception of fading relevance.

Yet our Navy remains as important to America's security as it ever was. The problem is that the Navy itself can't see it. The service suffers from the destructive nostalgia that afflicted the Army a decade ago, the desire to perfect a force to fight the wars of the past.

Nonetheless, our Navy remains the lead service for security affairs in the Indian Ocean. The Air Force will have a role in crises, while the Army and Marines will be needed to fight the region's ground campaigns of tomorrow (they're coming), but our naval presence is the indispensable military and strategic tool required by the Indian Ocean's strategic environment.

We have lost our focus on the control of the seas.

Half a millennium ago, the Indian Ocean proved to be the soft underbelly of the Ottoman Empire. Obscure naval battles off the coast of India secured the spice routes for Europe and triggered the long Ottoman decline. Today, the Indian Ocean is the weak link in Western security, a distant theater whose sea lanes carry not only oil, but vital trade, from the Suez Canal to the Straits of Malacca. No other region is so critical and so vulnerable. If we look beyond the terrible toll of the tsunami, there is much to be hopeful about. Far too little attention has been paid to the Thai government's position that, while it welcomed foreign recovery expertise, it did not need post-tsunami financial aid. Only a generation ago, Thailand was dirt-poor; today, it's proud of its ability to self-recover.

India has become a prized source of top-flight human capital. Afghanistan's proving that democracy can work in the absence of superhighways and investment bankers. South Africa is pioneering a dynamic multiracial society on a continent old-school thinkers blithely write off. And Indonesia, for all its problems, relishes its new democracy and its tolerant forms of Islam.

The future is waving its arms and shouting, but we see only the past.

First in uniform, then as a civilian, I've visited most of the countries on the Indian Ocean littoral, from Burma to Mozambique. I've become convinced both of the need to view the region as a unity and of the criticality of intelligent American engagement.

Only last month, I completed a book (*New Glory,* due out next summer) that argues for a shift in our strategic priorities and a fundamental rethinking of the way we view the world. My conclusion was that the Indian Ocean lies at the heart of postmodern strategy. I didn't expect the disaster of the century to underscore my point.

The tsunami's devastation raised a signpost to the twenty-first century's future. Does our government have the strategic literacy to read it?

Money for Hate

New York Post

January 10, 2005

The Saudi Arabian government and individual Saudis have spent billions of dollars spreading Wahhabi extremism and fostering hatred. No expense is spared to vilify Israel or the West. But when it comes to easing the misery of their fellow Muslims, the world-champ hypocrites in Riyadh just ain't interested.

As of last week, the Saudis had pledged a pitiful $20 million to the tsunami-relief effort. That's a Saudi prince's bar-and-bordello budget for a weekend in Paris. Even the devout Muslims of Indonesia's devastated Aceh province don't qualify for Saudi charity. The images of peerless suffering aren't enough to open *any* Arab wallets, for that matter.

It takes hatred to do that.

American government aid, private donations, and military operating costs will approach a billion dollars before we're finished. The Aussies, the Japanese, and even the Germans have pledged at least five hundred million bucks each. But the policy of the Saudis and their oil-rich neighbors can be summed up in eight words: Big bucks for bigotry, peanuts for human suffering.

It isn't supposed to be that way. The Koran *demands* generous giving to needy Muslims as one of the faith's central pillars. Doesn't matter a bit to those holier-than-thou Saudis. They set themselves up as the arbiters of Islamic purity and perfection, but they demonstrate less moral integrity than prostitutes and thieves.

Outside of the Middle East, no population has been as eager to follow the Arab lead on Islamic practices as the Muslims of Aceh. They already had a thriving Koranic school in Mecca in the fifteenth century, where Acehnese mullahs making the Haj could study Islam's subtleties at the source. The Acehnese still turn to Meccan madrassas today, in preference to Indonesian traditions.

So much for Saudi Arabia's sense of Islamic brotherhood.

I realize it would be uncomfortable for bloated Saudi sheiks and Riyadh's feckless military to contribute to the relief effort personally but couldn't they at least hire a few transport planes to ferry their unused helicopters to Banda Aceh? Actual Saudis wouldn't need to get their hands dirty. They could hire hard-working Filipinos to do the labor, as they do with everything else.

I don't agree with Osama bin Laden on much, but he's right that the Saudi government is despicable.

How the Saudis, with all of their self-righteousness and preaching about Islamic duties, can neglect the basic obligation of charity demanded by the Koran is so far beyond any recognizable sense of morality that words can't capture the shabbiness.

Saudi hypocrisy is an old story. Even before the financial demands of a swelling population cut into the budgets of the lesser princes, the Saudis talked holiness and practiced corruption. Ask the Palestinians, who hate the Saudis with a passion.

The Saudis and their fellow travelers still hold up the plight of the Palestinians as a bloody flag. But stingy Saudi charity barely kept the Palestinians from starvation. It was to Riyadh's benefit to keep the Palestinians miserable (of course, there's always plenty of money for anti-Israeli terrorists).

The Gulf Arabs are little better. Dubai is spending billions to reinvent itself as Orlando without the charm (Ouch!). Qatar harbors al Jazeera, which has been airing conspiracy theories blaming the United States and India for the tsunami. Qatar's emir, who can barely waddle across a ballroom without panting, hasn't been making any big sacrifices for his devastated fellow Muslims, either.

This column doesn't indulge in fantasy: I haven't suggested that the Arabs should donate to the Hindus, Buddhists, or Christians whose lives were shattered by the tsunami. Evil infidels are evil infidels, after all. But I expected the Arabs to do more for their coreligionists.

Silly me.

Meanwhile, U.S. Navy and Marine helicopters work around the clock to feed the starving—without asking for anybody's religious credentials. As predicted by the *Post*, Aceh's fundamentalist mullahs are already preaching that Allah punished the people for being insufficiently rigorous in their behavior, for being too tolerant. The same mullahs explain away Western aid as a plot.

But the people will know who helped them and who did not.

The tsunami revealed far more than the awesome power of nature. It revealed the hollowness of Saudi-Arabian Islam.

When Democracy Fails

USA Today

January 11, 2005

Democracy is the most humane and desirable form of government yet devised by humankind. From Afghanistan to Ukraine, democracy's recent successes have exceeded expectations. It deserves American support wherever it has a chance of taking hold.

The problem is that it doesn't always work.

As the vital Iraqi elections approach, there is more reason for sober optimism than for preemptive declarations of failure. More than 80 percent of the country's population is anxious to vote, with only foreign terrorists and an embittered minority of Sunni Arabs actively hostile to the balloting. But we need to think beyond the polls to understand how new democracies fail.

Pakistan has been the greatest disappointment among the major states that tried democracy. It should have been a contender, having begun its nationhood with a legacy of British legal traditions, an educated political class, and a vigorous press. Instead, Pakistan became a swamp of corruption, demagogy, and hatred. Those who believe in democracy need to recognize an ugly truth: Military government remains Pakistan's final hope—and even that hope is a slight one.

This is painful for us to accept. Well-intentioned Americans with no personal experience of the outrageous criminality that came to characterize every one of Pakistan's major political parties rebel against the notion that any military government can ever be good. Certainly, military regimes are despicable. General Pervez Musharraf's government, albeit imperfect, is the sole exception in the world today.

Pakistan is an artificial country, cobbled together from ethnically different parts and flooded early on with Muslim refugees from India who still form a distinct social and political bloc. The Pathans of the northwest frontier have more in common with their Afghan neighbors than with the Sindhis on the other side of the Indus River, whose culture reflects that of Mughal India. The Punjabis of Lahore inhabit a different civilization from the tribesmen of Baluchistan. Pakistan's Kashmiris are something else entirely.

Instead of seeking unity, Pakistan's political parties exploited internal divisions for short-term advantage. Well-educated political families, such as the Bhuttos, took a page from the Chinese nationalists, telling Westerners exactly what we wanted to hear. Preaching democracy and the rule of law abroad, they looted shamelessly at home. And they blamed the colonial powers, then America, for the destruction of a once-promising society. No matter their political allegiance, Pakistan's party bosses stole everything in sight, reducing the country to stinging poverty and stunning violence. It wasn't just the remote frontiers that became lawless, but even Karachi, Pakistan's largest city.

In order to win elections, one party after another pandered to Muslim extremists. English lessons faded from the classroom, robbing the country of a great advantage it had enjoyed in a globalizing world. About three thousand schools funded by the government were found to be nonexistent "ghost schools." Rural landholders and party hacks had pocketed the money. Fundamentalist madrassas filled the educational vacuum.

I recall standing in a classroom in the Murree Hills, a oncelovely hill station dating to colonial days, as a young man lectured me about America's theft of Pakistan's wealth. That was what he had been taught. Yet I could see over his shoulder the hideously eroded mountainsides stripped of timber with the connivance of local officials. Elsewhere, I saw poverty in the shadow of the extravagant wealth of political insiders. Pakistan's elite had robbed the country of its future.

In traveling through Pakistan, one thing became unmistakable: The least corrupt institution was the military. The military government attempting to rescue Pakistan is the country's last hope. The alternatives are chaos and terror. We may wish it were otherwise: Military government is repugnant. But the world is more complex than we try to make it. Perverted democracy brought ruin upon more than one hundred million Pakistani Muslims. We all are paying the price.

At present, Musharraf's government is a useful ally in combating terror, but its greater contribution lies in preventing the country from collapsing into chaos. We all should hope that the day will come when Pakistan's military government becomes obsolete. But for now we must do two things: resist the cynical pleas of the displaced politicians who devastated their own homeland, and learn what we can from democracy's failure on the banks of the Indus.

The two essential lessons are pertinent to Iraq.

• First, democracy faces an uphill struggle in tribal cultures where blood ties trump national interests.

• Second, democracy has no worse enemy than corruption.

If held on schedule, the Iraqi elections will be the most openly staged in the Arab world. But if Iraq cannot rise above the culture of corruption endemic to the region and cannot persuade Shiite and Sunni Arabs, Kurds, Turkmen, Assyrians, and others to form political alliances that transcend ethnicity and religious identity, it's unlikely democracy will take root and endure.

The world doesn't need another Pakistan, where only bayonets hold the state together. If anyone dooms democracy in Iraq, it won't be the foreign terrorists, but a corrupt political elite. The politicians pave the way for the generals.

Instant Amnesia

New York Post

March 22, 2005

I spent last week in Europe watching acrobats perform. There were no high-wires or circus tents—just left-wing intellectuals contorting themselves into bizarre shapes as they "explained" the changing Middle East.

A few Euro-papers raised the possibility that Bush might have been right about some things—only to knock down that notion with excuses so convoluted even the writers and editors couldn't begin to believe them. They were trying, desperately, to save face.

The commonly agreed alibi runs that the Middle East was changing on its own, that Anglo-American actions had little or no effect, that the outbreak of democracy has been on the way for years, that the Arabs did it themselves.

Oh, really? Guess our troops overlooked the warehouses full of multiparty ballots when they took Baghdad.

The *Independent,* a Brit rag that's been hilariously wrong about Iraq, talks around the icky little details—such as that minor impediment to democracy, Saddam Hussein. *The Iraqis were headed for free elections on their own. No reason at all to praise Bush.*

Dead Kurds? *Not our kind.*

Saddam's slaughter of the Shi'as? *Can't quite remember, old man.*

Torture chambers? *My dear fellow, you must mean Abu Ghraib.*

Saddam's wars of aggression, the employment of poison gas, and the network of mass graves? *Talking about that sort of thing simply isn't done. Anyway, the true aggressors are George Bush and his henchman Tony Blair.*

One starts to suspect a movement to nominate Saddam for the Nobel Peace Prize.

Presented with irrefutable evidence of the success of that incoherent cowboy in the White House, the brilliant minds of Europe are glummer than they've been since the Berlin Wall came down (that *really* hurt).

What intellectuals long for is an audience. And ever fewer people are paying attention. The workers and peasants have lost their faith in the central committee.

It's even getting tough to stage a decent anti-American protest. Despite the overblown media coverage, the "massive" rallies on the eve of Iraq's liberation were small compared to those of the glorious Cold War years when Moscow still provided a beacon of hope and American troops defended Jean-Paul Sartre's right to defend Comrade Stalin.

Last week, on the second anniversary of the start of Operation Iraqi Freedom, the European Left called for mass demonstrations to protest the American "occupation" of the Middle East. The turnout was pathetic.

My wife and I passed through London on demo day. The temperature was an unseasonable seventy degrees, and the sky was Texas blue—perfect weather for a protest.

Instead of attracting hundreds of thousands, the antifreedom rally was a bust. Londoners were basking in the sun, filling the outdoor cafes around Covent Garden. The burning issue of the day was whether to have beer or wine at lunch.

Strolling down Piccadilly toward Hyde Park, we saw the disappointed protesters straggling home, their signs as slack as their spirits. They came in three sad flavors: Dreary kids of the sort who blame "the system" when they can't get a date; aging lefties struggling to believe that the Soviet collapse was a hallucination, and Middle Eastern expats outraged that Coalition soldiers had done what they lacked the courage to do themselves.

I don't recall a single protester calling for *more* democracy in the Middle East. Nobody protested Syria's occupation of Lebanon or the Damascus regime's program of assassinations and terror. Not a single earnest undergraduate demanded free elections in Iran. No one criticized that great human-rights advocate Abu Musab al Zarqawi.

The protesters represented a forlorn hope that the new Middle East would fail. They found little sympathy among a population that had been promised an American defeat, only to find Washington winning again. There was more interest in the tale of the young British soldier who won a Victoria Cross in Iraq than there was in the demonstration.

Europeans are masters of instant amnesia. When they find themselves shamed by history, they simply move on. That's what they're doing now.

In France last week, there were more than ten times as many strikers protesting a possible lengthening of the thirty-five-hour work week than there were antiwar protesters.

Germans are far more concerned with unemployment levels last seen in the 1930s than they are with Iraq. And the Italian left's brief moment of delight in the accidental shooting of a hot-dogging agent by American troops has already passed.

And the French government, terrified of being shut out of the new Middle East, is standing shoulder-to-shoulder with its cherished ally and old friend, the Bush administration.

C'est la vie.

Lebanon's Peril

New York Post

March 31, 2005

Syria's troops are going home. Before Lebanon's spring elections. Damascus made the promise in writing. To the United Nations.

The question now is: How much damage does Syria intend to do on the way out?

Although a commitment from Damascus to the U.N. has a whiff of a pimp's promise to a hooker, international pressure will force the Syrians to honor their word. The problem lies in what the agreement omits. Getting the twelve thousand or so remaining Syrian troops out of Lebanon certainly matters. But ridding the country of Bashar Assad's five thousand-plus intelligence operatives is what really counts. And Damascus has been coy about their removal.

Syria's troops are bums with guns—largely undertrained draftees with unreliable equipment. They can't act without being seen by all. They'd be hard to use effectively.

The intel and security boys are another matter. Some function overtly, an acknowledged presence. But many work in the shadows. And there's no place on earth where the shadows grow longer and darker than in the Middle East.

If the intelligence personnel—overt, covert, and clandestine—aren't removed, the Syrian menace remains as grave as ever. Their agents don't merely spy and report. They bribe, bully, blackmail—and kill.

Syrian intel operatives were behind the assassination of Lebanon's former prime minister, Rafik Hariri. Even if they worked through Hezbollah or contract killers, Syrian agents doubtless sponsored the recent terror bombings in Christian enclaves as well.

What does Syria want? Enduring control of Lebanon, its people, its foreign policy, its wealth, and its strategic location. Assad and his cronies regard Syria as Saddam Hussein regarded Kuwait: an integral part of the homeland, hewn off by outside powers.

How will Syria try to get what it wants? Subversion. Terror. Resurrecting yesteryear's fears and hatreds. By bribing, blackmailing, and murdering. By igniting a new civil war, if Damascus can get away with it.

Who will do it? Those intelligence operatives, if they stay behind. Along with Hezbollah dead-enders who want nothing to do with true democracy, civil liberties, or a just peace with Israel.

Like the twenty-first-century IRA and Saddam's Ba'athists, Hezbollah has become a deadly mafia whose immediate goals are self-perpetuation and power.

Even if there's a formal withdrawal of Syrian intel agents, it's extremely unlikely that the undercover operatives would go home. And Syria will continue pulling the strings in Lebanon's own penetrated and compromised security services—which need to be purged.

What will happen if Lebanon's democracy appears on the verge of triumphing, despite Syrian mischief? If the Assad regime can't possess Lebanon, it will do its best to wreck it—to reignite the violence of twenty-five years ago to "prove" that Syria's presence was essential for peace.

What Assad the Lesser can't have, he'll try to destroy.

Given the remarkable strides the Middle East has made since Iraq's elections—with suggestions of more progress to come—we can't afford to let Damascus get away with a partial withdrawal or any other form of delay or compromise.

The Lebanese want all of the Syrians out. They want freedom and independence. That's the deciding factor. Every Syrian soldier, agent, and scheming official must go.

If Assad and his henchmen try to destabilize Lebanon, the Syrian government must pay a painful price. Even if that requires military action.

Thus far, Assad has literally gotten away with murder in Iraq by feigning innocence and intermittent cooperation. Our reluctance to call him to account may have led him to believe that he can pull a sleight-of-hand trick in Lebanon, withdrawing troops publicly while attacking the country in the netherworld of terror.

There's an impressive international consensus for getting the Syrians out—lock, stock, and hookah. Terrified of being deprived of influence in the changing Middle East, even the French have aligned themselves with America on this issue. Assad will try to divide us, to cut backroom deals. We must hold the French to an Anglophone standard of reliable behavior—no secret handshakes between Paris and Damascus.

Our successes in the Middle East have changed the region's political direction. Freedom and democracy are gathering momentum. But the course of reform could still be reversed among the failure-haunted Arabs. Lebanon is the next potential crisis and a critical test of our will. President Bush must continue to make our resolve explicitly clear, if we hope to prevent the ruin of Lebanon's convalescent society and economy.

If the Syrian government attempts to destroy Lebanon, the Damascus regime itself must be destroyed.

Champion of Faith— and Freedom

New York Post

April 3, 2005

From the Cuban Missile Crisis to President Reagan's resounding "Mr. Gorbachev, tear down this wall!" there were plenty of supposed turning points in the Cold War. Personally, I believe the tide turned on October 16, 1978, when a Polish cardinal, Karol Jozef Wojtyla, became Pope John Paul II.

It was a pivotal moment for humankind, but a dark day for the Kremlin—the geriatric Politburo must have clutched the remains of their shriveled hearts. It was a glorious day for the Catholic Church, as the Vatican took an unmistakable stand against the godless religion of Communism. It was also a momentous recognition of the role the Polish people long had played in the struggle for freedom, faith, and justice.

The mid-1970s had seemed a new dark age. After painful American losses, much of Indochina had fallen to Communism. The West suffered through oil crises, economic doldrums, and political terrorism. No outsider grasped how rotten the Soviet system had grown. Around the world, leftist revolutionaries believed the future was theirs.

Then the College of Cardinals broke with tradition to choose a new pope from behind the Iron Curtain. By doing so, they accomplished what vast armies and the threat of nuclear weapons could not do: Gave hope to hundreds of millions of the oppressed, unhinging the Soviet empire from within.

Suddenly, it was Christ vs. the Kremlin—and Jesus had a home-court advantage.

I was a young soldier in Germany when the new pope was chosen. We were outnumbered by the barbarian hordes across the inner-German border. Our equipment was aging and most of our NATO partners were incapable of actually fighting a war. Then we gained an unexpected ally. One who didn't need a single tank.

There's an apocryphal story from the days when Stalin ruled the Kremlin. Molotov, his foreign minister, raised the matter of the Vatican's resistance to a Soviet move. Stalin snorted and asked, "How many battalions does the Pope have?"

Stalin's successors found out.

I recall that we soldiers were delighted at the choice of Cardinal Wojtyla, a Pole, as the new pope. But we merely saw it as a nose thumbed at Moscow. We failed to understand the colossal impact.

One Polish-American PFC among us got it, though. For him, it was as if the Red Sea had parted to lure in Pharaoh's chariots.

The Soviets got it, too. Within three months, Soviet Foreign Minister Andrei Gromyko—hardly a devout Catholic—traveled to Rome for an audience with John Paul II. We'll never know precisely what was said between those two men who didn't need an interpreter—the pope was a splendid linguist—but Gromyko could not have been happy with what he heard.

In June 1979, Pope John Paul II made his first pastoral visit to Poland. Beloved from his days as archbishop of Kracow and his tenure as cardinal, he was greeted with scenes of fervent adulation. It was about the Catholic faith. But it was about other things, too.

Solidarity already haunted the Gdansk dockyards. The pope's secular counterpart, Lech Walesa, would rise from the ranks of the proletariat to denounce the "workers' paradise." The pope's visit was a catalyst for all that would come after.

As John Paul II stood in Victory Square in Warsaw, declaring that "it is not possible to understand the history of the Polish nation without Christ," his multitude of listeners heard it as an anathema pronounced on Communism.

A country that had been wiped off the map for nearly two centuries by its neighbors, Poland had survived as an idea, its identity preserved by its Catholic faith and its language. Now the people who had saved Christendom from Mongols, Turks, and Muscovite barbarians heard a call to rise to the struggle again.

What could the Soviets and their cronies do in the face of such a powerful, unarmed enemy? They tried to kill him. Working through the Bulgarian security services—who did some of the Kremlin's nastiest dirty work—the KGB moved a disturbed young Turk across the strategic chessboard.

The assassination attempt failed. And the man of peace who had taken his apostolic message to the developing world—where he proved as effective an opponent of Communism as he was in Poland—survived as a living reproof to Soviet savagery.

Shortly after Mehmet Ali Agca tried to kill the pope, the Kremlin cornered the Polish military into suppressing the Solidarity trade and freedom movement. The convalescing pope asked for prayers for the Polish nation. The world knew what he meant. Nor could the Russians prevent him from returning to Poland in 1983. The KGB didn't dare stage another assassination attempt.

The tide of history turned with stunning speed. In 1975, Communism was on the march around the globe. By 1985, confronted with the strategic pickup team of John Paul II, Ronald Reagan, and Margaret Thatcher, the Soviet empire faced a mortal crisis.

For Protestants (such as I am) and those of other faiths, the pope's theology sometimes seemed out of step with the times and pressing human needs. But that son of a Polish army NCO killed in 1941, the university drama student who labored in a quarry under the Nazi occupation and felt the call of the priesthood in war's midst, had no interest in fitting his faith to the times. He called for the times to return to a higher faith.

Whatever his theological legacy may be, John Paul II did God's work in helping the West win the Cold War without the need to fight World War III. For the Poles, he was a modern Moses, parting the blood-red Communist sea and nodding toward the promised land of freedom. He was one of the greatest men of the twentieth century—and perhaps the best soul his troubled times produced.

Pope John Paul II may have been the head of the Catholic Church, but we all were blessed to have him present among us.

A Dirty Frame

New York Post

April 27, 2005

The United Kingdom is our crucial military ally. Australia, with its feisty love of liberty and strategic location, grows more important to us every day. Canada treasures the role of abused spouse. But no country is more important to our future than Mexico.

With oil, a growing economy, a huge expat population in the United States (legal and illegal), its leadership role in Latin America, and a population of over a hundred million—more than three times Canada's—Mexico should top our list of strategic interests. Instead, we pay more attention to South Korea and show more respect for Qatar.

Our fates are intertwined. For better or worse. It only makes sense to do what we can to make our relationship healthier.

It's a challenge. Mexico's a country where politicians steal everything in sight, and then blame us for local poverty. Drugs sold by Mexican cartels kill more Americans than terrorists do in Iraq. Even the presidency of Vicente Fox—the first opposition candidate to hold the office since the Mexican Revolution—has been a lost opportunity.

Now our neighbor to the south faces a political crisis that will determine the country's future. At the center of the storm is a single man, Andres Manuel Lopez Obrador, the mayor of Mexico City and the most popular politician in the country.

President Fox and his conservative party, PAN, have united with their bitter rivals in the PRI, the party whose control of the state lasted longer than the Communist Party's rule in Moscow:

No one in the establishment wants Lopez Obrador to run for president next year. Because he'd win. And he owes nothing to the kingmakers.

As I write, the mayor has returned to the office from which the federal government tried to bar him for "criminal activities." He may already be under arrest. And what crime did Hizzoner commit? He built a hospital access road on a strip of private property.

Wrong? Yep. But given Mexico's whopping corruption at the top, this is akin to arguing that an American can't run for president because of a parking ticket.

Lopez Obrador's real "crimes" are that he's popular, incorruptible, and a champion of the people.

For almost a century, Mexico's politicians have made beautiful promises to their impoverished fellow citizens. Then they stuffed their own pockets, counting on the safety valve of illegal emigration to the United States to keep society from exploding.

Along comes Lopez Obrador, to the in-crowd's consternation. He actually improves the lot of the poor. He lives in a simple apartment, not a mansion. And he seems to be a genuine man of conscience.

The inner workings of the Mexican political system are opaque even to Mexicans. We never know what deals are being cut. But we can hear what the men who've failed Mexico say for our consumption.

Washington has been warned that Lopez Obrador is "another Hugo Chavez," the Venezuelan colonel who dresses up as Castro. It's a lie. Lopez Obrador is more of a cross between William Jennings Bryan and Huey Long, an "every man a king" kind of politician who puts at least a drumstick, if not an entire chicken, in every pot.

And he isn't antibusiness, either. Just anticorruption.

But even if Lopez Obrador were a leftist demagogue, we need to stop and ask ourselves why recent elections in Latin America have installed left-wing governments in office.

The truth is that the populations between the Rio Grande and the Rio de la Plata are sick and tired of broken promises and poverty. They're not voting for extremist philosophies. They're voting against those in power, against those who failed them.

Our position on Lopez Obrador will be a test. If Mexico's established powers bust him on phony charges and we stay mum, we'll have betrayed our own rhetoric about spreading democracy—while alienating Mexicans who view the United States more positively than ever before in their history.

Which brings us to the big lies told about Mexicans who live and work within our borders. The nuttiest fable is that Mexican immigrants want to "take back the Southwest" for Mexico. On the contrary, having experienced the decency of American society, those immigrants, legal and illegal, want to make Mexico more like *El Norte*.

No one wants to live in a society where bribes determine your fate.

The paradox of illegal immigration is that immigrants want to stay here because they've learned to value the rule of law. Mexicans come here because the United States offers opportunities and a level of justice they can't find at home. They're fleeing poverty, corruption, and degraded lives. Why on earth would they want to turn Texas into Jalisco?

What's really changing Mexico is Mexican exposure to the society, economy, and constitutional integrity of the United States. Even the illiterate now realize that things don't have to go on as they always have south of the border. Mexicans may be changing the United States, but our impact on Mexico is incomparably deeper. And Mexican pols are scared.

If he isn't assassinated—another grim Mexican tradition—or jailed on trumped-up charges, Lopez Obrador will be Mexico's next president. He's the people's choice. We must support fair treatment of him now. As president, he might not make us happy every day— but he could be the best thing that happened to Mexicans since they whipped the French army at Puebla on *Cinco de Mayo*.

Mesmerized by Iraq and the War on Terror, we neglect the neighbor whose future will have the greatest influence on our own. No foreign policy development would be better for the twenty-first-century United States than a prosperous, rule-of-law Mexico.

Standing by the Little Guys

New York Post

May 10, 2005

Every summer, we were reminded of Soviet crimes. Each weekend brought a different ethnic festival to the Pennsylvania coal towns. Whatever our family heritage, we gathered to eat kielbasa and pierogis, blinis and halupkies.

Folk-dance clubs from Saint This-or-That sweated through their costumes while accordions gasped. The adults drank beer all day and into the night.

But there was more. At a table between the beer tent and the ice-cream stand, a Lithuanian priest sold books on the armed resistance against the Soviets. Texts recounted the deeds of partisans who refused to lay down their arms when World War II ended.

As a polka band played across the park, Polish-Americans handed out pamphlets that kept the dream of a free nation alive. When their weekend arrived, Ukrainians lionized the freedom fighters who battled Stalin's commissars right into the 1950s.

Their tortured homelands remained alive in America, in church basements and parochial schools, in bars and at mass. The small-but-stubborn light of freedom burned against the Soviet darkness.

Those summer weekends shaped my life. As an Army officer, I would travel through the decomposing Soviet Union and then witness the strife Moscow instigated in the empire it had lost.

In Latvia in 1990, the Soviet Union still ruled. Nominally. But the Latvians and their Baltic neighbors had already grabbed freedom with both hands. And they weren't going to let go.

In the jewel-box city of Riga, a new museum chronicling Communist atrocities was second only to Auschwitz in its gut-punch power. Other exhibitions celebrated Latvia's cultural renaissance between the world wars, an astonishing display of creativity crushed by the Red Army.

The Nazis had come after the Soviets. Then the Russians returned. A third of Latvia's population perished—executed, starved, or devoured by the Gulag—a loss rate comparable to the ravages of the Black Death. Latvian men were beaten or shot for the crime of wearing eyeglasses—intellectuals were dangerous. Rape was used to break the people's will. The secret police settled in, imposing bureaucratic order on oppression. By the time I arrived, no Latvian wanted to speak Russian to me, preferring to stumble along in English or even German.

A few years later, during a brief thaw with Moscow, I got inside the Russian military archives and held the map Molotov and Ribbentrop used to negotiate their pact. Poland had been divided with a crayon, Baltic freedom ended with a scrawl.

My travels took me to Georgia, too, a land of stunning mountains and daunting hospitality. Centuries before, the Georgians had welcomed the czar's armies as fellow Christians and allies against Turkish and Persian invaders. But the Georgians didn't want any part of the Bolsheviks. The Red Cavalry crushed the people's dreams of freedom under their hooves.

Contrary to Vladimir Putin's grotesque claim, the collapse of the Soviet Union was no tragedy. It was a triumph for humankind. But Moscow's malevolence didn't end in 1991. I saw first-hand how the Russian security services worked to cripple newly independent states, with special efforts made to divide the Caucasus. Chechnya was only the bloodiest of Moscow's many crimes.

The "new, democratic" Russia tried to dismember Georgia. For a decade, Georgians suffered from weak governments, Kremlin interference, and unwanted Russian garrisons. The state became a kleptocracy.

At last, the people took matters into their own hands, staging a peaceful revolution that inspired later uprisings as far away as Lebanon.

But Moscow hasn't given up. It still regards the entire former Soviet empire as its "legitimate sphere of influence." As always, Russia's ambitions are mightier than its resources. If the world looks away, the results will again be tragic.

That's why President Bush's visits to Latvia and Georgia were vital. America finally took a stand against Russia's renewed aggression.

To us, these were brief stops, minor footnotes to history. But to the people of the Baltic states and the Caucasus, they confirmed their right to independence. Our president didn't mince words. He denounced the tragic outcome of the Yalta summit and stated clearly that the Soviets had been unwanted occupiers.

Bush's words and deeds mattered immensely. We must make up for time lost during the Clinton years, when incompetent "friends of Bill" insisted that our future lay with Russia—which was bound to become a model democracy. The newly independent states were treated as nuisances. And Moscow began to lust for a restored empire.

While cooperating rationally with Moscow, Bush made a vital course correction. First by supporting popular revolutions in Ukraine and Kyrgystan, and now by digging his heels into the soil of two brave countries—despite the Kremlin's protests—our president brought us back to the American tradition of sticking up for the little guy.

When Bush stood on the reviewing stand with Putin, he honored the single positive achievement of the Soviet era, the defeat of Nazi Germany. But when he bracketed the Kremlin's circus of nostalgia with visits to Latvia and Georgia, he honored something far greater: the triumph of freedom.

Myths of Globalization

USA Today

May 23, 2005

Every generation has its illusions. One of ours is that "globalization"—the internationalization of trade, services, investment, and information-sharing spurred by the internet—will shatter states and change humankind for the better. Although globalization itself is real enough, the visions imposed upon it by idealists and con men alike only make it harder to grasp what's happening—and what isn't.

Among the many myths surrounding globalization, two stand out: The notion that this phenomenon is new and, more dangerously, the claim that globalization will lead to an age of utopian peace. Those who see globalization as unprecedented simply don't know their history. Those who imagine that greater understanding, courtesy of the internet, will deliver an idyllic peace don't know humanity.

The first claim, that globalization is a wondrous child without historical parents, is the easiest to demolish. Greek culture of the age of Alexander influenced India's hairstyles, while eastern silks were sold in Caesar's Rome. Chinese porcelain and coins more than a thousand years old turn up in East Africa. Europeans of the Middle Ages paid a premium for pepper harvested a continent away. The Islamic world brokered trade between the West and the Far East. And that was before the discovery of the Americas.

There are more parallels with the past than differences. When Portuguese warships wrested control of the Indian Ocean from the

Ottomans and their clients at the dawn of the sixteenth century, they provided a model of strategic hegemony that remains in place today. Then, Lisbon's caravels and carracks controlled the spice trade. Today, U.S. Navy carriers guarantee the oil trade. The commodities have changed, but not the strategic geography.

Globalization today may proceed at a swifter pace, generate greater wealth, and touch more lives, but its essence is at least 2,500 years old. Over the centuries, the process has changed international relationships profoundly, but it has never changed human nature.

Which brings us to the second myth—one that also has ancient roots—that globalization will bring about peace. The human desire to believe in a worldly paradise is as old as it is understandable. And it always proves illusory, foundering on humanity's capacity for mischief, our deadly good intentions, and our ineradicable selfishness. Just as hippie communes fell apart because somebody had to do the dishes, predictions that war will become "unthinkable" fail because they embrace a dream and ignore human reality.

Historical eras of relative peace never came about because competing cultures agreed to cooperate, but because both sides were exhausted by war or because a hegemonic power laid down the rules. No peace lasted.

Predictions that humankind "learned its lesson" echoed in every age. On the eve of World War I, Western thinkers said that European wars were a thing of the past, that new weapons were too terrible, that societies had grown too enlightened, that international trade made war economically suicidal, and that workers of France, Germany, Austria-Hungary, Britain, Italy, and Russia had too much in common to march against each other. August 1914 saw a euphoric embrace of war.

Likewise, the collapse of the Soviet Union meant the "end of history." Democracy would sweep the world and put an end to conflict. Russia itself would become a Jeffersonian ideal. Well, democracy may still triumph at some future date, but the wreckage of the USSR failed to produce the Age of Aquarius. Instead, we saw bloodbaths in the Balkans, civil wars and genocide elsewhere, and a flood of passions the Cold War had dammed up.

We need not celebrate the human taste for violent solutions, but pretending the appetite doesn't exist only makes conflicts likelier and deadlier. As 9/11 should have taught us, today's hyperglob-alization means the globalization of insecurity. Our new enemies think as internationally as any statesman or corporate CEO.

Every claim that globalization equals peace ignores the facts. Suggestions that the world is flat may be right, but not in the ways intended. The new flat-worlders aren't the information-age aristo-crats rising above their fellow citizens. They're the millions of frightened believers who reject science and social change, while debasing religion to superstition. The inquisition is back.

That's the international phenomenon that should occupy our thoughts: The dynamic movements in world religions insisting their gods are intolerant and vengeful. If information is power, fanati-cism is nuclear power. Far from uniting humanity, globalization has made billions of people newly aware of economic disparities. Glob-alization threatens inherited values and traditional societies. And the internet, for all its practical utility, has been the greatest tool for spreading hatred since the development of movable type for the printing press.

Islamist fanatics, neo-Nazis, and pedophiles now can find each other with startling ease. Those who hid in dark corners a dozen years ago are all but unionized today. The real global brotherhoods of the internet age are conspiracies of hatred. This is an age of new possibilities for the most talented humans. Yet it is also an age of bigotries reborn, with digital propaganda as the midwife.

Yes, our future is rich with new possibilities, but it will take a firm sense of reality to maximize those opportunities. The latest edi-tion of globalization may do many things, positive and negative, but it will not change human nature. Another enduring lie is that the future belongs to the dreamers. It belongs to those who go forward with open eyes.

Return of the Tribes

New York Post

June 1, 2005

Today, the Dutch vote on the proposed European Union constitution. They're expected to reject it, as the French did Sunday. But whatever the result of the referendum, something's happening in Europe that international elites swore was impossible.

Tribes are back.

In Europe, they're called nations, which sounds more distinguished. But the French voters who refused to submerge their identity in a greater European state behaved as tribally as any Hutus or Tutsis in central Africa—or any Arab clan in Iraq.

Certainly, there are practical issues at stake. The French fear an invasion of their welfare state by hardworking East Europeans. They dread hints of a market economy and Turkey's prospective membership in the EU. The Dutch are still reeling from the failure of their multicultural experiment and the grisly rise of Islamic fundamentalism.

But the underlying cause of the voter shift from continental integration to the *nouveau* chauvinism erupting from Paris to Moscow is far cruder and more explosive: the undiminished importance of group identity, of primal belonging.

If anything should strike us about this turn from Greater Europe back to a Europe of competing parts, it's how wildly the intellectuals were wrong and how ineffectual elite power monopolies proved in the end. For a half-century, Europe's approved thinkers insisted that a new age had begun, that historical identities were dying. The wealth and power of a borderless Europe would rival, if not exceed, that of the United States.

Instead, we see a squabbling, grasping continent. Far from feeling solidarity with their Polish or Hungarian counterparts, French farmers view them as the enemy. Labor unions in Germany and France have turned Slavic job-seekers into bogeymen who'll rob the daily bread from the native-born.

The Dutch feel doubly under siege, invaded by an immigrant community that rejects their values, while simultaneously in danger of being gobbled up by a leviathan Europe that would seize control of their destiny.

For Europe's political elites—accustomed to docile, bought-off populations—the turn against further EU integration has been an enormous shock.

The German vote that thumped Chancellor Gerhard Schroeder last month was a vote against globalization and a European meta-identity. In his first public appearance after Sunday's "Non!" vote, President Jacques Chirac looked like a walking corpse.

Satisfying to watch? You bet. But the pleasure we can take in the humiliation of Schroeder and Chirac masks the fact that, for all their rhetoric and anti-American posturing, they were do-nothing, status-quo leaders whose authority never rose above the nuisance level. We may come to miss their fecklessness and gourmet-level pandering as nationalism swells among their electorates.

Whenever Europe's nationalist tide flows back in, the innocent drown.

The EU is far from Europe's first attempt at integration. The medieval church exercised transnational authority until the Reformation galvanized German identity. The multicultural Habsburg empire split in two, thanks to primitive nationalism. After the Great War, its Austro-Hungarian remnant shattered under nationalist pressures.

Group identity is indestructible. Despite genocide, Armenia rose again. Poland's back. The phony Yugoslav identity died in a storm of bullets, leaving behind antique nations. The Soviet empire dissolved into bloody nationalism. Irish pubs have conquered the world, but it's hard to find an EU-themed watering hole.

Forget the genetic arguments against racial purity. Ignore the historical facts. What matters is who men and women think they are. Belief is *always* stronger than truth. It certainly would appear rational for Europeans to bury their differences and subscribe to a greater, unified identity. But humankind isn't rational. That's been the crucial lesson of our time.

What man or woman on that old, bloodstained continent says, "I'm a European" with the same conviction he or she says, "I'm French" or "I'm Polish" or "I'm Russian"? The last time we heard that Europe had overcome its national identities was on the eve of World War I.

France may not invade Germany this summer, but we need to escape the illusion of a new, pacifist Europe too sophisticated to repeat past errors. This is the continent that perfected genocide and ethnic cleansing, the source of history's grimmest wars.

Europe may be good for some ugly surprises as its states struggle with faltering economies, declining birthrates, angry Islamic minorities, and a lack of opportunity for the young that resembles the plight of the developing world. Expecting Europe's nationalities to behave is as foolish as hoping to beat the house in Vegas.

We may discover that Europe has changed less than any other part of the globe, that all the bureaucrats in Brussels can no more suppress the local tribes than could the Roman legions. For all of our concern about a European superstate, we may live to regret the return to a Europe of nations.

The Smart Way to Aid Africa

New York Post

June 8, 2005

Yesterday, Prime Minister Tony Blair lobbied President Bush for more aid to Africa, and the two leaders agreed to an ambitious program to ease the debts of deserving nations. The obvious question for Americans was "What's in it for us?"

Certainly, there are moral reasons to help that tortured continent. But set those aside; here's what we get out of doing the right thing:

Countering Islamist extremism: Despite the bombings of our embassies in Kenya and Tanzania back in the '90s, terrorism has made few inroads in East Africa—the continent's key strategic terrain.

Long present along the Indian Ocean coast, Swahili Islam has yet to be poisoned by Wahhabi venom. But the extremists are on the move. And social, political, and economic disparities nurture the seeds of hatred. Terrorists view Africa as a realm of opportunity.

The problem isn't out of control. Not yet. But the time to act is now. We must assist those states that are doing their best to help themselves. Our habit of waiting for a crisis to explode is too expensive today.

Building markets and securing resources: African economies are small compared to those of East Asia or even Latin America. But that only means they have more room to grow. Would you rather have gotten in on Cisco Systems in 1989 or 1999? Those who take a long-term view of Africa's potential—as South Africa, the regional powerhouse, does—will do well for themselves by doing good for others.

Human capital: The first exploitation of Africa's human capital was the slave trade. The twenty-first century could turn that old injustice around by allowing Africa's untapped human capital to interact freely with the global economy. Forget the negative stories we all hear. Firsthand experience taught me that Africa is rich with human potential—the most important resource of the future.

OK. But, beyond debt relief, how can we help? Without enriching corrupt officials and throwing tax dollars away?

Concentrate our efforts: By trying to do a little bit of everything, we end up doing nothing sufficiently well to make a decisive difference.

President Bush's initiative to help African and Caribbean states fight AIDS is a powerful program that hasn't received the acknowledgement it deserves. But as we fight AIDS today, we need to envision Africa's tomorrow.

Emergency assistance will still be necessary, but it's time for the United States to specialize in a single type of *continuous* foreign aid.

Educate the people: Nothing would be of more use to Africans than a long-term, comprehensive commitment from the United States to help them educate themselves at every level, from primary school through advanced-degree programs.

If you want to reduce disease, educate the people. If you want to break down violent rivalries, provide unbiased education. If you want to build economies, train workers. If you want to foster democracy, promote literacy.

In short, if you want to help Africa stop being a basket case, concentrate ruthlessly on education. Let the Europeans do the feel-good projects. Let celebrities give away granola bars. Stick to the mission of helping people learn.

Some African countries are significantly ahead of others in educational progress, but every one of them could use our help. Governments may be wary—despite their rhetoric, political bosses like to keep the poor ignorant (a rule that applies to our own inner cities as much as it does to Africa). But the people desperately want education.

When I visited Mozambique—one of the world's poorest countries—no one asked me for a handout. They asked about books and scholarships.

Even South Africa suffers from educational lost generations, thanks to the decades-long freedom struggle.

If we concentrated on the former English and Portuguese colonies, it could make a greater difference than any other form of aid—while working to our long-term strategic advantage.

But we would have to do it right. That means weathering criticism from demagogues and avoiding waste. Meaningful educational assistance isn't about state-of-the-art classrooms built by carpetbagging contractors. It's about qualified, adequately compensated teachers. Don't subsidize show projects. Train teachers and provide basic facilities. And insist on nonideological textbooks.

Such a commonsense approach would meet resistance both in Africa and here at home. Some countries would demand to control the aid money themselves. The answer should *always* be no. Cooperation, yes—blind trust, uh-uh. Been there, done that, lost the silk T-shirt.

Africa's elites have stolen enough. If a country isn't serious about helping its people, our aid should go to states that genuinely want to make progress.

Here at home, we would have to fight off no end of interest groups with pernicious agendas. Just as we would need to resist left-wing propaganda in African textbooks, we would have to stick to hard science in any textbooks we funded. No creationism from the right, and no loopy political correctness from the left. Africans need facts, not fantasies.

If any rule applies globally, it's that education is the key to the future. Islamist extremists have taken that message to heart. In Africa, they fund religious schools that teach medieval hatred. Without an alternative, parents send their children to the bigots.

While we need to be wary of well-intentioned rock-star demands for hurling money into an African mosh pit, we're foolish not to do more for a continent whose awful press disguises enormous potential. If we give wisely now, we will profit greatly tomorrow.

Africa is as hungry for knowledge as it is for food. If we help provide the education, the continent will learn to feed itself.

Pyrrhic Terror

New York Post

July 8, 2005

It was inevitable. Terrorists struck again. In one of the West's great capitals. Killing innocent civilians. Winning the day but losing the greater struggle.

Yesterday, during the morning rush, Islamist terrorists triggered bombs on three of London's Underground trains and a signature double-decker bus. They killed thirty-seven people and severely wounded approximately a hundred, injuring as many as a thousand. They brought the city to a halt, interrupted the start of the G-8 summit, and dominated the headlines once again.

And they damaged their own cause far more than the magnificent city they bombed.

At present, the footage of bloodied victims obscures valuable lessons. About how little the terrorists have learned and how limited their resources have become. About how much progress Western governments have made in coping with attacks. And about our enemies' hunger for publicity.

Once again, the terrorists demonstrated tactical skill, the ability to coordinate attacks against a carefully chosen series of targets. Reasoning correctly that Britain's security apparatus would focus on the G-8 summit in Scotland, they saw a window of opportunity.

They also grasped that London's restrictions on private vehicles in the city center made the public transportation system an especially lucrative target. And although the attacks were planned to interrupt the G-8 meeting, Wednesday's announcement that London would host the 2012 Olympics may have moved up the date of the strikes. The terrorists upstaged two big events at once.

So far so good for al Qa'eda's European tentacles. Now consider how counterproductive their attack was:

• Instead of intimidating the heads of state at Gleneagles—from South Africa's Thabo Mbeki to Mexico's Vicente Fox—the terrorists reminded them all of the need for unity. If you catch a rerun of Tony Blair reading their joint statement, study the worried face of Jacques Chirac. He knows it could have been Paris.

• The terrorists expect a repeat of Madrid, with British support for free Iraq collapsing. But Londoners aren't madrileños. During the Blitz, they withstood massive Nazi terror attacks night after night. They've endured decades of IRA bombings. The English intelligentsia will find a way to blame America, but the British people will not yield to terror.

• They've spoiled the party for all those sympathizers in the West who had turned their attention away from Abu Ghraib for five minutes to demand more aid for Africa. As President Bush pointed out, the terrorists disrupted a summit focused on poverty. Africans watching events unfold will realize that their continent stands to lose far more than London did. Even a rock star or two might figure this one out.

• Despite the drama of the attacks, it's revealing that the terrorists couldn't do more. 7/7 *wasn't* 9/11. It wasn't even Madrid. Not every attack can be prevented, but Britain's tough antiterror efforts clearly limited what the terrorists could achieve.

The terrorists did all they could to maximize damage, detonating their bombs in confined spaces where blast effects are enhanced. Yet the terror cells in Spain assembled much greater quantities of explosives than the terrorists in Britain were able to do. And they couldn't construct dirty bombs employing radioactive material or biological weapons. The terrorists weren't nearly as potent as they would have liked to be.

The world also witnessed a superb British performance. The planning and drills worked. The initial press conference held by London's emergency-response authorities was orderly, sober—and inspiring. It was a classic illustration of the British lion's coolness under fire.

The battlefield always looks messy, but this time the headquarters swiftly gained control. London's response to the attack appears to have been a model of how to do it right. Buses were running last night, and the Underground planned to resume operation today.

• Even before the London bombings, terrorist leaders had begun to reveal a great potential weakness: They've become addicted to celebrity. From Osama bin Laden to Abu Musab al Zarqawi, they've manipulated the global media with finesse and even brilliance in the past, but now they appear to be trapped in celebrity culture.

They can't stand to lose the spotlight for fifteen minutes. With the headlines shifting to Africa's needs and global warming, the London attacks were as much a tantrum as Tom Cruise jumping around on Oprah's sofa.

The terrorists understand that the global media are their sole remaining hope to turn the tide. 9/11 rebounded terribly on them, bringing an angry America into their refuges—and they can't dislodge us. The beheading videos backfired, too, once the novelty wore off and Muslims grew embarrassed. 7/7 will be another strategic reverse, confounding their hopes to divide the civilized world and reviving our unity instead.

The terrorists need to stay in the news to stay in the game, to keep the recruits and money flowing. Above all, the London bombings were a publicity stunt. Voices on the left will soon tell us that the War on Terror has failed, citing yesterday's attacks, but the terrorists know just how well our efforts are working.

London will return to business as usual. But Iraq and Afghanistan won't. We're not going to back down. Terrorists will draw blood for years to come, but they will never rule another state.

It's going to take time, but in the end their fellow Muslims will destroy the terrorists—if the casualty count in London were broken down by religion, dozens of Muslims would be on the roll of victims.

Islamist terror isn't a sign of a great religious revival. It's a cult in love with death, not with any god. In the end, it's terror for terror's sake. Since 9/11, more Muslims have been its victims than Christians or Jews.

Americans—especially New Yorkers—feel a solidarity beyond words with our British cousins. But the best thing we can do isn't to offer pity but to renew our own determination to combat terror for "as long as it takes."

Don't mourn. Fight back.

Not So Anti-American

New York Post

August 10, 2005

"I think Mr. Osama does many good things," Hassan told me two weeks ago. "I think Mr. Bush is to blame for these problems. What do you think?"

We were sitting under the thatched roof of a "hotel" that lacked electricity and running water on the Muslim-dominated coast of Tanzania. The Indian Ocean shone blue beyond grim shanties. Discarded now, socialist doctrine had done deep damage to a society already hindered by Islam.

So I wasn't surprised by Hassan's opening gambit. On the contrary, I had been pleased by how rare anti-American views are in East Africa. But I figured I'd found an America-hater at last.

I was wrong. Hassan was just a nervous young man showing off for a moment. He promptly moved on from Monsieur bin Laden to admiring questions about the American system of government.

Hassan's dream—shared with nearly every young Muslim I met in East Africa—was a scholarship to the United States.

Critics may carp that surveys show unusually strong pro-American sentiment in Kenya and Tanzania, but experience has convinced me that serious anti-Americanism abroad is wildly exaggerated by pollsters with agendas and a sensation-hungry media.

From Indonesian cities declared "hotbeds of Islamic fundamentalism" to that darkest of continents, Europe, I've found far more visa-seekers than would-be suicide bombers. After about thirty seconds of blowing off steam, my interlocutors from Sulawesi to Strassbourg only wanted to know how to get a green card.

Don't be fooled: America remains the most inspiring symbol in the world. A minority of a minority may actually prefer punitive religion, gender apartheid, poverty, and filth, but much of the superficial rhetoric you hear directed against our country is a sign of jealousy and longing.

There are real America-haters out there, of course. The worst are deadly, and they'll menace us for decades to come. But there are no long lines of would-be émigrés outside of any Saudi, Iranian, or Chinese embassies. No Africans or Latin Americans dream of building a better life for their families in Russia or Syria.

The American dream is still very much alive. For countless human beings around the world, the United States remains *the* shining city on a hill.

We forget how blessed we are. Having seen bitter poverty, disease, miserable corruption, and life reduced to the most basic needs, I find it increasingly hard to put up with complaints about our country from spoiled professors and actors grown rich in a society they disdain (it makes me want to add a personal touch to their lattes). Even conservatives often underestimate the transformative genius of America and the power of our ideas.

We live in the one country on earth where pessimism is *never* warranted.

I've spent a month in a different part of Africa each of the last three years. And I've met one truly ferocious anti-American on that continent. She was an absolute nut case who reminded me of those domestic leftists who blame America for their self-wrought misfortunes and personal discontents.

On the other hand, I've been taken aback by African fury toward "imperialist" Arabs and militant Islam. Nashville at its most patriotic has nothing on one educated Kenyan who all but volunteered to swim to Pakistan and kill Osama bin Laden single-handedly.

Foreign correspondents, academics, and even some of our diplomats will disagree with the claims made in this column. A few will sincerely believe that the world despises America.

Let me tell you why my experience has been different from theirs. It's simple: We speak with different people.

Diplomats listen to politicians. Academics confer with their fellow academics. And journalists—especially the lazier sort—crib from local journalists or interview politicians and academics.

Imagine trying to form a picture of America by interviewing only Ted Kennedy, Ward Churchill, and Dan Rather.

Myself, I avoid embassies, rarely interview politicians, and seek out students, not professors. I like to listen to shopkeepers, mullahs, and missionaries, to workers, businessmen, medical personnel, and the local equivalent of Joe Sixpack. And I never claim to be a journalist. That reveals a very different picture of any society.

Take your own poll. The next time you go on vacation or a business trip to a developing country, stroll off the resort or skip the lunch at the hotel restaurant. Don't be afraid. Work past the touts who prey on tourists everywhere and wander the streets. Just for an hour or two. And let conversations happen.

Once you get past the preliminaries, you may experience something marvelous: yearning fellow human beings helping you see afresh how blessed you were to be born, or to have become, a U.S. citizen.

You are the envy of the world.

Sure, anti-Americanism is out there. I know it. Maybe one of these years I'll find it in some Saudi madrassah or French ministry. Along the way, I'll be listening to the dreams of those millions who adore a country they've never even seen.

The Other Jihad

USA Today

August 24, 2005

The mosque stood empty beside the road in a Christian town in Kenya. Funded by Saudis, it wasn't meant for worshippers. It was meant to stake a claim.

The mosque annoyed the locals. Windows were broken. A goat grazed in the garbage-speckled yard. Yet that shabby mosque was part of an extremist campaign that threatens widespread strife in the years ahead.

On a trip to Kenya and Tanzania last month, I saw recently built mosques wherever I went. Even along the predominantly Muslim coast, there were far more mosques and madrassahs than the worshippers needed. I counted seven mosques along one street in a Mombasa slum—most of them new but neglected.

The construction boom is part of what my personal observation convinces me is "the other jihad," the slow-roll attempt by fundamentalists from the Arabian Peninsula to reclaim East Africa for the faith of the Prophet. We dismiss Osama bin Laden's dream of reestablishing the caliphate, Islam's bygone empire, as madness. But Saudis, Yemenis, Omanis, and oil-rich Gulf Arabs are every bit as determined as bin Laden to reassert Muslim domination of the lands Islam once ruled.

No region is as vulnerable as Africa. The differences between the Saudi ruling family and bin Laden aren't so much about goals as about methods. The Saudis were furious over the 1998 embassy bombings in Nairobi and Dar es Salaam not because of the vicious-ness of the acts, but because the attacks threatened to call the West's attention to quiet subversion by fundamentalist Wahhabis in the region.

For the Muslims of the Arabian Peninsula, ties to Africa's Indian Ocean coast go back more than a millennium. By the four-teenth century, trading cities such as Kilwa (now a ruin) and Mom-basa were opulent outposts of Islam. One dream shared by the House of Saud and Islamist terrorists is the reclamation of the old Swahili Coast, where their ancestors grew rich trading ivory, gold, and slaves.

Arabs still regard black Africans as inferior, fit only to be sub-jects. As a result, their charities don't fund clinics, universities, or sanitation systems. They just keep on building mosques, staking graphic claims to a once and future empire of faith.

Even in the United States, Saudi-funded Quranic schools encourage religious apartheid. While events have forced their mul-lahs to tone down public hate-speech directed toward the West, Saudi madrassas never encourage young people to integrate into their host society. They praise rigid separation.

In East Africa, this takes the form of pressuring the young to devote themselves to studying the Quran. This prevents Muslims from getting a practical education. As a result, they remain unqual-ified for the best jobs, which are taken by Christians with university degrees, further exacerbating antagonism.

The Saudis and their accomplices know exactly what they're doing. They don't want a "separate but equal" system. Separate and unequal does the trick, creating a sense of deprivation, of being cheated, among Muslims and driving a wedge down the middle of fragile societies. The last thing the bigots of the Arabian Peninsula want to see would be prosperous, patriotic, well-integrated Muslim communities in Africa.

Nor is this slow-motion jihad confined to the coast. It takes still uglier forms in the interior. Saudi money and arms smuggled from Yemen keep tribal strife alive in northern Kenya, Uganda, Sudan, Ethiopia, and of course, Somalia.

During my stay in Kenya, nearly a hundred tribal people were massacred near the Ethiopian border. The religious undertone of the slaughter—which included the executions of schoolchildren—was played down. The Kenyan government fears a wider conflagration and quietly accepts its inability to control its northern borders. But extremist sentiment is growing, while Kenya's policy of benign neglect collapses.

The jihad in eastern Africa stretches from the butchery in Sudan down to Tanzanian villages where poverty was exacerbated by decades of socialism. It takes multiple forms, from a name-calling contest with émigrés returning to Somaliland from the West to support for separatist movements on Zanzibar and Pemba islands.

No one has called the Saudis or their partners to account. This matters. Kenya and Tanzania have largely avoided the succession of tragedies that crippled Africa in the postindependence era. But the tension between Kenya's Christian majority and Muslim minority, or between Tanzania's roughly equal factions, never quite disappeared. Now, Arab money threatens to undermine the fragile unity of these struggling, yet hopeful states.

Religious freedom goes only so far. Building mosques and madrassas would be tolerable were their purpose not frankly subversive. A strong society such as our own can overcome such hate-based shenanigans. But the stakes could not be higher and the danger could not be greater for the struggling states of eastern Africa.

The violent jihad waged by those who hijacked Islam in the Middle East is our immediate challenge. Even so, terrorists from the Horn of Africa have already been implicated in the London subway bombings and other attacks. The time for engagement is now—not after widespread radicalization has destroyed the future for millions of Africans and drawn still more states into the maelstrom of terror.

Global War on Women

USA Today

September 27, 2005

The greatest social revolution in history is under way all around us: the emancipation of women. Advanced in our own society, elsewhere the battle for women's rights lies at the heart of colossal struggles over the future of great religions and civilizations.

The Washington establishment would shrink from any such claim, but the Global War on Terror is a fight over the social, economic, and cultural roles of women. The core issues for the terrorists are the interpretation of God's will and the continued oppression of women. Nothing so threatens Islamic extremists as the freedom Western women enjoy.

The sudden transition of women from men's property to men's partners in our own country unleashed dazzling creative energies. In the historical blink of an eye, we doubled our effective human capital—and made our society immeasurably more humane. Our half-century of stunning economic growth has many roots, but none goes deeper than the expansion of opportunities for women.

But such unprecedented freedom threatens traditional societies. Behavior patterns that prevailed for millennia are suddenly in doubt. Relationships that granted males the power of life and death over female relatives have disappeared from successful cultures. Defensively, the failing cultures left behind cling harder than ever to the old ways amid the tumult of global change.

The true symbols of the War on Terror are the Islamic veil and the two-piece woman's business suit.

The math is basic. No civilization that excludes half its population from full participation in society and the economy can compete with the United States and its key allies. Yet Middle Eastern societies, especially, have dug in their heels to resist change. Some, such as Turkey, Pakistan, and Iran, have tumbled backward.

Islamist terrorists have formed the last, great boy's club, meeting in caves and warning girls to stay out—or, in the case of the 9/11 hijacker Mohammed Atta, demanding that women be kept from his grave to avoid polluting it. Their vision offers women fewer rights by far than those enjoyed by the wives of the prophet Mohammed. They are women-hating sadists for whom faith is an excuse. Their fears are primal.

The good news is that the forces of oppression can make plenty of tactical mischief but can't achieve strategic success. No society in which women are veiled and sequestered can achieve the dynamism and force of one in which women are senators, judges, CEOs, doctors, and military pilots. Freedom will win, if not swiftly.

The bad news is that this is a truly global struggle involving not only Islamist thugs terrified by female sexuality, but also reactionary forces in our own society. The Global War Against Women is still being waged on the home front, too.

Without questioning the integrity of those who believe that life begins at conception, the struggle to overturn *Roe v. Wade* can also be viewed as an attempt to turn back the clock on women's freedom. Opposing such a reversal isn't a matter of thinking abortion admirable, but of accepting the magnificent revolutionary principle that no man has a right to tell any woman what she can or cannot do with her body.

Attempts to interfere with another citizen's liberty are worthy of Osama bin Laden, not of Americans.

Likewise, the ideologically driven reluctance of the Food and Drug Administration to approve the "morning-after pill" for general use is a vestige of patriarchal tyranny that would please Abu Musab al Zarqawi, al Qa'eda's leader in Iraq. Longing to restore the tyrannical pattern that governed social relations down the ages, our extremists demand that women's options be restricted, that their bodies be treated as chattels of the state.

Nor should we be surprised that women stand among those who would deny rights to other women. Their counterparts are the African crones who demand that young girls undergo genital mutilation just as they did, or the women of the Middle East who insist that wearing a chador protects them. They are the champions of the small morality of rules over the greater morality of freedom.

The greatest moral advance has been the attainment of basic human rights by women. It's also the most threatening development to those daunted by change, who cling to a mythologized past and fear the future—whether in a Saudi-funded madrassa or protesting outside a U.S. Planned Parenthood clinic. Around the world, troubled souls continue to insist that women are the source of sin and must be kept in line for their own good. Theirs is a prescription for suffering, dreariness, and stagnation.

In traveling the globe, I've witnessed far more instances of the mistreatment of women than I care to recall, but the one that always leaps to mind is local and superficially benign: In the southern heat of a Washington summer, it's common to see a male Middle Eastern tourist comfortably dressed in a polo shirt and shorts trailed by a staggering woman wrapped from head to toe in flapping black robes, eyes peering out through a mask. It offends me to meet that image in my country—or anywhere.

We do not think of our troops abroad as fighting for women's rights. But they are. This is the titanic struggle of our time, the liberation of fully half of humanity. Islamist terror is only one aspect of it. But we can be certain of two things: In the end, freedom will win. And no society that torments women will succeed in the twenty-first century.

Survival Strategy: Middle Eastern Islam, Darwin, and Terrorism

Armed Forces Journal

February 2006

As the Christmas holiday approached, it was time to talk about terrorism. I spent part of a December afternoon in a sterile conference room symbolic of strategic thought in Washington ("Avoid the virus of originality!"). Following a discussion of Middle Eastern Islam's power to generate suicide bombers, a miffed senior official challenged the notion that religion had anything whatsoever to do with the phenomenon.

As sincere as he was wrong, his view of the world was typical of our intelligence and policy communities. The official insisted that faith wasn't really a motivating factor because his agency's compilation of data on suicide bombers revealed that most had either personal grievances—perhaps a relative killed, abused, or imprisoned—or simply a sense of humiliation. Mistaking the trigger for the entire gun, he clung to the last century's rationalist view of the world. The official just could not make the leap of faith required to accept religion as a strategic factor.

He was standing in a downpour, insisting it wasn't the rain that was making him wet. Suicide bombers had worldly grievances, and that was that. The promise of paradise made no difference. It was typical mirror-imaging, all about the usual suspect factors dear to the academic world and Washington think tanks. The official refused to reflect on the obvious: A wide variety of populations around the world have grievances, from Chinese peasants to the minority population of New Orleans, from indigenous populations in Latin America to the Africans tormented by Zimbabwe's Robert Mugabe. Yet neither the Irish Republican Army nor Sudan's Christian tribes, not Falun Gong or Corsican separatists produced suicide bombers. While the world beyond the Muslim heartlands has generated terrorists aplenty, the phenomenon of suicide bombing remains overwhelmingly Islamic and Middle Eastern.

Religion isn't only a matter of personal faith, but of social and psychological context as well. While we struggle to deny it, the religious environment of today's Middle East is acutely conducive to violent self-sacrifice, to willing death in violent jihad. Tumbling backward from its bitter confrontation with the modern world, Middle Eastern Islam's culture makes paradise a given for the believer who sacrifices his life in the struggle against the infidel, the Crusader, the Jew, or the apostate. (On the other hand, Western atheist suicide bombers are in notably short supply.) The suicide bomber need not even appear to have been especially religious as remembered by his acquaintances: The Middle Eastern Muslim's belief in paradise after death is as casual and pervasive as was the medieval European's faith in the existence of a hell with horned devils. The reward of paradise is assumed.

Suicide bomber X or Y certainly may feel that his people have been shamed or that his sister has been embarrassed, and that he must respond violently to the antagonist in question. Yet while plenty of other cultures generate hyperviolent behavior under stress, none but Middle Eastern Islam has given rise to the cult of the suicide bomber. The promise of paradise, with its literal treats, is undeniably a crucial determinant, whether at the subconscious or conscious level. The culture of contemporary Middle Eastern Islam makes death an appealing option.

Still, after the Koran and the hadiths have been studied and analyzed, after allowances have been made for the mesmerizing personas of terrorist chieftains and all the practical catalysts for action have been calculated, the question remains: Why has the cult of the suicide bomber developed so swiftly today, and why is it rooted in the Middle East and not elsewhere (from Indonesia to Kosovo, Muslims behave violently but not suicidally)?

The answer is timely, given the current fuss about intelligent design versus the theory of evolution in our own country: Suppose that Darwin was right conceptually, but failed to grasp that religion is a highly evolved survival strategy for human collectives?

FAITH AS A STRATEGIC FACTOR

Once a human collective expands beyond the family, clan, and tribe, decisive unity demands a higher organizing principle sufficiently powerful to entice the individual to sacrifice himself for the common good of a group whose identity is no longer defined by blood ties. A man or woman will die for the child of his or her flesh, but how can the broader collective inspire one stranger to volunteer his life to guarantee the survival of a stranger whose only tie is one of abstract identity?

No organizing principle, not even nationalism (a secular, debased religion), has proven so reliable and galvanizing as religious faith. Religion not only unites, it unites exclusively. Throughout history, religious wars have proved the cruelest in their execution and the most difficult to end satisfactorily (toss in racial differences and you have a formula for permanent struggle). The paradox is that, in pursuit of a "more godly" way of life, human beings have justified the slaughter of millions of other human beings down the centuries.

Even in adversity or miserable defeat, religious identity has allowed human collectives to survive when linear analysis would foretell their inevitable disintegration. Without their powerful monotheism and the conviction that they are chosen by their god, would any Jews survive today as practitioners of their faith? Even in the Diaspora and in the course of two millennia of pogroms that culminated in a massive, organized genocide, Jews withstood the worst that humankind could direct at them. Their survival and ultimate triumph cannot be explained by the safe, academic (and politically correct) factors beloved of our analysts. Faith provided the unity—even in geographical separation and during immense suffering—to preserve the genetic collective.

Could anything but a powerful new faith have united the backward tribes of Arabia into the conquering armies that exploded out of the desert thirteen centuries ago to conquer so much of the world in Allah's name? From the beginning of the sixteenth century into the early twentieth, European conquerors justified them-selves—not always cynically—in terms of the apostolic spread of their redemptive faith. Religious fervor fueled phenomenal courage not only among missionaries, but among the Victorian era's "martyr officers," from Gordon in Khartoum to Conolly in Bukhara. In Rome's centuries of decline, her legions were held together more by the cult of Mithras (and their own self-interest) than by allegiance to any caesar.

And faiths are never more ferocious than when they're cornered. The responses of the human collective to an external threat can be delayed by various practical factors, from physical weakness to internecine struggles, but when the empire of faith strikes back, it does so ruthlessly. The crusades were, indeed, barbaric acts of aggression, rampaging from the Iberian Peninsula to the banks of the Jordan (and the conquest of the New World may be viewed as the last and grandest Christian crusade). But the crusades did not occur in a strategic vacuum: They were Europe's response to the Islamic jihad that had taken Muslim warriors to the Marne and dis-possessed Christianity of all of its birthright cities—not only Jerusalem, but Alexandria, the cradle of Christian thought and doc-trine, Antioch, Damascus, Philadelphia, Ephesus, and so on.

It's often been noted that the first crusade achieved an aston-ishing military upset by not only reaching the Holy Land but con-quering Jerusalem (where the crusaders indulged in a stunning massacre not only of Muslims and Jews, but of eastern-rite Chris-tians, too). The issue raised less frequently is: How were the frag-mented European powers—deadly rivals—able to unite long enough to conquer so many of the wealthiest cities of the then-dominant Islamic world? Could any factor other than faith have excited and sustained such unity? Greed might have been satisfied closer to home. Even beyond the historian's observation that the pope sought to exploit crusading ventures as a means to staunch the endemic bloodletting in Europe itself or Marxist arguments about surplus population, and allowing that there was plenty of dis-unity and calculation among the crusaders and their various back-ers during their two centuries in the Levant, the phenomenon of the crusades cannot be explained without the fuel of faith.

However false they judge the tenets of religion to be, even non-believers recognize the power of faith to shape (or misshape) individual lives. Cynics may snort at the notion of harp-wielding, nightgowned angels with feathered wings, declaring religion nothing but a con to keep the workers and peasants in line, but they cannot deny the psychological comfort provided by the promise—true or false—of a better life beyond the mortal flesh. Religious conviction is a mighty force in the life of a man or woman of faith, and no scientist would argue against the empirical data to that point. Why is it, then, that we are so anxious to avoid recognizing the far greater impact of religious beliefs shared by an embattled human collective?

Threatened faiths lash out. They have done so from first-century Palestine through the Albigensian crusades, from Stalinist purges (Marxism was the degenerate religion of Europe's twentieth-century intellectuals) through intercommunal bloodlettings in post-independence Africa and on to the vicious backlash from defeated Islam today.

Even religious wars within faiths reek of biological survival strategies. The oppressive dominance of Latinate Christianity summoned the north-European Reformation as a response (along with no end of massacres over the contents of the communion cup). The inextinguishable rivalry between Shi'a Islam, with its Persian heart, and the Sunni schools of the Arabs is also about group competition for survival and alpha status. While overarching faiths compete strategically, subordinate branches of any religion function as local survival strategies for their adherents. Despite all the aberrations that can be cited, the development and tenacity of organized religion is evolution at its purest and fiercest.

Beyond blood, nothing binds human beings together more powerfully than a shared religious creed. No heart is mightier or crueler than the one beating in the breast of the holy warrior. And no other factor provides so rich an excuse for mass murder as stern faith.

THE ANALYTICAL MISMATCH

The executive who argued that faith wasn't a consequential factor in the making of suicide bombers was an archetype: The well-educated Westerner who, even if he or she engages in perfunctory attendance at church or temple, has been thoroughly secularized in matters of education, intellect, and the parameters of permissible thought. Secular, analytical thought in the West today is every bit as close-minded as the worldview of the inquisitors who forced Galileo to recant. Its true believers have simply exchanged one set of rigid doctrines for another.

Without the personal experience of transformative faith, it's nearly impossible for analysts to comprehend the power of religious belief as a decisive motivating factor. One of the most dangerous asymmetries we face is the mismatch between our just-the-facts-ma'am analysts and the visionary ferocity of our enemies.

Merely recognizing the problem isn't enough. Overwhelmingly, analysts active in the intelligence community or in Washington think tanks (to say nothing of those bizarre mental prisons, university campuses) face a terrible challenge in adjusting to the intellectual demands posed by Islamist terrorism. Approaching the problem with a maximum of integrity would mean discarding virtually every theory they have been taught. Understanding the rhapsodic violence of Abu Musab al Zarqawi or even the seductive rhetoric of Osama bin Laden requires us to jettison the crippling heritage of the Enlightenment and much of the rationalist tradition.

Whenever I brief that we are at war with devils, heads nod dully, passing off the terminology as aimed at a theatrical effect. But it isn't. The devils are real. The Western intellect simply cannot bear to see them.

WHAT WILL IT TAKE?

Religion is, to say the least, a volatile topic. Even those national leaders willing to come to grips with the need for a tough response to Islamist terror take great pains to assure the world that ours is not a religious war and that the Muslim faith is as peaceful as a new-born sheep in a meadow full of wildflowers. Islam is, of course, an umbrella faith, covering forward-looking movements as well as reactionary, violence-prone sects. But we nonetheless must come to grips with the extent to which Middle Eastern Islam itself has become the problem—not only the cause of structural failure, but an impetus for confessional violence (defensive violence, in the

Darwinian context, since it seeks to preserve the threatened community—although it's savagely aggressive from our perspective).

We shy away from a fundamental question of our time: What if Islam is the problem?

Some months ago, an Army general made headlines through his politically incorrect remarks about Islam and Christianity. A devout religious believer, he spoke in a church, in uniform. My personal response to the media's self-righteous, self-important horror was twofold: Yeah, the guy displayed poor judgment by letting loose at a religious event with his fruit salad on his chest. But I also recognized that, as a believer himself, that general was vastly better equipped to grasp the nature of our enemies than our legions of think-tank experts and timid analysts. Put bluntly, it takes one to know one.

If we are serious about understanding our present—and future—enemies, we will have to rid ourselves of both the plague of political correctness (a bipartisan disease so insidious its victims may not recognize the infection debilitating them) and the failed cult of rationalism as the only permissible analytical tool for understanding human affairs. We will need to shift our focus from the individual to the collective and ask forbidden questions, from inquiring about the deeper nature of humankind (which appears to have little to do with our obsession with the individual) to the biological purpose of religion.

The latter issue demands that we set aside our personal beliefs—a very tall order—and attempt to grasp three things: why human beings appear to be hardwired for faith; the circumstances under which faiths inevitably turn violent; and the functions of religion in a Darwinian system of human ecology.

The answers we are likely to get will satisfy neither secular commissars nor their religious counterparts, neither scientists schooled to the last century's reductionist thinking nor those who insist on teaching our children that the bogeyman made the dinosaurs. We are at the dawn of a new and deadly age in which entire civilizations are threatened by the dominance of others. They are going to default to collective survival strategies that will transform their individual members into nonautonomous parts of a whole. We are going to find that, after all, we may not be masters of our individual wills, that far greater forces are at work than those the modern age insisted determined the contours of our lives. Those greater forces may be god or biology—or a combination of the two—but they are going to have a strategic impact that dwarfs the rational factors on which our faltering thinking still relies.

Applied to human affairs, rationalist thought too easily becomes just another superstition. Even the unbelievers among us are engaged in religious war.

The Atlantic Century

Parameters

Autumn 2003

Throughout the previous decade, strategists and statesmen asserted that we were about to enter the "Pacific Century." Global power and wealth would shift to East Asia. American interests, power, and investments would follow. The Atlantic would become a dead sea strategically, its littoral states and their continents declining to marginal status. Economic opportunities, crucial alliances, and the gravest threats would rise in the east, as surely as the morning sun.

An alternative view of the evidence suggests that the experts were wrong. Although the United States will remain engaged in the Far East—as well as in the Middle East, Europe, and nearly everywhere else—the great unexplored opportunities for human advancement, fruitful alliances, strategic cooperation, and creating an innovative, just, and mutually beneficial international order still lie on the shores of the Atlantic. The difference is that the potential for future development lies not across the North Atlantic in "Old Europe," but on both sides of the South Atlantic, in Africa and Latin America.

Especially since 9/11, the deteriorating civilization of the Middle East has demanded our attention. But we must avoid a self-defeating strategic fixation on the Arab Muslim world and self-destructive states nearby. Any signs of progress in the Middle East will be welcome, but the region overall is fated to remain an inexhaustible source of disappointments. While Africa suffers from an undeserved reputation for hopelessness (often a matter of racism couched in diplomatic language) and Latin America is dismissed as a backwater, the aggressive realms of failure in the Middle East always get the benefit of the doubt. When the United States places a higher priority on relations with Egypt than on those with Mexico or Brazil, and when Jordan attracts more of our attention than does South Africa, our foreign policy lacks common sense as much as it does foresight.

Our obsession with the Middle East is not just about oil. It's about intellectual habit. We assign unparalleled strategic importance to the survival of the repugnant Saudi regime because that's the way we've been doing things for half a century, despite the complete absence of political, cultural, or elementary human progress on the Arabian Peninsula.

Certainly, the United States has genuine strategic interests between the Nile and the Indus, and the threats from the region's apocalyptic terrorists and rogue regimes are as deadly as they are likely to be enduring. But we must stop pretending there is a bright, magical solution for the darkest region on earth, if only we Americans could discover the formula. The Middle East will remain a strategic basket case beyond our lifetimes. We will need to remain engaged, but we must be careful not to be consumed. If you are looking for hope, look elsewhere.

Apart from crisis intervention and measured support for any promising regimes that may emerge in the region (such as, perhaps, an independent, democratic Kurdistan), we need to begin shifting our practical as well as our emotional commitments away from the Middle East—and even away from Europe and northeast Asia—in order to help Africa and Latin America begin to realize their enormous strategic potential. Our past lies to the east and west, but our future lies to the south.

This is not a utopian vision. On the contrary, the returns of such a shift in our commitments would be practical and tangible. Turning our focus to Africa and Latin America would be the strategic equivalent of a "dogs of the Dow" approach, investing in "stocks" that are out of favor and unwanted, and placing our resources where the potential returns are highest, instead of continuing to throw them at strategic investments with, at best, marginal rates of return.

Nor is this about forging a neoclassical American empire. Rather, it's about creating strategic partnerships to supercede our waning relations with continental Europe and about structuring alternatives to an overreliance on the states, populations, and markets of East Asia. Although the United States, where all the relevant cultures converge, would be the most powerful member of an Afro-Latin-Anglo-American web of alliances, this would be a new kind of informal, democratic network, based on shared interests, aligning values, cultural fusion, and mutual advantage.

Turning our attention to Africa and Latin America is also the right thing to do, although that will not impress the advocates of Realpolitik. For them, the argument would lie in the security advantages, the profit potential in developing human capital, the expanded markets, and the enhancement of American influence even beyond our current "hyper-power" status.

Old Asia and Old Europe have devoured American lives and consumed our wealth. The regressive societies of the Middle East are sick—and contagious—with hatred, jealousy, and congenital disrepair. Whenever the United States is forced to engage cultures whose glory days are behind them, we win, but we often pay a bitter price.

America always has done best on frontiers, from our own West through technological frontiers to our pioneering of the society of the future, in which gender, racial, and religious equality increasingly prevail (to the horror of our enemies, foreign and domestic). And the great human frontiers of the twenty-first century lie to our south.

As this essay is written, President Bush visits Africa, having asked Congress to increase our funding for counter-AIDS initiatives in Africa and the Caribbean to $15 billion. The administration is contemplating the dispatch of Marines to Liberia, and the people of that long-abandoned country are begging for the Yankees to come and stay. During a visit to Zimbabwe last winter, the commonest question asked of me was, "Why, please, does the American Army go to Iraq, but not come here? We *want* you to come and free us, sir."

Of course, Zimbabwe is a problem for the Commonwealth of Nations, but what's striking in much of Africa is the desire for American involvement that one encounters below the level of bureaucrats and intellectuals still blinded by the ideology of the liberation struggle. The people of sub-Saharan Africa harbor the most pro-American sentiments of any population outside of our own country. Even in francophone Ivory Coast, last autumn's violence resulted in signs, written in English and held aloft by demonstrators, begging Uncle Sam to rescue them from Paris and its support for Islamic insurgents.

One of the many unintended consequences of the 9/11 attacks, as well as of al Qa'eda strikes in East Africa, has been the sudden realization in Washington that Africa matters. At present, the focus is heavily on security issues. But as the administration is already learning, enduring security is inseparable from development, opportunity, justice, and the rule of law. In the long term, President Bush's journey to Africa could prove of even greater strategic significance than our war-on-terror campaigns in Afghanistan and Iraq.

In an unfortunate symmetry, however, the same terror events that led to a new appreciation of Africa's relevance stopped the President's initiatives to improve relations with Mexico and the rest of Latin America dead in their tracks. The hopes of Mexico's reformist President Vicente Fox became unintended victims of 9/11, and recent elections decreased the number of seats in the legislature held by Fox's National Action Party. Fox, whose country may be the most important of all foreign powers for America's security, economy, and society, was forgotten amid the dust and rubble of the World Trade Center Towers.

Nonetheless, much of Latin America is on the threshold—or already across the threshold—of genuine reforms and profound cultural changes. For the first time, traditional political parties throughout Latin America are losing the power to resist the popular will—and the popular will wants real democracy, economic opportunity, and an end to the plague of corruption. There are now two generations of Latin American technocrats, almost a critical mass, educated in the United States. Miami is the informal financial and cultural capital of Latin America. Yet the United States pays more attention to Pakistan than it does to all of the countries south of the Panama Canal. We bribe our enemies, while ignoring our greatest potential friends.

Latin America's family secret is that everybody really wants to be a gringo, though it dare not be said in public. The "Yankee go home" era is over, except for the dwindling revolutionary hardliners who have failed the continent as badly as did their nemeses, the *caudillos,* the strongmen, and the land barons. Latin Americans don't want to Latinize the United States—they want to Americanize their own countries by creating responsible governments, lawful economies, and social regimes that respect human rights and human dignity. Yet the United States shows greater respect for Saudi Arabia, a regime founded on the principle of religious intolerance that permits no political dissent, routinely abuses human rights, and denies the most elementary freedoms to its female citizens. It would be hard to design a more counterproductive, nearsighted foreign policy.

During the buildup to Operation Iraqi Freedom, a fascinating constellation of allies emerged. When President Bush, British Prime Minister Tony Blair, and Spain's Prime Minister Jose Maria Aznar posed in front of the cameras after their minisummit, an unwitting world got a snapshot of a strategic triumvirate of North Atlantic powers positioned to change the world and their own situations for the better, if only they could continue to work together (both Britain and Spain should be viewed as members of a great Atlantic community, not primarily as European states). Indeed, if Portugal could be persuaded to join the group, you would have the ideal combination of North Atlantic democracies to work with Latin America and Africa in the coming decades.

The linguistic and cultural ties are there, as is a surprising degree of goodwill on the part of previously colonized populations. While the most oppressive and corrupt colonial powers of the twentieth century, notably France, watch their influence fade in Africa

(President Bush's visit to Senegal was calculated to show the flag in a developing power vacuum), the British legacy has been profoundly different. The French, Belgians, and others left behind a system of corrupt economies in service to statist governments. The British left behind a belief in the rule of law, democracy, and human betterment.

Despite the suffering and tribulations of black Africans in British colonies, the colonized learned to value the colonist's ideals for his own country even as they despised and fought against the colonist himself. The vile Apartheid regime in South Africa and the white-supremacy policies of Ian Smith's Rhodesia could not destroy the legacy of the missionary school's lessons about the Magna Carta, elected parliaments, and fair play. Those colonized by the British kept more than the sport of cricket for themselves. They also kept a belief in constitutions.

The Spanish legacy in Latin America was much harsher, but Spain's rule was cast off almost two hundred years ago. The old wounds healed, while the cultural affinities remain. Indeed, in much of the twentieth century, it was Spain, slumbering under the Franco regime, that wasn't moving forward. Now, with Spain vibrantly democratic and economically successful (for the first time in four centuries), Madrid has rediscovered its long-lost empire and seeks to engage it in emulation of Britain's Commonwealth.

In Prime Minister Jose Maria Aznar, Spain found a visionary. Although his party may suffer because of his unpopular support for the war to depose Saddam Hussein, he did not let opinion polls dictate his actions. Aznar did what he believed to be necessary and right, not only in the sense of ridding the world of a dangerous dictator, but in recognizing that Spain's greatest potential for market expansion and diplomatic influence lies in working constructively with the United States, its fellow Atlantic power, rather than slavishly following the dictates of continental states with profoundly divergent interests. Spanish investors have sunk billions into Latin America, and they are in for the long haul. They want cooperation, not confrontation, with the United States.

Aznar recognizes that the best route to an Atlantic future runs through Washington. While fashionable anti-Americanism in the streets of Spain may limit intense cooperation in the near term, in the longer term ever more Spaniards, chafing under European Union restrictions dictated by Paris and Berlin, will see opportunity to the west, not east. And it is hard to imagine any coalition that would be better for Latin America than a strategic partnership between the United States and Spain.

The Portuguese legacy is the most peculiar under consideration here. Portugal was the first European colonial power and the most enduring. Although Lisbon withdrew from Brazil in the mid-nineteenth century, it continued to occupy its African colonies into the 1970s. The prevalent postcolonial model would suggest that Portugal has no role to play for the present, given the degree of alienation manifested by recently liberated colonies. But Portugal's small size and lack of strategic power paradoxically offer it recuperative advantages. Mozambique and Angola, for example, do not fear creeping recolonization from the Iberian Peninsula—they're more concerned about South African "economic imperialism." Portugal has a surprisingly laissez-faire relationship with its former colonies, where its cultural influence is still felt profoundly and welcomed. Should Portugal recognize its future where its past greatness lay, in Africa and South America, it could serve as an essential bridge between its former colonies and other states in the Atlantic strategic network.

The United States, however, offers the model of success others wish to emulate. While the empty hubris of much of the Arab world leads it to anathematize all things American, the populations of the South Atlantic continents admire the social and economic success of the United States, our cultural totems, and our political values.

Certainly, a significant—though shrinking—number of leftists and populists in Latin America cling to yesterday's image of a ruthless, interventionist Uncle Sam bringing his guns to bear on behalf of the United Fruit Company. But the average citizen yearns for his or her voice to be heard as the voices of citizens are heard in the United States. They want a fair shake, economically and legally. They hate the corruption that torments their lives and robs them of their potential. They despise their inheritance of nepotism and a rigid class system. And, thanks to the information revolution and increased economic migration, they now know that things are better elsewhere.

Centuries of Latin American awareness that things were wrong were not enough. The people of Latin America also needed to know that change was possible, that things truly could be different. Now they know. And we will see decades of heady change south of the Rio Grande.

The people of Latin America do not want another Juan Peron or Fidel Castro. They want their FDR and JFK.

In sub-Saharan Africa, the reluctance to embrace the United States and its ideals is generational. The leaders and intellectuals who waged Africa's long independence struggle were shaped by the decades in which socialist solutions and communist rhetoric seemed indispensable tools of liberation. Now, even though statist socialism has collapsed or turned capitalist everywhere else, many of those aging heroes of the independence movement—even giants such as Nelson Mandela—cannot fully overcome the prejudices of their youth. And with sadly few exceptions, most notably Mandela, the old maxim that successful revolutionaries fail at governing certainly has been proven by the African experience.

The first European conquest of Africa was accomplished with guns. The second European conquest was achieved through the inspiring rhetoric and practical folly of Marxism-Leninism and related theories of "rational" social organization. Today, Africans must achieve a third conquest of their continent by themselves, a liberation from the poisonous cant of their liberators. The progress some African countries have made in just the last ten years in embracing practical, humane solutions to societal problems has been remarkable. But vicious wars and genocide make headlines, while African initiatives that slowly improve economies, gradually increase literacy, limit the spread of AIDS, or battle against corruption do not. Journalists flock to scoundrels, not to dull, dutiful bureaucrats.

In much of Africa, the transition from the revolutionary generation and its tainted protégé generation is already under way. Africa has been allowed to fall so far that progress will be slow and wildly uneven, but the willingness to embrace the rule-of-law and market economics is there, impeded only by the corrupt political class in far too many sub-Saharan countries. And the old, automatic anti-Americanism is passing from the scene where it has not already disappeared entirely.

Instead, younger Africans increasingly see the United States as a model of a racially integrated society in which blacks are accorded opportunity and dignity. It is impossible to overstate the contrast in African eyes between uniformly white European politicians on state visits to Africa and the arrival of Colin Powell or the sight of Condoleezza Rice standing beside the American president.

Where can sub-Saharan Africans turn for models, for support, for friends? To the north, the Islamic world is profoundly bigoted against them, religiously and racially. Muslims were the original slave traders, the worst exploiters, and except for the Belgians, the most savage oppressors of sub-Saharan Africa. Today, the collision between North African Islam and black African Christianity is not only a matter of daily violence, from Nigeria to Sudan, but of growing confrontation and conflict. Indeed, the new "church militant" is emerging in Africa, and the struggle with expansionist Islam may lead to the most savage religious wars of our century. This is the dynamic that should most concern us about the continent's future, since Africa's religious fault line is largely a racial divide as well—a combination that, historically, has made for especially virulent hatreds and merciless wars. The African deserts, grasslands, and cities where Christianity and Islam collide already offer a textbook example of Samuel Huntington's theory of the "clash of civilizations."

If the Islamic world's North African crusaders are viewed as implacable enemies of Christian Africa, then the populations of sub-Saharan Africa cannot turn to Europe and their former colonial masters for social or political models. Even Britain, which has an enormous, positive role to play in Africa's future, remains a racist, stratified society, despite much progress since the 1960s. On the continent, states such as France and Germany are rabidly racist, and despite protestations to the contrary from Paris and Berlin, the people of Africa know it. (A recent, severe miscalculation by President Chirac of France occurred when he insisted on hosting Zimbabwe's dictator Robert Mugabe in Paris, even though the European Union had imposed a travel ban on Mugabe. The visit was so deeply resented by the half-starved population of Zimbabwe that it guaranteed the French will not be welcome between the Zambezi and the Limpopo for a long time to come.)

Indeed, one of the key lessons Africans have drawn from comparing foreign societies is that, while anyone can become an American, no one can become French, or German, or Swedish. Of course, the global popularity of black American sports and entertainment figures helps, too. But they do not play the primary role we often imagine for them. The people of Africa don't just want good music and jump shots. They want good government. And jobs. And justice. The Statue of Liberty is still a better draw than Beyonce Knowles.

We don't think of Latin America and Africa as similar, despite their cultural ties and geographic proximity. Yet, the identical dreams of the average residents of Monrovia or Mexico City are to claim the best of America for themselves.

This vision of affinities and strategic connectivity between the Americas and Africa isn't new. It's the vision Fidel Castro tried—and failed—to apply thirty years ago. Castro simply connected the historical lines on the map. His mistake was to see Havana as the nexus, when the lines actually converge in New York City.

For all his many faults and stubborn cruelty, Castro was one of the great visionaries of our time (and whether we like it or not, he did as much good for Cuba as harm; his great mistake was outliving his virtues). He recognized that the slave trade from Africa to the New World hadn't created a one-way street (or sea lane), but that the chronically underestimated African influence on the Americas paved the way for the development of mutual strategic ties. Culture opened the door for power and influence.

Castro had the vision but lacked the resources to implement it successfully—although his forces repeatedly defeated the Apartheid-era South Africans in Angola. The United States had the resources but, blinded by the prejudices and priorities of the Cold War, failed to grasp the vision. We saw only an attempt to spread communism with a Cuban accent, while Castro was trying to build strategic bridges across the seas that once carried slave ships.

Indeed, for all the oppression and problems of Cuban society, it offers the best example of racial integration outside of the United States; by some practical measures, integration is even more advanced in Cuba. Castro understood that he could offer a model no one else was advertising (and thirty years ago, integration certainly had not progressed as far in the United States as it has today). He didn't just offer soldiers and doctors to Africa. Castro tried to offer a model of empowerment. His was, perhaps, the greatest strategic dream of the last half-century. His failure must be bitter to him.

Now we have inherited Castro's dream of transatlantic peoples bound together by culture, common interests, and mutual aspirations. Americans have the resources to do what Castro and his expeditionary forces could not achieve. But will we have even half the vision of that aging revolutionary in fatigues?

Whenever Africa comes up in a Washington conversation, eyes roll, shoulders shrug, and an entire continent is dismissed with a few phrases about AIDS, civil wars, genocide, and corruption. The unspoken message is that Africa is hopeless, that it's "just the way those people are."

But it's *not* just the way "those people" are. Africa is the way brutal colonization, fatal borders, the struggles of the Cold War, foreign ideologies, and finally, utter neglect have made it. Few of the arms used in those wars or tribal massacres were made in Africa. European governments—most notably France again—not only didn't fight corruption in their former colonies, they fostered it as a tool for continuing their control. French presidents and prime ministers have a long tradition of mutually profitable, personal relationships with African dictators. Indeed, corruption as a form of exploitation may have done even more damage to post-independence Africa than any other catastrophe prior to the advent of AIDS.

And what about AIDS? Has the disease doomed Africa to failure and backwardness? Considering the scope of the human devastation, with HIV infection rates that may range as high as 60 percent in some populations, unrestrained pessimism may, indeed, be in order. Tens of millions of Africans have died or will die, leaving millions of orphans behind. Professionals, the educated, and skilled workers are especially hard hit, since they have the disposable income to acquire more sexual partners. Military establishments are being gutted by AIDS.

Yet the effects of catastrophes are rarely linear. On the contrary, human collectives react unexpectedly to disasters, and the greater the scope of the loss, the more nonlinear the ultimate reaction may be. AIDS is, unquestionably, so great a tragedy for today's Africa that its devastation cannot be measured simply in the number of deaths. But that does not mean that the reverberations in tomorrow's Africa will necessarily take negative forms.

Consider a historical event that may have been even more lethal to a continental population: The Black Death, which reached the edges of Europe in 1346, is believed to have killed between one-third and two-thirds of the continent's inhabitants. Nothing known to human history killed so high a proportion of victims with such speed. A linear extrapolation would have predicted Europe's economic collapse, a faltering culture, and, at best, centuries of slow recovery.

The real results were decidedly nonlinear. Despite recurrent bouts of the plague, modern Europe was born in the disease's shadow. The epidemic fatally weakened the feudal system, opened Europe's cities to fresh blood, undercut Rome's religious monopoly, challenged the tradition of static, Aristotelian knowledge, and led to a flowering of the arts. The labor shortage created by the Black Death laid the foundations for collective bargaining and put talent at a new, far higher premium.

Instead of triggering a European collapse, the Black Death exploded the established order and was followed by the Renaissance, Europe's voyages of discovery, the Reformation, foreign colonization, the scientific revolution, and the rise of the West to centuries of global domination.

This observation is not intended to make light of the vast misery caused by AIDS in Africa (or elsewhere), but only to warn that those who assume that disaster can only lead to further disasters are wrong. Catastrophe, paradoxically, unleashes human creativity and great energies. Out of the many imaginable post-AIDS scenarios for Africa, one certainly would be economic and governmental failure. But an alternative scenario could see an Africa reborn. We simply do not know. But the smart money will always bet on human ingenuity, innovation, and will.

AIDS could lead to militarized societies based along tribal lines, or to the breakdown of tribal control, to the rise of violent millenarian sects, or to more egalitarian societies, to an opening of markets or their collapse. The results simply are not predictable at this point. But it is fair to observe that our continued insistence that Africa can only fail runs the risk of becoming a self-fulfilling prophecy.

Saints, con men, politicians, and smart investors see opportunity in disaster. The correct question isn't whether or not there are opportunities in Africa, but which of the many opportunities Africa offers its people and the world are the most promising. In the Arab world, we play down the negatives. In Africa, we ignore the positives. As a nation proud of our rationality, we are behaving very irrationally, indeed.

Consider, briefly, the most promising major country on the continent—South Africa. If you only read the statistics from afar—HIV-infection rate, 30 percent or higher; unemployment rate, 40 percent or higher; up to three million AIDS orphans; low levels of literacy; astronomical crime rates—you would conclude that South Africa is on the brink of becoming a failed state. The visitor, on the other hand, sees a coalescing multiracial society that has done an astonishing (if still imperfect) job of overcoming historical hatreds. Much of the infrastructure is world-class. The government is serious about fighting corruption, improving living conditions for the poor, and expanding educational opportunities. South African boardrooms are no longer populated only by white faces, and South African firms invest in the rest of the continent and beyond (earlier this year, for example, South African Breweries bought Miller Breweries in the United States, and SAB-Miller also has extensive investments in China). Elsewhere, some Africans fear South African "economic imperialism." And the infamous "white flight" of the early days of majority rule has reversed itself, with emigres returning to South Africa from abroad.

Despite many grave challenges, South Africa appears programmed for success on a continental scale. Events still could derail the country's future, but it now appears that South Africa, not Nigeria, is destined to become the continent's leader and moral beacon. Indeed, any Africa policy that does not strive for close relations with South Africa as a fundamental objective could achieve only partial, localized successes.

As noted above, the liberation generation and its protégés continue to suspect the United States of all sorts of deviousness, too often breaking out into ludicrous public accusations. But those men and their rhetoric will pass. We need to lay the groundwork now to work with the practical men and women who will succeed to government posts and positions of leadership in business across the next generation. What is especially striking to an American visitor to South Africa is how similar our two countries are, in so many respects, from a multiethnic society, to a can-do frontier spirit, to the varieties of landscape. We share elementary values, an English constitutional heritage, and a belief in the future (as opposed to Europe's fixation on the status quo). We are natural allies.

Elsewhere on the continent, the United States has already established a military presence in the northeast, on the Horn of Africa, in formerly French-occupied Djibouti. If we are both wise and humane, we will assist Liberia on Africa's west coast, considering—if the people of Liberia approve—the establishment of a permanent naval and Marine base in the country. In the continent's southern third, however, we need to allow South Africa to take the lead, to continue its effort to build regional military cooperation among democratic states, while we explore ways in which we can work more closely with Angola on the Atlantic coast and Mozambique, Tanzania, and Kenya on the eastern coast. In the north, more and more former French colonies will turn toward us, especially those that are black and majority Christian. Through a strategy of "triangulation," of positive engagement (with a limited permanent presence) in converging spheres of influence on Africa's west coast, east coast, and in the southern cone, we and our allies would be well-positioned to help Africa and thereby help ourselves throughout this century.

This is not a recommendation for trying to do everything but a suggestion that we have neglected even the minimum commitments that could bring us enormous strategic advantages. After all, seen from one perspective, the United States is simply the most successful African country.

Less need be said here about Latin America, since so much has been written elsewhere on the subject, at least in comparison to our neglect of Africa. But the same admonition applies: The routine Washington response to the mention of Latin America, as with Africa, suggests that "those people" just can't put all the pieces together. Although many arguments might be made about the complex history of Latin America—multiple histories, really—what matters is the here-and-now and the future. And, despite setbacks, much of Latin America has begun to change, profoundly, over the past generation.

Mexicans have gone from blaming the United States for everything that goes wrong to blaming their own political leaders and their own society. One gets the feeling from Chile that its opinion leaders believe all parties concerned would be better off if Chile could swap places with California. In Colombia, the elite finally has begun to take responsibility for the country's internal war with its narco-guerrillas and paramilitaries (in the past, the poor were drafted to die, the lower-middle class supplied the combat leaders, and the elite decamped to their mansions in greater Miami).

The election of a labor leader Washington feared as Brazil's head of state resulted in increased dialogue, responsible economic policies, and a surprising personal rapport between the leaders of our two nations. After their turn-of-the-millennium economic collapse, Argentines don't want another demagogue. They want fair, transparent government, and they just might get it. Venezuela is led by a populist who yearns to be Fidel Castro, but the democratic system that put him in office also restrains his most authoritarian impulses—the repeated street crises in Caracas are a rough form of democracy in action. And Mexico, which defined itself through much of the last century as the anti-United States, now recognizes the criticality of working constructively with Washington on multiple fronts, from fighting crime to economic immigration to fostering democracy elsewhere in the Western hemisphere. Unfortunately, Washington's attentions are elsewhere.

We have much to repair in our relations with Latin America. Some of the errors that long plagued our relationship have been theirs, but not a few have been our own. Arrogance and condescension toward our southern neighbors need to be banished from our diplomatic fashion show. We need to begin to build a serious, long-term partnership of equals—not yet equal in wealth, or in quality of government, or in raw power, but equal in our human dignity and our popular aspirations. Working together, we can develop our mutual potential far more efficiently and rapidly than by continuing along our far-too-separate paths.

Imperial Spain looked to Latin America for the silver in its mountains. We must look toward Latin America for the gold in its population. In a century when Europe's populations are aging toward fiscal and societal crises (the truly old Europe) and our ties with East Asia may become more limited, rather than expanding, even America's progressive immigration system will not be able to supply all the human power needed to fuel our continued economic expansion. It will not be a matter of "exporting American jobs," but of creating new jobs elsewhere that generate wealth for both host states and the United States.

For the next several decades, Africa will need its talent to focus primarily on internal development, but the better-educated, more urbane pools of talent in Latin America are the natural resource to which we can turn. Especially given the deepening cultural impact of American Latinos on our own society, we will have in place human bridges that no other country will be able to match. Even Spain, which will play an ever greater role in much of Latin America, will have only a shared language and heritage in common with local populations, while we will have their relatives—carrying American passports.

As with Africa, if we look only for problems in Latin America, we will have no difficulty in finding so many that we might easily convince ourselves to stay home. But the current trend in the wake of Operation Iraqi Freedom to downplay our recent differences with France, Germany, and other European powers is wrongheaded. Increasingly, continental Europe's interests, values, and aspirations diverge from our own. Certainly, we will continue to work together productively in many spheres. But the United States and Europe are growing apart, not converging.

The future—our future—lies elsewhere, in those long-neglected realms where human wastage has been blithely dismissed and every local misfortune was seized upon as proof that "they" simply weren't in our league. We have been seduced into playing nineteenth-century European great-power politics in the twenty-first century; indeed, considering our current involvement in the Middle East, one is tempted to claim that we're playing twelfth-century European power politics.

To the extent strategic requirements allow, we need to reduce our commitments to Europe, as well as combating our psychological dependence on the Eurocentric worldview. We are the children of Mark Twain, not of Proust. Like Huck Finn, we need to avoid Aunt Polly's attempts to put too many table manners on us. We always need to light out for new frontiers. And the human frontiers of the twenty-first century are in our own country, in Latin America, and in Africa.

Try a simple experiment. Lay out a map of the world. With a pencil and ruler, connect the United Kingdom, Spain, and Portugal with all the countries in the Americas or in Africa to which they have historical or cultural ties. Next, connect the countries of Africa to those states of the Western Hemisphere to which they have ethnic and cultural ties. Now connect the United States to the countries in Latin America and Africa to which we have ties of population and culture. You have just drawn the most promising strategic network of this century.

It is time for the United States to begin making Castro's dream a reality, leaving behind his socialist baggage and replacing it with respect for the popular will, individual rights, and truly free markets. We need to begin to bind together North America, Latin America, Africa, and the Atlantic powers on Europe's western frontier in a mutually beneficial, ocean-spanning network of rule-of-law democracies. Our history laid the foundation. Now we need to build the Atlantic Century.